Towards Financial Superpower

Towards Financial Superpower

China's Financial Industry and Its Road to Internationalization

Lerong Lu

OXFORD
UNIVERSITY PRESS

OXFORD
UNIVERSITY PRESS

Great Clarendon Street, Oxford, OX2 6DP,
United Kingdom

Oxford University Press is a department of the University of Oxford.
It furthers the University's objective of excellence in research, scholarship,
and education by publishing worldwide. Oxford is a registered trade mark of
Oxford University Press in the UK and in certain other countries

Published in the United States of America by Oxford University Press
198 Madison Avenue, New York, NY 10016, United States of America

British Library Cataloguing in Publication Data

Data available

Library of Congress Control Number: 2025933837

ISBN 9780198948537

DOI: 10.1093/9780198948568.001.0001

Printed and bound by
CPI Group (UK) Ltd, Croydon, CR0 4YY

The manufacturer's authorised representative in the EU for product safety is Oxford University Press España S.A. of El Parque Empresarial San Fernando de Henares, Avenida de Castilla, 2 – 28830 Madrid (www.oup.es/en or product.safety@oup.com). OUP España S.A. also acts as importer into Spain of products made by the manufacturer.

This book is dedicated to the Lu family (吕氏) from Quanzhou, Fujian, China—my ancestral roots. In particular, I honour my ancestor, Lu Huiqing (吕惠卿, 1032–1111 AD), a distinguished politician, scholar, and key reformist of the Northern Song Dynasty. His significant contributions to the 'New Policies' legal reforms—pioneering socio-economic measures to improve state administration and promote stability—and his service as Vice Chancellor of Imperial China from 1074 to 1075 inspire my work and reflect the enduring legacy of our lineage.

Preface

The book provides a holistic and in-depth analysis of the financial industry and its regulatory frameworks in the People's Republic of China. It covers the latest developments and industry practices in China's banking sector, capital markets, and emerging central bank digital currencies (CBDCs). Additionally, it examines the legal and regulatory environments underpinning China's financial industry, including its regulatory agencies, financial safety net, and specialized financial courts. Through detailed case studies, the book critically assesses the strengths and weaknesses of financial institutions and markets in the world's second-largest economy, addressing if and when China might become the next global financial superpower.

The topic of the financial industry, from both practical and regulatory perspectives, has been widely debated since the Global Financial Crisis of 2007–2008, but the discussion is mostly framed within a Western context. However, China now boasts one of the largest and most dynamic financial systems in the world. Among the top 100 banks globally ranked by total assets, China alone has 20 of the largest lenders, compared to 11 from the United States, 8 from Japan, 6 each from the United Kingdom, France, and South Korea, 5 from Australia, and 4 from Germany. In terms of the top ten global stock markets measured by market capitalization, China has three of the largest markets (Shanghai Stock Exchange, Shenzhen Stock Exchange, and Hong Kong Exchanges), second only to the United States (which holds the New York Stock Exchange and NASDAQ). China is actively opening its financial markets by reforming its securities law and introducing stock connect schemes with exchanges in the United Kingdom and Switzerland. Moreover, China has the most advanced Fintech sector, and its CBDC pilot project (digital yuan or e-CNY) is already being rolled out on a national scale, contributing to the rise of the Chinese yuan as a new global currency. Despite the remarkable rise of China's financial industry, its detailed operating mechanisms and regulatory regime remain less known to readers in the West.

Therefore, this book is a timely study of China's financial industry, capturing the fast-changing and dynamic nature of China's financial institutions and markets from three unique angles: financial marketization, financial globalization, and financial innovation. First, since the late 1970s, China has been advancing its market-oriented reforms, gradually replacing state control with market mechanisms in economic activities. This book examines the effects of these free-market economic reforms and financial liberalization. Second, the book discusses how China's financial industry proactively responds to major economic and geopolitical crises in the twenty-first century, such as the Global Financial Crisis of 2007–2008, the COVID-19 pandemic, and the trade war, which pose external threats to the growth of the Chinese economy. China's eagerness to integrate into the global economy is evident in its efforts to promote the international connectivity of its stock exchanges and the global use of the Chinese yuan through the Belt and Road Initiative and the CBDC trial. Third, the book evaluates the impact of technological innovations on China's financial industry. Technology is transforming global finance, with big data, cloud computing, artificial intelligence (AI), and blockchain being widely deployed in most aspects of financial businesses. This book discusses the great potential of Fintech and the CBDC experiment in China.

This book is a must-read for anyone studying the practice and regulation of China's financial industry. It will be particularly useful for financial lawyers, bankers, management consultants, fund managers, and corporate executives involved in international banking and financial markets. This interdisciplinary work also interests Law and Economics students, professors, researchers, think tanks, and policymakers who study financial economics, financial regulation, and the Chinese economy.

This book results from over ten years of research experience in China's financial industry and its regulation. I began this journey by writing my PhD thesis on shadow banking in China from 2013 to 2017 as a doctoral candidate at the University of Leeds. Since then, I have been researching various topics related to China's financial industry, including banking regulation, capital markets law and regulation, Fintech, and CBDC, during my tenure at King's College London and the University of Bristol from 2017 to 2024. Through my research, I have witnessed the rapid rise of Chinese financial markets, institutions, and Fintech in the 2010s and early 2020s, along with the associated risks and regulatory challenges.

For the publication of this book, I would like to express my gratitude to the following individuals. First, I thank my students and colleagues who assisted with material collection and preliminary research, particularly Ningyao Ye, Lingsheng Zhang, Ci Ren, Hang Chen, Shunqi Yang, and Jiujing Ye. Second, I am deeply indebted to my family. Without their love, encouragement, and support, this book would not have been possible. I dedicate this book to my family, especially my wife and children. Third, I thank the editors at Oxford University Press for their immense support, professionalism, and patience during the publication process. Finally, I appreciate the editors from Thomson Reuters (Sweet & Maxwell)[1] and LexisNexis[2] for the permission to reproduce parts of papers published in their journals. The materials in this book are current as of July 2024, when the writing was completed. However, any errors or inaccuracies are solely my responsibility.

Lerong Lu
Xiamen, China
July 2024

[1] The following material was first published by Thomson Reuters, trading as Sweet & Maxwell, 5 Canada Square, Canary Wharf, London, E14 5AQ, and is reproduced by agreement with the publishers: Lerong Lu, 'The Rising Star in the East: Unveiling China's Star Market, the Registration-Based IPO Regime, and Capital Markets Law Reform' (2020) 31 *International Company and Commercial Law Review* 394–412; Lerong Lu, 'Building a Eurasian Capital Market: Understanding the Operating Mechanism and Legal Framework of Shanghai-London Stock Connect' (2020) 35 *Journal of International Banking Law and Regulation* 67–74 (with Ningyao Ye); and Lerong Lu, 'Shadow Banking for Cash-Strapped Entrepreneurs: A Study of Private Lending Agreements Under Chinese Contract Law' (2018) 3 *Journal of Business Law* 215–228.

[2] Lerong Lu, 'PRC Securities Law 2020: Promoting More Efficient and Transparent Capital Markets in China' (2021) 3 *JIBFL* 237. This article was first published in the March 2021 issue of *Butterworths Journal of International Banking and Financial Law*, ISSN: 0269-2694; and Lerong Lu, 'Black Swans and Grey Rhinos: Demystifying China's Financial Risks and the Financial Regulatory Reform' (2018) 9 *JIBFL* 594. This article was first published in the October 2018 issue of *Butterworths Journal of International Banking and Financial Law*, ISSN: 0269-2694.

Contents

List of Figures

List of Tables

List of Abbreviations

ABC	Agricultural Bank of China
ADR	American depositary receipt
AI	artificial intelligence
AIIB	Asian Infrastructure Investment Bank
AMC	asset management corporation
AML	anti-money laundering
BigTech	largest technology company
BIS	Bank for International Settlements
BOC	Bank of China
BOCOM	Bank of Communications
BRI	Belt and Road Initiative
BRICS	Brazil, Russia, India, China, and South Africa
BSE	Beijing Stock Exchange
CBDC	central bank digital currency
CBIRC	China Banking and Insurance Regulatory Commission
CBRC	China Banking Regulatory Commission
CCB	China Construction Bank
CCP	Communist Party of China
CDD	customer due diligence
CDR	Chinese depositary receipt
CERF	carbon emission reduction facility
CFC	Central Financial Commission (China)
CFT	combating the financing of terrorism
CFWC	Central Financial Work Commission (China)
Chengyu Financial Court	Chengdu-Chongqing Financial Court
China Clear	China Securities Depository and Clearing Corporation Limited
ChiNext	Growth Enterprises Market of Shenzhen Stock Exchange
CIRC	China Insurance Regulatory Commission
CPPCC	Chinese People's Political Consultative Conference
CSRC	China Securities Regulatory Commission
DCEP	Digital Currency Electronic Payment (China)
DCSS	dual class share structure
DGS	Deposit Guarantee Scheme
DIFMC	Depository Insurance Fund Management Co., Ltd. (China)
EBA	European Banking Authority
EU	European Union
FCA	Financial Conduct Authority
FDIC	Federal Deposit Insurance Corporation (US)

Fintech	financial technology
FSB	Financial Stability Board
FSCS	Financial Services Compensation Scheme (UK)
FSDC	Financial Stability and Development Committee (China)
FSN	financial safety net
G7	Group of Seven
GDP	gross domestic product
GDPR	General Data Protection Regulation (EU)
GDR	global depository receipt
HDB	Hainan Development Bank
HKEX	Hong Kong Stock Exchange
ICBC	Industrial and Commercial Bank of China
ICO	initial coin offering
IMF	International Monetary Fund
IOSCO	International Organization of Securities Commissions
IP	intellectual property
IPO	initial public offering
LOLR	Lender of Last Resort
LPR	Loan Prime Rate
LSE	London Stock Exchange
LTV	loan-to-value ratio
MLF	Medium-term Lending Facility
MYBank	Zhejiang E-Commerce Bank
NASDAQ	National Association of Security Dealers Automated Quotations (US)
NDRC	National Development and Reform Commission (US)
NEEQ	National Equities Exchange and Quotations (China)
NET	National Electronic Trading System (China)
NFRA	National Financial Regulatory Administration (China)
NIFC	National Interbank Funding Centre (China)
NPC	the National People's Congress (China)
NPL	non-performing loan
NYSE	New York Stock Exchange
OMO	open market operation
OTC	over-the-counter
P/B ratio	price-to-book ratio
P/E ratio	price-to-earnings ratio
PBoC	People's Bank of China
PE	private equity
PICC	People's Insurance Company of China
PIPL	Personal Information Protection Law (China)
PRA	Prudential Regulation Authority (UK)
PSBC	Postal Savings Bank of China
PSL	Pledged Supplementary Lending
QFII	qualified foreign institutional investor
R&D	research and development
Repo	repurchase agreement

RMB	Renminbi
ROA	return on asset
RQFII	RMB Qualified Foreign Institutional Investor
RRR	required reserve ratio
RWA	risk-weighted asset
SAFE	State Administration of Foreign Exchange (China)
SCNPC	Standing Committee of the National People's Congress (China)
SLF	Standing Lending Facility
SLSC	Shanghai–London Stock Connect
SME	small and medium-sized enterprises
SOE	state-owned enterprise
SRDI	specialization, refinement, differentiation, and innovation
SSE	Shanghai Stock Exchange
STAQ	Securities Trading Automatic Quotation (China)
Star Market	Science and Technology Innovation Board of Shanghai Stock Exchange
SZSE	Shenzhen Stock Exchange
UK	United Kingdom of Great Britain and Northern Ireland
UKLA	UK Listing Authority
US	United States of America
USDT	Tether
VC	venture capital
VIE	variable interest entity
WB	World Bank
WTO	World Trade Organization

Chapter 1
Overview of China's financial industry

This introductory chapter explains the book's background and analytical framework, laying a foundation for the further analysis of China's financial industry and its regulatory frameworks in the rest of the book. It consists of three sections. Section 1.1 discusses the recent developments in the Chinese economy and the role played by the financial industry in the overall economy. Section 1.2 identifies the three key themes driving the rapid rise of China's financial industry: financial marketization, financial globalization, and financial innovation. Section 1.3 maps out the book's analytical framework by addressing the question: if and when China is becoming the next financial superpower, and introduces how the book will answer this question. It provides an outline of the contents of the following chapters.

1.1 The Chinese economy and its financial industry

China is on track to become the next superpower in the world. The phenomenal rise of Chinese economy in the twenty-first century has drawn extensive discussion among economists, legal scholars, political scientists, and international relationship experts. According to the International Monetary Fund (IMF), China accounted for 18.82% of the world's economic output, measured by GDP based on purchasing power parity (PPP), in 2023.[1] It makes China the largest economy on our planet, followed by the United States that represented 15.42% of global GDP. Even based on the nominal sum of GDP, China, with an annual growth rate of over 4%, is very likely to overtake the United States, which has a growth rate of 1.9%, by 2035 to become the largest economy.[2] China's increasing economic might is proportionate to the

[1] International Monetary Fund, 'IMF Data Mapper—China, People's Republic of', https://www.imf.org/external/datamapper/profile/CHN.

[2] *South China Morning Post*, 'China GDP to surpass US around 2035, years later than previously expected, Goldman Sachs predicts' (by Ji Siqi, 9 December 2022), https://www.scmp.com/economy/china-economy/article/3202752/china-gdp-surpass-us-around-2035-years-later-previously-expected-goldman-sachs-predicts.

Towards Financial Superpower. Lerong Lu, Oxford University Press. © Lerong Lu (2025).
DOI: 10.1093/9780198948568.003.0001

size of its population, as the country has 1.41 billion people or one-fifth of the world's population. Clearly, the study of Chinese economy is of great importance given its enormous size and increasing interaction with other parts of the world. China and India, both populous nations with rapid economic progress, have contributed to over 50% of global economic growth in the aftermath of the COVID-19 pandemic.[3]

The expansion of Chinese economy has profound impacts on itself and the rest of the world due to its dual roles as both producer and consumer in the global economy. For example, Chinese consumers buy a lot of goods and services from large corporations in developed countries. In 2022, the German automaker Mercedes-Benz saw 37% of its sales and 18% of its revenue coming from China.[4] The French luxury group LVMH which is well-known for its Louis Vuitton handbags and Moet champagnes made almost 30% of its revenue in China, compared with 27% in Americas.[5] Not to mention China's well-known status as the world's factory, given its powerful productive power, logistics, and supply chain. Over 95% of Apple's iPhones and iPads are manufactured in China, as the US electronic giant's partner Foxconn employs over 500,000 workers in its Shenzhen factories.[6] The leading electric vehicle maker Tesla produces around one million cars each year at its Gigafactory in Shanghai, more than any of its other factories in California, Texas, and Berlin.[7] In addition, China is the largest commodities importer in the world. In 2022, it bought 1.1 billion tonnes of iron ore from other countries, 65% of which coming from Australia.[8]

This book is focused on the most dynamic part of the Chinese economy, which is its financial industry. It examines the rapid growth of Chinese commercial banks, financial markets, and central bank digital currencies, as well as the country's financial regulatory frameworks over the past four decades

[3] International Monetary Fund, 'World Economic Outlook' (April 2023), https://www.imf.org/en/Publications/WEO/Issues/2023/04/11/world-economic-outlook-april-2023.

[4] *Reuters*, 'Cutting ties with China is "unthinkable", Mercedes-Benz CEO tells Bild am Sonntag' (29 April 2023), https://www.reuters.com/business/autos-transportation/cutting-ties-with-china-is-unthinkable-mercedes-benz-ceo-tells-bams-2023-04-29/.

[5] *Reuters*, 'LVMH flags strong Chinese rebound, U.S. slowdown' (by Mimosa Spencer and Silvia Aloisi, 13 April 2023), https://www.reuters.com/business/retail-consumer/lvmh-sales-lifted-by-strong-chinese-rebound-first-quarter-2023-04-12/.

[6] *Forbes*, 'Apple's reliance on China poses a problem for the company' (by Steve Banker, 19 January 2023), https://www.forbes.com/sites/stevebanker/2023/01/19/apples-china-problem/.

[7] *South China Morning Post*, 'Tesla's Shanghai factory delivers fewer electric cars as upgrade ahead of new Model 3 launch disrupts production' (by Daniel Ren, 9 October 2023), https://www.scmp.com/business/china-business/article/3237342/teslas-shanghai-factory-delivers-fewer-electric-cars-upgrade-ahead-new-model-3-launch-disrupts.

[8] *CNN*, 'Australia's exports to China hit record high as relations thaw' (by Laura He, 5 May 2023), https://edition.cnn.com/2023/05/05/economy/australia-china-exports-record-intl-hnk/index.html.

since the start of China's market-oriented economic reform in the late 1970s.[9] The financial industry plays a vital role in matching the supply and demand of capital, enabling the efficient allocation of financial resources in society and increasing economic productivity. The study of China's financial industry is a very interesting and important subject for economists and other social scientists, for the following two reasons.

First, it is all about the gigantic size of Chinese financial institutions and financial markets and their increasingly leading position in the world. Among the top 100 banks in the world valued by total assets, China alone has 20 of the largest lenders, compared with 11 from the United States, 8 from Japan, and 6 from the United Kingdom, 6 from France, 6 from South Korea, 5 from Australia, and 4 from Germany.[10] In terms of top ten global stock markets measured by market capitalization, China has three largest markets (i.e. Shanghai Stock Exchange, Shenzhen Stock Exchange, and Hong Kong Exchanges), catching up quickly with the New York Stock Exchange and NASDAQ in the United States.[11] China is actively opening its financial markets by reforming its securities law and introducing stock connect schemes with exchanges in the United Kingdom and Switzerland. Moreover, China has the most advanced Fintech sector, and its central bank digital currency (CBDC) pilot project (digital yuan or e-CNY) is already being rolled out on a national scale, contributing to the rise of the Chinese yuan as a new global currency.[12] Despite the spectacular rise of China's financial industry, its detailed operating mechanism and regulatory regime is less known to the readers in the West.

Second, China's financial industry is unique as it is situated within a special economic and political environment that is distinctive from most countries. The Chinese economy is officially labelled as the socialist market economy, being governed by the world's largest communist party—the Communist Party of China (CCP). In this sense, China is sometimes regarded as a country with state capitalism by scholars.[13] The financial industry has been the

[9] China's economic reform is guided by the 'reform and open-up policy' proposed by Deng Xiaoping from 1978 to 1992. See Yuyan Zhang, *Reform, Opening-up and China's Changing Role in Global Governance* (Springer, 2021), p. 3.

[10] S&P Global, 'The world's 100 largest banks, 2023', https://www.spglobal.com/marketintelligence/en/news-insights/research/the-world-s-100-largest-banks-2023.

[11] Statista, 'Largest stock exchange operators worldwide as of September 2023, by market capitalization of listed companies', https://www.statista.com/statistics/270126/largest-stock-exchange-operators-by-market-capitalization-of-listed-companies/.

[12] For the discussion of Fintech in China, see Lerong Lu, *Global Fintech Revolution: Practice, Policy, and Regulation* (Oxford University Press, 2024), p. 52.

[13] Kellee S. Tsai, 'The Political Economy of State Capitalism and Shadow Banking in China' (The Hong Kong University of Science and Technology IEMS Working Paper No. 2015-25).

pinnacle of modern capitalism, generating the most added value in developed countries like the United States and the United Kingdom. It is, therefore, interesting to find out how the financial industry operates in an economy with strong socialist elements. So far, the financial industry has been growing robustly in China, forming an organic part of the socialist market economy. Both the CCP and Chinese government have fully recognized the need to build the nation with a strong financial sector, given that the financial sector is the lifeblood of a nation's economy and a crucial component of China's core competitiveness.[14] There are a lot of special characteristics in China's financial industry, such as a strong role of state in financial institutions and a preference of financial stability over other economic objectives like growth and competition. Such features will be observed throughout the discussion in this book. Evidently, China offers a unique case study for understanding the practice and regulation of the financial industry, potentially presenting a new path for global economic development. This book significantly contributes to the current literature on financial industry practice and regulation, which is predominantly centred on Western countries, including the United States, the United Kingdom, and the European Union (EU).

1.2 Financial marketization, financial globalization, and financial innovation

In this book, we will focus on three key themes underlying the recent developments in China's financial industry. First of all, the rapid growth of financial institutions and markets in China largely results from the marketization or deregulation process, like what other economic segments in China have experienced over the past four decades (1978–present). Financial marketization means that China has been actively liberalizing its financial industry by removing entry barriers and regulatory red tapes, as the financial industry has been dominated by state-owned institutions. Through a series of reforms, China invites more private and international players into the arena. There have been an increasing number of privately owned banking institutions like WeBank and Shanghai Huarui Bank that were launched during the 2010s. Moreover, most public companies that obtained a listing recently

[14] In October 2023, during the central financial work conference held in Beijing and chaired by President Xi Jinping, the importance of building a nation with a strong financial sector was emphasized. See *Xinhua*, 'Central financial work conference is held' (1 November 2023), https://english.news.cn/20231101/e027c8d2e7994fd590957c7152d4f4fa/c.html.

have been private corporations rather than state-owned companies. Financial marketization echoes China's overall market-oriented economic reform when the free market is gradually replacing the state to play a key role in the socialist market economy.

After the founding of the People's Republic of China in 1949, China experienced the socialist movement as the new government exercised tight control over the economic operation and other aspects of the society for three decades (1949–1978). As a result, banks and other financial institutions, like any other private enterprises, had been either ordered to close or put under state control. For a long period of time, the People's Bank of China (PBoC) served as both a central bank and a commercial bank.[15] As the only bank and superior financial institution in China, the PBoC, controlled by the Ministry of Finance, held over 90% of national financial assets and processed most financial transactions in the country. In terms of financial markets, most stock, future, and commodities exchanges had been closed during the same period. There is no place for the trading, speculation, and investment activities as financial resources were organized centrally by the government under the plan economy. From 1949 to 1978, minimal financial activities were conducted by individuals and private enterprises, due to the operation of a state-monopolized financial system with the sole purpose of serving the socialist economic production and distribution. Most citizens only had access to some basic banking services like savings and money transfer, provided by state-owned institutions and credit cooperatives. Ration coupons were issued to urban citizens to buy a quota of rice, flour, meats, cooking oil, cloth, and bicycles. The Chinese currency, Renminbi (RMB), was used on a limited scale since there were not many commodities freely circulating in the economy.

Since the late 1970s, China has launched a series of market-oriented economic reforms to reduce the state control in economic operation and let markets play a greater role in the financial industry.[16] As a result, various new financial institutions were established by central and local governments, private entrepreneurs, and foreign investors as the state gradually ceded ground to the market in the banking and finance sector. The Shanghai and Shenzhen stock exchanges have opened business for trading since the early 1990s. Thus, the central planning economy has given way to the socialist market economy that we see today. The new economy has multiple players, from state-owned

[15] Franklin Allen, Xian Gu, and Jun Qian, 'The People's Bank of China: From 1948 to 2016' in Rodney Edvinsson, Tor Jacobson, and Daniel Waldenström (eds), *Sveriges Riksbank and the History of Central Banking* (Cambridge University Press, 2018), pp. 418–453.

[16] William Byrd, *The Market Mechanism and Economic Reforms in China* (Routledge, 1991), p. 19.

enterprises to privately owned businesses and other enterprises of mixed ownership. Now private businesses in China account for over 60% of national GDP and 80% of employment in the urban regions.[17] The rise of private capitalism has greatly transformed China's economic outlook, as the raised productivity makes it the world's second-largest economy from the beginning of the twenty-first century. At present, the financial industry has been an organic part of the socialist market economy. The increased commercial activities call for more institution-based and market-based financing channels. Throughout the 1980s and 1990s, various kinds of banking institutions, securities brokers, and insurance companies have sprung up in China. China now has over 4,600 banking institutions, including the 'big four' banks, a dozen national joint-equity commercial banks, hundreds of city commercial banks, and thousands of rural banks.[18]

Despite the trend towards deregulation and marketization reform, China's financial industry remains subject to significant state influence, and in some cases, direct state control. A lot of prominent banking, securities, and insurance institutions have central or local governments as their majority shareholder. For example, ICBC, the largest Chinese commercial bank, has the Ministry of Finance and Central Huijin Investment Ltd. (the central government's investment vehicle) as its main shareholders, holding 31.14% and 34.71% of the bank, respectively.[19] In practice, the Chairmen and CEOs of the big four banks, who are appointed by the central government, enjoy vice-ministerial administrative powers and therefore are often perceived as government officials rather than real bankers. It is the same for other large financial institutions backed by the state. In addition, all stock exchanges in mainland China (Beijing, Shanghai, and Shenzhen) are membership-based public legal entities and fall under the direct management of the China Securities Regulatory Commission (CSRC).[20] They do not operate independently like London Stock Exchange and New York Stock Exchange which are incorporated bodies and listed publicly. Therefore, unlike the UK Financial

[17] World Bank, 'How much do state-owned enterprises contribute to China's GDP and employment?' (by Chunlin Zhang, 15 July 2019), https://documents1.worldbank.org/curated/en/449701565248091726/pdf/How-Much-Do-State-Owned-Enterprises-Contribute-to-China-s-GDP-and-Employment.pdf.

[18] The big four refers to the Industrial and Commercial Bank of China (ICBC), the China Construction Bank (CCB), the Agricultural Bank of China (ABC), and the Bank of China (BOC). See Lerong Lu, 'Private Banks in China: Origin, Challenges and Regulatory Implications' (2016) 31 *Banking and Finance Law Review* 585 at 586–587.

[19] ICBC, 'Particulars of shareholding of the top 10 ordinary shareholders of the bank' (31 December 2021), https://www.icbc-ltd.com/ICBCLtd/Investor%20Relations/Share%20Information/Shareholding%20Structure/.

[20] Shanghai Government, 'Brief introduction of Shanghai Stock Exchange' (18 July 2023), https://www.shanghai.gov.cn/nw47986/20200824/0001-47986_108559.html.

Conduct Authority or the US Securities and Exchange Commission, the CSRC has significant influence over stock exchange's daily operations and used to fully determine the quota and outcome of most IPO applications. It serves as clear evidence of the strong regulatory power unique to China's financial industry.

The second key theme in the recent history of China's financial industry is the government's significant efforts to enhance its internationalization and interconnectedness with the global economy. China joined the World Trade Organization (WTO) in December 2001, facilitating its trade in products and services with the rest of the world.[21] The rapid growth of China could not be achieved without its close economic cooperation with other countries across Asia, Europe, Africa, Americas, and Oceania. Financial globalization implies the integration of Chinese financial markets and institutions into the global arena. Just like other economic sectors, policymakers believe that China's financial industry should become more open and interconnected with the global system. However, Chinese leaders are also cautious about the growing influence of foreign capital and the external risks posed by international financial markets, which may be beyond their control. This includes incidents such as the Global Financial Crisis of 2007–2008, financial turmoil during the COVID-19 pandemic, and geopolitical tensions with the United States. Such external risks are likely to affect the financial stability in China and the interest of Chinese investors given the increasingly tight economic link between China and the world.

We have seen China's great efforts in opening up its financial industry since the turn of the twenty-first century. Just to provide a few examples. Stock exchanges in mainland China have established cooperative connect schemes with exchanges in Hong Kong, London, and Zurich. These initiatives facilitate direct access for investors to each other's capital markets and allow companies to pursue fast-track secondary listings in another country.[22] Moreover, as part of the 'Belt and Road Initiative' (BRI), China established the Asian Infrastructure Investment Bank (AIIB), a multilateral development bank and international financial institution aimed at collectively improving economic and social outcomes in Asia, especially the funding of large infrastructure projects.[23] Headquartered in Beijing, AIIB has 109 countries joining

[21] WTO, 'China—Member information', https://www.wto.org/english/thewto_e/countries_e/china_e.htm.

[22] Ningyao Ye and Lerong Lu, 'Building A Eurasian Capital Market: Understanding the Operating Mechanism and Legal Framework of Shanghai-London Stock Connect' (2020) 35 *Journal of International Banking Law and Regulation* 67–74.

[23] Asian Infrastructure Investment Bank, 'About AIIB', https://www.aiib.org/en/about-aiib/index.html.

as members, positioning it as a potential rival for the more established international financial institutions, including the World Bank (WB) and the IMF. The WB and IMF are Western-style institutions that are predominately supported by the United States. The rise of AIIB and other financial institutions in Asia, to some extent, contributes to a more balanced international financial order in the near future.

Not to mention China's ambition for the internationalization of RMB as a global reserve currency. As of July 2023, RMB represented only 2.23% of international payments, in contrast to dominant currencies such as the US dollar (59.21%), the Euro (13.61%), the British pound (5.65%), and the Japanese yen (5%).[24] Clearly, the Chinese currency is underrepresented in the global financial system, despite China's weighty contribution to one-fifth of the world's GDP. China aims to make the wider use of RMB for both international commerce and national reserve of other countries. This is evidenced by signing the bilateral agreements of RMB usage with member countries joining the BRI. Also, China is leading the experiments on its CBDC with built-in capacity of being a global currency for cross-border use.[25] However, there is a long way to go for the internationalization of RMB and China's overall financial industry. It has faced setbacks as some Western countries view the rise of the RMB and China's financial power as more of a threat than an opportunity. This confrontation has intensified in recent years, particularly in light of the growing China–US geopolitical tension and strategic competition.

The third key theme in the book is about financial innovation in China, in particular, its thriving Fintech sector and the world-leading CBDC project. Fintech refers to the application of innovative technologies like artificial intelligence (AI), blockchain, big data, and cloud computing in financial services.[26] The book attempts to assess the impacts of technological innovations on China's financial industry, transforming the practice and regulation of financial activities. China has rapidly emerged as a global leader in financial innovation, showcasing the country's transition from a manufacturing-based economy (known as the world's factory) to a more modern, service-based economy. For instance, China accounted for over 75% of Bitcoin mining and

[24] Statista, 'Most used currency in the world for international payments in SWIFT from January 2019 to July 2023, based on share in total transaction value', https://www.statista.com/statistics/1189498/share-of-global-payments-by-currency/.

[25] Lerong Lu and Lingsheng Zhang, 'Could the "Dragon" Now Fly Beyond Borders? Contextualizing Regulatory Aspects and Risks for China's CBDC Cross-Border Use' (2022) 14:S *Tsinghua China Law Review* 19–44.

[26] Lerong Lu, *Global Fintech Revolution: Practice, Policy, and Regulation* (Oxford University Press, 2024), p. 11.

a large proportion of crypto trading activities before the government ban in 2021.[27] At the peak, China had over 3,000 peer-to-peer lending platforms matching lending transactions worth billions of yuan each day. Moreover, China's mobile payment industry is second to none. Thanks to the world-class telecom infrastructure and a high smartphone adoption rate, China has embraced a cashless society with over one billion citizens using Alipay and WeChat Pay mobile payment services on a daily basis.[28] More recently, China has accelerated experiments with digital yuan, or the DC/EP project, as the country's CBDC. As the first major economy to roll out CBDCs on a large scale, this development contributes to China's economic strength and the internationalization of RMB.[29] China, as an ancient civilization that invented paper money (banknotes) during the Song dynasty in the eleventh century, is once again taking a lead in the digital finance age.

1.3 The book's analytical framework and chapter outline

It seems certain that China is on its way to become the world's next superpower, as the country is exercising more economic, political, and cultural influence over the world in the twenty-first century. Superpower is a prestigious status achieved by a small number of countries over the nineteenth and twentieth centuries like the British Empire, the United States, and the Soviet Union.[30] There are other similar concepts denoting strong economic and political powers. For instance, the Group of Seven (G7) is the intergovernmental political and economic forum that represents seven most advanced industrialized countries including Canada, France, Germany, Italy, Japan, the United Kingdom, and the United States. G7 is heavily involved in the setting of today's international economic order as they have a great say in the international organizations such as the United Nations, WB, IMF, and the Bank for International Settlements (BIS). The BRICS is another intergovernmental organization that includes the most important developing countries

[27] *CNN*, 'Bitcoin mining: China's government is cracking down' (by Laura He, 24 May 2021), https://edition.cnn.com/2021/05/24/investing/bitcoin-mining-china-crackdown-intl-hnk/index.html.

[28] Lerong Lu, 'Decoding Alipay: Mobile Payments, A Cashless Society and Regulatory Challenges' (2018) 33 *Butterworths Journal of International Banking and Financial Law* 40–43.

[29] Lerong Lu and Lingsheng Zhang, 'Could the "Dragon" Now Fly Beyond Borders? Contextualizing Regulatory Aspects and Risks for China's CBDC Cross-Border Use' (2022) 14:S *Tsinghua China Law Review* 19–44.

[30] After the Second World War, the British Empire went into decline throughout the rest of the twentieth century, marked by the process of decolonization and the independence of its former colonies. In 1991, with the dissolution of the Soviet Union at the end of the Cold War, the United States emerged as the sole superpower at the beginning of the twenty-first century.

Table 1.1 The world's largest economies by nominal GDP in 2024

Rank	Country	GDP (million US$)
1	United States	28,781,083
2	China	18,532,633
3	Germany	4,591,100
4	Japan	4,110,452
5	India	3,937,011
6	United Kingdom	3,495,261
7	France	3,130,014
8	Brazil	2,331,391
9	Italy	2,328,028
10	Canada	2,242,182

Source: International Monetary Fund.

such as Brazil, Russia, India, China, and South Africa. BRICS are established to challenge the political and economic dominance of the wealthier nations like G7. The size of emerging economies is quickly catching up with the developed countries. Based on Table 1.1, China is now the world's second-largest economy in 2024, India ranks fifth, and Brazil holds the eighth position. By the middle of the twenty-first century, the world's economic order is likely to be significantly different from today, driven by the rise of China and India, the two most populous nations in Asia.

The book's analytical framework revolves around a central question: if and when China is poised to become the next financial superpower. This question is important not only for China and its people but also for readers in the West and other countries, given the close economic ties between China and the rest of the world. In the twenty-first century, no one working in business and finance can completely avoid dealing with China. In answering this question, the book discusses various dimensions that contribute to the rise of China's financial industry. It covers not only the infrastructure, legal, and regulatory environments of the financial industry but also the practices of financial institutions and markets. The regulatory agencies and institutional arrangements are discussed in Chapter 2, the financial safety net and crisis management in Chapter 3, and the financial courts and dispute resolution mechanisms in Chapter 7. The practices of financial institutions and markets are explored in detail, including the banking sector and shadow banking in Chapter 4, capital markets and securities regulation related to IPOs and stock trading in Chapter 5, and Fintech and CBDC in Chapter 6. Additionally, Chapter 8 is dedicated to case studies analysing China's efforts to promote the internationalization of its financial industry, including international financial centres, stock connect schemes, and cross-border enforcement of securities laws. The comprehensive treatment of the subject matter will provide readers with an in-depth understanding of how China's financial industry operates, how it is being regulated, and the implications of its rise for the rest of the world. The book offers valuable insights for law and finance practitioners, corporate executives, management consultants, professors, students, policymakers, and think tanks.

Chapter 2
China's financial regulatory agencies

2.1 Introduction

China has quickly emerged as a main player in the global financial arena. It has some of the largest commercial banks and stock exchanges in the world. The state-dominated financial industry is undergoing a great transition towards a more market-based sector with multiple players and increased competition. The financial marketization process discussed in Chapter 1 has unleashed the growth potential of China's financial industry with improved efficiency in allocating financial resources. It is a key driver in the country's economic growth in the twenty-first century. However, the deregulation and the rise of free market also increase the possibility of bank runs and other types of financial crises which used to be rare in a socialist economy. Clearly, China's financial regulatory framework has been built upon the state-centred banking system dating back to the central planning economy. Although it has been constantly reformed during the four decades of economic reforms (1978–2018), the regulatory system is not always fully adapted to the industry growth and financial liberalization. The regime might sometimes restrict the further growth of its financial sector. Neither could it effectively cope with the rise of financial innovation and financial technology (Fintech) in the country, evidenced by the P2P lending crisis and the outright ban on crypto transactions.[1] Therefore, it is high time for us to examine the institutional structure of financial regulation in China, assessing its effectiveness, strengths, and potential drawbacks.

Chapter 2 examines China's latest financial regulatory architect by focusing on the changing institutional structure of financial regulation, while Chapter 3 continues to consider the building of a financial safety net (FSN) as crisis management mechanism. The Chinese government still has huge influence over the developments of the financial industry due to the country's distinctive economic and political environments. Therefore, it is natural

[1] *Financial Times*, 'Collapse of Chinese peer-to-peer lenders sparks investor flight' (by Gabriel Wildau and Yizhen Jia, 22 July 2018), https://www.ft.com/content/75e75628-8b27-11e8-bf9e-8771d5404543.

Towards Financial Superpower. Lerong Lu, Oxford University Press. © Lerong Lu (2025).
DOI: 10.1093/9780198948568.003.0002

to study the powerful state institutions governing banking and finance before the analysis of other market players like banks, securities firms, and Fintech corporations. After this introduction, Section 2.2 discusses China's overall financial regulatory objectives as regulators attempt to maintain financial stability, protect consumer interests, and promote industry competition. Section 2.3 introduces the reform of regulatory agencies and institutional frameworks. The chapter, then, assesses the functions of key regulatory institutions in China, including Central Financial Commission (CFC) and Central Financial Work Commission (CFWC) in Section 2.4, the People's Bank of China (PBoC) in Section 2.5, the National Financial Regulatory Administration (NFRA) in Section 2.6, and China Securities Regulatory Commission (CSRC) in Section 2.7. Section 2.8 draws a conclusion to this chapter.

2.2 The regulatory objectives

This section is concerned with the overall regulatory objectives for China's financial industry at the macro level. Regulatory authorities have their specific objectives at work as defined in their statutory mandates. For example, as the central bank, the PBoC is in charge of the making of monetary policies in order to maintain the stability of the currency value and thus promote economic growth.[2] As the capital markets regulator, the CSRC aims to maintain an orderly securities and futures market and ensure its operation is in line with relevant laws and regulations.[3] The monetary authority and financial regulators also have working priority at a certain time to address the mounting problems. However, financial regulation needs to be guided by an overarching set of principles to ensure its effectiveness. In the global context, investor and consumer protection, as well as financial stability, have long been the primary objectives of modern financial regulation.[4] The regulatory objectives in China's financial industry are as below.

2.2.1 The promotion of market competition and efficiency

First, it aims to inject more competition into the financial industry that is conducive to achieving better efficiency in capital allocation and helping China's economic reform towards a service-based economy. The objective of

[2] Law of the People's Republic of China on the People's Bank of China 2003, Article 3.
[3] China Securities Regulatory Commission, 'Overview', https://www.csrc.gov.cn/csrc_en/c102023/common_zcnr.shtml.
[4] John Armour et al., *Principles of Financial Regulation* (Oxford University Press, 2016), p. 61.

financial regulation is in line with the overall goal of China's market-oriented economic reform. The reform tends to let the market, or the invisible hand, play a larger role in the economy. The financial regulatory regime tends to strike a delicate balance of power between state and market in the operation of banking and finance. As discussed, China's financial industry is undergoing marketization to attract more private capital and foreign institutions to establish financial institutions and invest in financial markets.[5] The Chinese industry does need more players to break up the state monopoly in the banking, securities, and insurance sectors. In contrast to other economic segments where private enterprises now occupy a larger share than state-owned corporations (as private businesses accounted for 60% of national GDP), the financial industry is relatively conservative and largely dominated by state players. This is partly due to the strategic importance of the financial industry in the overall economy. As a result, the ruling party and government are unwilling to relinquish their control over banking and finance. Therefore, despite the goal to increase the level of competition and liberation in the industry, Chinese regulators by no means encourage private or foreign capital to assume a dominant role. In fact, regulators continue to protect state interests in the industry, or at least provide state players with preferential treatment in some cases. This has become clear when large private financial group attempts to challenge the position of state institutions. In November 2020, Ant Group, the world's largest fintech company owning the mobile payment network Alipay, was asked to suspend its $34.5 billion IPO due to regulatory concerns about its lending model and capital adequacy.[6] It was subsequently instructed to transform its business into a financial holding company, subjecting it to stricter prudential regulations similar to those applied to Chinese banks. Clearly, balancing the power between private and state players has remained a key task for Chinese regulators.

2.2.2 The maintenance of financial stability

Second, the regulation of China's financial industry has a primary focus on the maintenance of financial stability. Financial stability, or the wider economic and social stability, has always been a top priority for Chinese

[5] See Chapter 1, Section 1.2 'Financial marketization, financial globalization, and financial innovation'.

[6] Lerong Lu and Lingsheng Zhang, 'Regulating Fintech Corporations Amidst Covid-19 Pandemic: An Analysis of Ant Group (Alipay)'s Suspension of IPO and Business Restructuring' (2021) 42 *Company Lawyer* 341–343.

government. Preventing and mitigating financial risks, especially the systemic financial risks, remain a perpetual priority in financial regulatory work. Such risks can manifest suddenly, exhibiting the spill-over effect with great complexity and interconnectivity. Once contagion spreads in the financial industry, it can have a destructive influence on the national economy and social development. Accordingly, China has made efforts to establish a cross-department coordinated mechanism to protect financial stability, which is led by the CFC.[7] China has been promulgating its national Financial Stability Law to ensure that financial institutions, financial markets, and financial infrastructure consistently fulfil their essential roles. The Law aims to enhance the financial system's resilience against risks, promote its service to the real economy, prevent individual or regional risks from escalating into systemic ones, and maintain a systemic financial risk-free baseline.[8] Preventing financial risks and maintaining financial stability is also a key area of work for the PBoC, apart from its role in making monetary policies.[9] The regulators aim to build a comprehensive mechanism covering both ex-ante crisis prevention and ex-post crisis handling. As a result, China's financial industry remains stable and resilient, despite experiencing radical reforms and turbulent incidents, such as the Global Financial Crisis of 2007–2008, the COVID-19 pandemic, and China–US geopolitical tensions.

2.2.3 The protection of consumer and investor interests

Third, China's financial regulation aims to protect the consumers' fund safety and other legitimate interests. Regulators place significant emphasis on consumer protection for two reasons. On the one hand, China has the largest number of financial consumers in the world due to its 1.4 billion population. On the other, as a socialist regime, the Chinese government has a special responsibility to safeguard people's financial interests. This is reflected in the name of China's central bank as it is called the People's Bank. Moreover, enhancing consumer protection contributes to financial stability as well. When savers have confidence in their banks, bank runs are less likely, as they view banks as a safe place to deposit funds. China's deposit insurance offers each saver the protection of up to RMB 500,000 in the event of

[7] Reuters, 'China's He Lifeng named to key post in Central Financial Commission' (6 November 2023), https://www.reuters.com/world/china/china-appoints-he-lifeng-head-office-central-financial-commission-cbank-2023-11-06/.

[8] Financial Stability Law of the People's Republic of China (Draft, 2022), Article 2.

[9] Law of the People's Republic of China on the People's Bank of China 2003, Article 2.

bank insolvency or other crisis.[10] China is proposing to set up the national Financial Stability Guarantee Fund to deal with financial institutions in distress, with contribution from both private and public sectors such as the PBoC's relending facilities.[11] Regulators are actively engaged in financial consumer education to enhance consumers' knowledge and risk awareness. For example, in October 2023, the National Administration of Financial Regulation (NAFR), in collaboration with the PBoC and CSRC, organized a financial education month and released a total of twenty-eight typical cases of financial consumer rights protection, covering banking, securities, insurance, payment, and other fields.[12] In order to maintain the integrity and stability of the financial system and to foster public confidence, it is crucial to protect consumers in financial services.

2.2.4 The resolution of mounting financial risks

China now has a gigantic financial industry worth trillions of dollars. Its banks and insurance companies are among the largest in the world. It also holds three of the most active stock exchanges (Beijing, Shanghai, and Shenzhen stock exchanges) and thousands of public companies. Fintech firms have sprung across the country including top global players such as the Ant Group. The rapidly growing size of the financial industry, coupled with fintech innovations, has produced various financial risks endangering China's financial stability and economic growth. Some unpredictable financial risks in China are described as 'black swans' while other predictable elements are referred to as 'grey rhinos'.[13] The phrase 'black swan' denotes highly unexpected risks, and it has been popularized by Nassim Nicholas Taleb's book of the same name in 2007.[14] Some black swan incidents over the past decade include the Trump presidency in the United States, the UK vote to leave the European Union (Brexit), and the outbreak of the COVID-19 pandemic. In contrast, the term 'grey rhino', invented by Michele Wucker, has been used to describe large and predictable risks that are often ignored.[15] One typical

[10] Deposit Insurance Regulation, Article 5.

[11] Financial Stability Law of the People's Republic of China (Draft, 2022), Article 29.

[12] National Administration of Financial Regulation, 'NAFR, PBOC, and CSRC issued typical cases on the protection of financial consumers' rights and interests' (10 October 2023), https://www.cbirc.gov.cn/cn/view/pages/ItemDetail.html?docId=1130937&itemId=4099.

[13] Lerong Lu, 'Black Swans and Grey Rhinos: Demystifying China's Financial Risks and the Financial Regulatory Reform' (2018) 33 *Butterworths Journal of International Banking and Financial Law* 594–597.

[14] Nassim Nicholas Taleb, *The Black Swan: The Impact of the Highly Improbable* (Random House, 2007).

[15] Michele Wucker, *The Gray Rhino: How to Recognize and Act on the Obvious Dangers We Ignore* (St. Martin's Press, 2016).

example of a grey rhino incident is the Global Financial Crisis of 2007–2008 which was preceded by some early warning indicators. Nonetheless, both metaphors have been used by the *People's Daily*, China's official media, to describe mounting financial risks in the country's financial industry.[16] Evidently, the speedy growth of the financial industry and widespread financial innovations have given rise to various financial risks that are either black swans or grey rhinos. This section considers some major financial risks in China's financial industry, such as asset bubbles, mounting debt, and capital flight.

The asset bubbles: China has observed a series of asset bubbles over the past decade. For example, the Shanghai Stock Exchange (SSE) Composite Index climbed from 2,000 points in July 2014 to a peak of 5,166.35 points in June 2015.[17] The stock market mania was partly driven by leveraged investment instruments, as investors had borrowed funds from either stockbrokers or shadow banks to purchase shares. In its heyday, the P/E ratio of ChiNext board (China's equivalent to Nasdaq) reached 130, considered more than twice a reasonable level for businesses with strong growth prospects. Contrary to stock markets in the United States and the United Kingdom where institutional investors play a main role in making transactions, retail investors in China account for 90% of daily trading. From June 2014 to May 2015, over forty million securities dealing accounts were opened by retail investors hoping to take a bet on the rising trend.[18] After the SSE Composite Index reached its peak in June 2015, it began to fall rapidly and lost 30% of its value within the next three weeks. In particular, the Index slumped by 8.49% on 24 August 2015 which was dubbed 'Black Monday'. Global financial markets were significantly affected by China's stock crash. The Dow Jones Industrial Average dropped 1,000 points when it opened on Black Monday.[19] There has since been a bear market for a few years, despite the government's stimulus measures to boost investment and stock market performance. As of November 2023, the SSE Composite Index was standing at around 3,000 which is below 60% of its peak in 2015.

[16] *People's Daily*, 'Effectively prevent financial risks' (17 July 2017), http://opinion.people.com.cn/n1/2017/0717/c1003-29407958.html.

[17] Lerong Lu and Longjie Lu, 'Unveiling China's Stock Market Bubble: Margin Financing, the Leveraged Bull and Governmental Responses' (2017) 32 *Journal of International Banking Law and Regulation* 146.

[18] *Bloomberg*, 'There are now more stock traders in China than Communist Party members' (30 June 2015), https://www.bloomberg.com/news/articles/2015-06-30/in-communist-china-stock-market-capitalists-now-rule.

[19] *CNN*, 'After historic 1,000-point plunge, Dow dives 588 points at close' (by Matt Egan, 25 August 2015), http://money.cnn.com/2015/08/24/investing/stocks -markets-selloff-china-crash-dow/.

Aside from the equity bubble, China's property market has been on a rising trajectory since the early 2000s. Although the rise in property prices seems to be a global phenomenon, China's problem is extremely serious. In 2017, thirteen global cities experienced double-digit house price growth, with eight of them located in mainland China.[20] The average housing prices for prime residential properties in Beijing and Shanghai are $1,500 and $1,580 per square feet respectively, while the figures for London and New York are $1,770 and $1,570. The rising urban population, income, employment, and other positive fundamentals have collectively driven real demand, leading to housing prices growing over 600% in major Chinese cities over the past decade. This has not only triggered people's discontent over housing affordability, but also has an impact on the safety and soundness of the banking system. This is because the majority of funds in the property market come from state-owned banks. Property developers derive their working capital from bank loans while property investors borrow mortgage loans to finance their purchases. Moreover, local governments rely heavily on selling land as a vital source of revenue. Hence, the question of how to curb rapid housing price growth while ensuring financial resilience and fiscal health remains an important and challenging task for policymakers and financial regulators. The financial risks stemming from the property market became extremely serious from 2021 to 2023 when both property sales volume and prices began to decline. Some leading developers, such as Evergrande and Country Garden, started defaulting on their corporate bonds and bank loans, plunging into a debt crisis.[21]

The debt problem: A series of asset bubbles have revealed other critical economic issues such as the mounting debt in China's financial industry. The stock market craze and the continuing property market boom have largely been fuelled by debt. Investors borrow considerable capital through official financial institutions or grey-market shadow banks to fund their asset purchases, multiplying their buying power and thus increasing the asset prices. China's shadow banking system is worth CNY4–5 trillion, providing enormous funding for entrepreneurs and investors who have limited access to official banks.[22] Besides, after the global financial crisis, the Chinese government launched several rounds of financial stimulus packages, most notably

[20] Savills, 'China dominates global city rankings for house price growth' (12 February 2018), http://www.savills.co.uk/insight-and-opinion/savills-news/228041-0/china-dominates-global-city-rankings-for-house-price-growth, accessed 15 July 2018.

[21] *Financial Times*, 'China property: Accelerating meltdown threatens other markets' (25 September 2023), https://www.ft.com/content/790ceab3-3169-445f-aade-733daa50bb07.

[22] Lerong Lu, 'Shadow Banking for Cash-Strapped Entrepreneurs: A Study of Private Lending Agreements Under Chinese Contract Law' (2018) 3 *Journal of Business Law* 215.

the 4-trillion-yuan stimulus plan, to inject liquidity into the real economy.[23] However, the liquidity created did not entirely reach where it was most needed. The additional money generated by quantitative easing flowed into certain state-dominated industries, such as iron and steel, causing an over-capacity issue and giving rise to zombie enterprises. This, in turn, led to a high ratio of bad loans for large lenders. The excessive cash contributed to the asset price explosion, indicating the misallocation of financial resources in the economy. The disorderly flow of capital hinders the effectiveness of monetary and industry policies.

The mounting debt has presented significant challenges to economic growth, exposing serious financial risks. The rising debt-to-GDP ratio around the world has raised concerns about the occurrence of the next global financial crisis. China is no exception. According to the IMF, China's debt-to-GDP trebled over past three decades, reaching a level of 270% in 2022.[24] The rampant credit expansion has been described as unsustainable by some commentators. An economist from Deutsche Bank warned that the probability of a financial crisis in China is as high as 13%.[25] Others justify China's mounting debt by pointing out that the country has the highest savings rate and current account surplus in the world. China's financial system has more credit compared to other countries, raising questions about the long-term sustainability of its debt-driven economic growth. Whether a Minsky moment materializes in the coming years remains to be seen.[26]

The capital flight: Capital flight has been another dark cloud over China's economy. In recent years, capital worth $3.8 trillion has left China for other places.[27] Chinese citizens and companies have been moving money out of the country for various reasons. Some companies are using funds to acquire overseas business ventures. For example, the automobile maker Geely Holding which owns Geely Cars, Volvo Cars, and Lotus acquired 10% of shares in Daimler that owns Mercedes-Benz.[28] The overseas mergers and

[23] Geoff Dyer, 'China authorises "massive" stimulus package', *Financial Times* (10 November 2008), http://www.ft.com/content/6e89710e-ae91-11dd-b621-000077b07658, accessed 15 July 2018.

[24] IMF, 'Introductory remarks to the Fiscal Monitor Press Conference' (by Vitor Gaspar, 11 October 2023), https://www.imf.org/en/News/Articles/2023/10/11/introductory-remarks-to-the-fiscal-monitor-press-conference-vitor-gaspar.

[25] Will Martin, 'Deutsche Bank: A major financial crisis is almost twice as likely in China as anywhere else in the world', *Business Insider UK* (11 December 2017), http://uk.businessinsider.com/deutsche-bank-china-debt-financial-crisis-probability-2017-12, accessed 15 July 2018.

[26] A Minsky Moment refers to the period preceding a full market crash. It occurs when investors participate in high-risk speculative activities and elevate credit risks during prolonged periods of prosperity. *See* Hyman P. Minsky, *Stabilizing an Unstable Economy* (McGraw Hill, 2008).

[27] Frank R. Gunter, 'Why China lost about $3.8 trillion to capital flight in the last decade', *Forbes Inside Asia* (22 February 2017), http://www.forbes.com/sites/insideasia/2017/02/22/china-capital-flight-migration/, accessed 15 July 2018.

[28] Peter Campbell, 'Geely builds $9bn stake in Mercedes owner Daimler', *Financial Times* (24 February 2018), http://www.ft.com/content/68c57048-18c1-11e8-9376-4a6390addb44, accessed 15 July 2018.

acquisitions require Chinese corporations to exchange a large amount of Renminbi (RMB) into foreign currencies. In recent times, a cohort of Chinese private conglomerates, including HNA, Anbang, Fosun, and Wanda, has actively pursued the acquisition of companies and other overseas assets. This international buying spree has encompassed Anbang's $2 billion purchase of New York's Waldorf Astoria, Dalian Wanda's takeover of Hollywood studio Legendary Entertainment for $3.5 billion, and HNA's $40 billion acquisition of stakes in companies such as Deutsche Bank and Hilton Hotel.[29] The acquisitions partly explain the large amount of outgoing capital leaving China.

Moreover, an increasing number of Chinese people studying, travelling, or emigrating to other countries has boosted the demand for foreign currencies. China has been the largest source of international students in universities in the United Kingdom, the United States, Canada, and Australia. For instance, during the 2021–2022 academic year, there were 151,690 students from China enrolled in British higher education institutions.[30] The tuition fees, student accommodations, living expenses, and travelling costs amount to tens of billions of pounds each year. Moreover, Chinese citizens made 136.8 million overseas trips in 2016 and spent $292 billion abroad.[31] Some Chinese citizens use crypto trading, such as Bitcoins, to exchange RMB for foreign currencies and evade the foreign exchange quota imposed by the authorities.[32] Clearly, the capital fight problem has eaten into China's enormous foreign currency reserves and creates depreciation pressure on the RMB, which has been a particular concern for Chinese regulators.

2.3 The reform of regulatory agencies and institutional framework

Preventing and mitigating financial risks, especially those threatening financial stability, has remained a top priority for China's financial authorities. In order to tame the financial risks of black swans and grey rhinos, China

[29] Tom Hancock and Lucy Hornby, 'China conglomerates suffer different fates in Beijing crackdown', *Financial Times* (23 February 2018), http://www.ft.com/content/8ed61466-186e-11e8-9376-4a6390addb44, accessed 15 July 2018.

[30] Study in the UK, 'International Chinese student guide to UK universities' (28 March 2023), https://www.studyin-uk.com/study-guide/chinese-student-guide-uk-universities/.

[31] Sally Peck, 'The truth about Chinese travellers', *The Telegraph* (25 July 2017), http://www.telegraph.co.uk/travel/destinations/asia/china/how-chinese-tourists-travel-etiquette-and-money/, accessed 15 July 2018.

[32] Lerong Lu, 'Bitcoin: Speculative Bubble, Financial Risk and Regulatory Response' (2018) 33 *Butterworths Journal of International Banking and Financial Law* 178–182.

has been carrying out a series of financial reforms, such as the restructure of the financial regulatory architecture. For a long time (2003–2018), China's financial regulatory system had been widely known as 'one bank, three commissions'. 'One bank' refers to the PBoC which oversees monetary policy, while 'three commissions' means the China Banking Regulatory Commission (CBRC), the CSRC, and the China Insurance Regulatory Commission (CIRC). These are responsible for conduct and prudential regulation in their respective areas.

However, the sector-based regulatory framework of 'one bank, three commissions' is considered too fragmented to detect and manage systemic risks in the entire financial industry as banking, securities, and insurance activities have become highly intertwined in practice. It resulted in unclear responsibilities, cross-regulation, and other regulatory loopholes in the old regulatory regime. For instance, the 2015 stock market crash highlighted the popularity of leveraged investment instruments that derive funding from both official banking and unofficial shadow banking channels.[33] There have been calls for further coordination and cooperation between banking and securities regulators to resolve the excessive use of margin finance in securities markets. Moreover, the insurance company Anbang Group's aggressive overseas M&A activities have been largely funded by the premium collected from policyholders. Anbang ranked among the world's largest insurers with around $300 billion in assets, holding stakes in hotels and financial firms across America, Europe, and Asia.[34] Its sudden downfall in 2017–2018, involving the state takeover of its business and the arrest of its founder, signalled the complexity in regulating China's financial giants and the need to reform its regulatory regime. The investment operations relying on debt and leverage generate huge credit, liquidity, and systemic risks, which can only be effectively regulated through the close collaboration of multiple regulators or the consolidation of regulatory powers into one agency.

In order to deleverage the financial industry and limit financial risks, China has been conducting financial reforms to streamline the regulatory framework. As of the end of 2023, the new central regulatory regime consists of four agencies: the CFC, the People's Bank of China (PBoC), the NAFR, and the China Securities Regulatory Commission (CSRC). Figure 2.1 illustrates the current regulatory bodies overseeing China's financial industry and

[33] Lerong Lu and Longjie Lu, 'Unveiling China's Stock Market Bubble: Margin Financing, the Leveraged Bull and Governmental Responses' (2017) 32 *Journal of International Banking Law and Regulation* 146–160.

[34] *The Economist*, 'The rapid rise and fall of the Anbang empire' (23 February 2018).

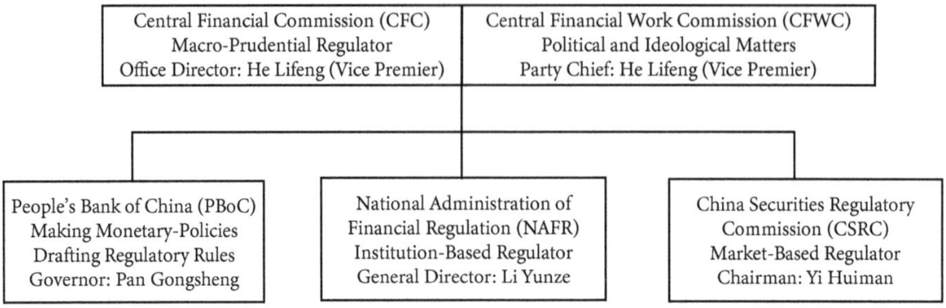

Figure 2.1 The institutional structure of China's financial regulatory system (2024)
Source: The figure is compiled by the author.

the persons in charge. The history, functions, and mandates of such regulatory agencies will be discussed in the following sections. Nonetheless, China's regulatory architecture is huge and complicated, which also includes local regulatory agencies like local governments' financial affairs offices that will not be covered here. Also, the institutional cooperation with international financial organizations (e.g. IMF, WB, BIS, FSB, and IOSCO) and the application of international regulatory norms like Basel accords will not be discussed here. They will be addressed in other parts of the book where it is necessary. Furthermore, the FSN will be discussed in Chapter 3, while the financial law courts and other dispute resolution mechanisms will be introduced in Chapter 7.

2.4 Central Financial Commission (CFC) and Central Financial Work Commission (CFWC)

At the pinnacle of China's financial regulatory regime is the CFC, which is responsible for overall supervising the financial system, ensuring financial stability, and achieving other strategic goals set by the ruling Communist Party of China (CPC) and the Chinese government.[35] In March 2023, the CFC was established by the 'Party and State Institutional Reform Plan'. The CFC replaced its predecessor—the Financial Stability and Development Committee (FSDC) of the State Council—as a super regulator for the financial industry. The CFC has an executive body called the CFC Office, with its director being China's Vice Premier He Lifeng, and the general office is

[35] The Central Financial Commission (CFC) is a commission of the Central Committee of the Chinese Communist Party (CCP), and it directly reports to the CCP. Legally speaking, it is a party organ but not a state institution.

located in the Beijing Financial Street. Having a vice premier as its direct leader has demonstrated the status of the CFC within China's institutional governance structure. The CFC commenced operations in September 2023. The CFC Office has recruited personnel from various financial institutions, including the PBoC, the Ministry of Finance, and the National Development and Reform Commission. Meanwhile, another important Party organ called CFWC was also launched in March 2023. Vice Premier He was also appointed as the Party chief for CFWC. The CFWC is in charge of political and ideological matters in the financial system, especially for state-owned financial institutions. The CFWC has been sharing the office and personnel with the CFC in Beijing. Given that both CFC and CFWC are party-led commissions, it is suggested that the CPC has strengthened direct and unified supervision, or control, over China's financial industry.

It is worth mentioning the FSDC as it played a vital role in China's financial governance and economic development from 2017 to 2023. In November 2017, the first cross-sector regulatory body, the FSDC, was officially launched.[36] The FSDC, dubbed as the super financial regulator, is a specialist committee under the central government and cabinet (State Council). As an inter-agency coordinating body, the FSDC has been tasked with the mandates of strengthening macro-prudential regulation and preventing systemic risks. It also ensures the resilience of China's financial industry in the face of evolving global challenges. Ma Kai, then the vice premier of China, served as the inaugural chairman of the FSDC, indicating the important status of this new organization. The functions and powers of the FSDC are similar to that of the Financial Policy Committee in the United Kingdom. The FSDC oversees urgent and important matters relating to financial stability and resilience. It facilitates high-level coordination between the different financial authorities. The FSDC's arrangement reflects its comprehensive regulatory approach, bringing together key regulatory and policymaking bodies. Representatives from the PBoC, the China Banking and Insurance Regulatory Commission (CBIRC), the CSRC, and other financial authorities collaborate within the FSDC to formulate consistent policies that address risks relating to financial stability. Furthermore, the FSDC actively engages with international financial organizations like the IMF, World Bank, and Bank for International Settlements, contributing to global financial governance dialogues and sharing China's experiences and insights in managing financial affairs. As China seeks to integrate further into the international

[36] Zhou Xin, 'China's super financial regulator headed by vice-premier more powerful than ministries', *South China Morning Post* (8 November 2017), http://www.scmp.com/news/china/economy/article/2119001/chinas-super-financial-regulator-headed-vice-premier-more, accessed 15 July 2018.

financial markets, the FSDC played an increasingly important role in aligning the national financial policies with international norms and best practices. In July 2018, the first meeting of the new FSDC was held and the then vice premier Liu He who is in charge of China's economic and financial affairs began to serve as its chairman.[37] The FSDC successfully performed its super regulatory role for five years before handing over power to the CFC in 2023.

2.5 The People's Bank of China (PBoC)

The PBoC was established in December 1948 to work as the central bank and monetary authority for the new People's Republic of China which was founded one year later in 1949.[38] The PBoC was consolidated upon three banks: the Huabei Bank, the Beihai Bank, and the Xibei Farmer Bank. From 1948 to 1952, in the period of national economic recovery, the PBoC started to establish a unified national banking system under the leadership of the Central People's Government.[39] Between 1953 and 1978, the PBoC was the only bank in the nation and oversaw both central banking and commercial banking operations.[40] All other banks within mainland China, such as the Bank of China, were either divisions of the PBoC or did not accept deposits. It managed currency circulation, provided credit, and functioned as the monetary authority and a centre for monitoring the implementation of the national economic plans. When China started to launch the market-oriented economic reform in 1978, the PBoC gradually restored its main role as the central bank and stopped its commercial banking operation.[41] Its non-central banking functions have been transferred to other banks like the restoration of Agricultural Bank of China (ABC), and the restoration of the People's Insurance Company of China (PICC) to resume insurance operations, and establishment of trust and investment companies as well as urban credit cooperatives.

In September 1983, the State Council decided to have the PBoC function as a central bank. The Chinese central banking law formally adopted on 18 March 1995 by the third Plenum of the eighth National People's Congress has since legally confirmed the PBoC's central bank status. Since

[37] China Government, 'The New FSDC Held the First Meeting' (3 July 2018), http://www.gov.cn/guowuyuan/2018-07/03/content_5303229.htm, accessed 15 July 2018.

[38] The People's Bank of China, 'Purposes and functions', http://www.pbc.gov.cn/en/3688066/3688080/index.html.

[39] The People's Bank of China, 'A brief history of the People's Bank of China', http://www.pbc.gov.cn/en/3688066/3688089/index.html.

[40] Ibid.

[41] Ibid.

then, the PBoC has been playing a vital and indispensable role in China's socialist market economy, in particular, the macroeconomic management. In 2003, the Chinese central banking law underwent major amendment by the National People's Congress, confirming the following major functions of PBoC:[42] (1) drafting and enforcing relevant laws, rules, and regulations that are related to fulfilling its functions; (2) formulating and implementing monetary policy in accordance with law; (3) issuing RMB and administering its circulation; (4) regulating the inter-bank lending market and the inter-bank bond market; (5) administering foreign exchange regulation and supervising the inter-bank foreign exchange market; (6) regulating the gold market; (7) holding and managing the foreign exchange and gold reserves of the state; (8) managing the state treasury; (9) maintaining the normal operation of the payment, clearing, and settlement systems; (10) providing guidance for the anti-money laundering (AML) work in the financial industry and being responsible for monitoring the movement of funds for the AML purpose; (11) being responsible for statistics, survey, analysis, and projection concerning the financial industry; (12) engaging in relevant international financial activities in its capacity as the central bank of the state; and (13) other functions and responsibilities prescribed by the State Council. Also in 2003, the CBRC was established to take over from the PBoC the functions of supervising banks, financial asset management companies, trust and investment companies, and other deposit-taking financial institutions.

The PBoC has its headquarters in Beijing with main responsibilities of formulating and implementing China's monetary policies, ensuring overall financial stability, and promoting sustainable economic developments.[43] The PBoC maintains several regional branches, situated in key cities such as Tianjin, Shenyang, Shanghai, Nanjing, Jinan, Wuhan, Guangzhou, Chengdu, and Xi'an. Furthermore, there are municipal sub-branches distributed throughout the country. The PBoC is responsible for the issuance and management of China's national currency—the Renminbi (RMB) or Chinese yuan. More recently, it has taken on the role of experimenting with the digital yuan, known as the Digital Currency Electronic Payment (DCEP) project, as China's next-generation central bank digital currency (CBDC).[44] Clearly, the PBoC holds exclusive authority to regulate the money supply, adjust interest rates, and intervene in foreign exchange rates, exerting substantial influence

[42] The Law of the People's Republic of China on the People's Bank of China, 2003, Article 4.

[43] The central banking functions, including its making and implementation of monetary policies, will be discussed in detail in Chapter 3.

[44] Lu, L. & Zhang, L., 'Could the "Dragon" Now Fly Beyond Borders? Contextualizing Regulatory Aspects and Risks for China's CBDC Cross-Border Use' (2022) 14:S *Tsinghua China Law Review* 19–44.

over China's overall economic operation. The PBoC is run by a board of directors, including its Governor Pan Gongsheng who is also the head of State Administration of Foreign Exchange (SAFE), three deputy governors, and a chief inspector.[45] Throughout its history, the PBoC has had thirteen governors since its foundation.[46] The State Council Institution Reform Plan in 2018 resulted in the PBoC being granted expanded powers in terms of prudential financial regulation and the authority to formulate laws and regulations in the areas of banking and insurance.[47]

The PBoC's responsibilities extend beyond traditional central banking functions defined by Western economists.[48] It actively participates in financial markets development, overseeing banking operations, and managing China's foreign exchange reserves which are the world's largest. As of October 2023, the PBoC held a total foreign exchange reserve of $3.1 trillion, along with other official reserve assets like IMF reserve position ($9.58 billion), Special Drawing Rights ($52.31 billion), and Gold ($142.17 billion).[49] The multiple roles that the PBoC plays shows its importance in shaping both domestic and global economic growth, given its diverse functions compared with central banks in liberal capitalism. Over the past four decades, the PBoC has changed over time to accommodate the complicated circumstances of China's quickly developing economy. It has supported the internationalization of the RMB, interest rate liberalization, and financial reforms. As China strives to accomplish financial openness and enhance its economic influence across the globe, the PBoC has played an instrumental part in the establishment of currency swap agreements, promotion of financial connectivity, and participation in international monetary cooperation. Compared with China's economic weight measured by GDP as a percentage of the world total (around 20%), the share of RMB in the global reserve portfolio is just 3%. This suggests that the PBoC has a long way to go in promoting the internationalization of the RMB. Nonetheless, the PBoC also faces difficulties, such as striking a careful balance between promoting economic expansion and mitigating financial risks. It is evidenced by a series of corporate and financial crises over past five years, like the failures of Anbang and Evergrande.

[45] The People's Bank of China, 'Management team', http://www.pbc.gov.cn/en/3688066/3688083/index.html

[46] The People's Bank of China, 'Former governors', http://www.pbc.gov.cn/en/3688066/3688086/index.html.

[47] Lerong Lu, 'Black Swans and Grey Rhinos: Demystifying China's Financial Risks and the Financial Regulatory Reform' (2018) 33 *Butterworths Journal of International Banking and Financial Law* 594–597.

[48] The PBoC's role in the making of monetary policies and managing economy will be discussed in Chapter 4, Section 4.2 'Central banking: devising effective monetary policy tools'.

[49] The State Administration of Foreign Exchange, 'Official reserve assets', https://www.safe.gov.cn/safe/2022/0207/20625.html.

2.6 The National Administration of Financial Regulation (NAFR)

In May 2023, the NAFR was officially established as a new central financial regulatory agency to enforce the financial laws and regulations and to supervise all parts of China's financial industry apart from the securities markets.[50] The securities markets are still regulated by the CSRC. The launch of NAFR, which is directly under the State Council of Chinese government, marks an important step in the country's institutional reform on financial supervision. The NAFR stands as a pivotal institution in China's financial regulatory system, wielding authority over the banking and insurance sectors. Figure 2.2 provides an illustration of the historical evolution of the NAFR over the past decades. It was created to replace the CBIRC as well as taking over some regulatory functions from the PBoC and CSRC. The NAFR is overseeing 400 trillion yuan ($58 trillion) of banking and insurance assets, making it one of the most powerful financial regulators in the world.[51] The executive body of NAFR consists of one general director, four deputy directors, and one chief inspector. The current general director is Li Yunze (May 2023 to present). With the headquarter located in Beijing Financial Street, the NAFR has thirty-six dispatched agencies in all Chinese provinces and municipalities.[52] One of the key roles of NAFR is consumer protection and public education. It will need to: (a) conduct consumer rights protection policy guidance, knowledge popularization, and consumer education activities; (b) guide the public to improve their ability to correctly understand and

Figure 2.2 The historical development of National Financial Regulatory Administration

Source: The figure is compiled by the author.

[50] The State Council of China, 'China establishes national financial regulatory administration' (18 May 2023), https://english.www.gov.cn/news/202305/18/content_WS6465bd1ac6d03ffcca6ed27f.html.

[51] Lee, Amanda, 'China's financial overhaul continues with banking veteran Li Yunze named party chief of new regulatory body', *South China Morning Post* (10 May 2023).

[52] National Administration of Financial Regulation, 'Institution introduction', https://www.cbirc.gov.cn/cn/view/pages/jigougaikuang/jigougaikuang.html.

access financial products and services; and (c) publicize relevant risk tips and typical cases to help the public enhance their awareness and ability to protect their rights according to law.[53]

The predecessor of NAFR is the CBIRC that has a relatively short life of five years (2018–2023). The CBIRC is an institution-based regulator supervising banking and insurance institutions, especially those with systemic importance. Established in 2018 as part of a comprehensive structural overhaul of China's financial regulatory framework, the CBIRC was formed through the merger of the CBRC and the CIRC.[54] This merger aimed to streamline regulatory functions, enhance efficiency, and fortify the supervision of financial institutions to foster stability and resilience in the sector. The CBIRC's creation emerged in response to the evolving complexities within China's financial sector. Mixed operation has become common for some largest financial groups in China whose businesses engage in banking, insurance, and investments, such as Ping'an Group and Citic Group. It makes the separation of regulatory agencies implausible in practice. Therefore, the merger of the CBRC and CIRC was a strategic move to address overlapping responsibilities, ensure a unified regulatory approach, and strengthen risk management in the banking and insurance industries. Prior to this consolidation, the CBRC and CIRC operated independently, focusing on their respective domains. The CBRC was set up in 2003 as China's independent regulator for the banking industry to address the problems like increasing bad loans, undercapitalization, and non-transparent business practices. The CIRC was established in 1998 to regulate the Chinese insurance products and services market and maintain legal and stable operation of the insurance industry. Both CBRC and CIRC were authorized by the State Council to perform their regulatory duties and enjoy the power as a ministerial institution. CBRC and CIRC ceased operation due to their merger in 2018, suggesting a significant step towards achieving a more integrated and comprehensive regulatory framework.

The CBIRC officially commenced operation on 8 April 2018, under the leadership of its inaugural Chairman, Guo Shuqing. As a seasoned financial expert with experience in both banking and insurance, Guo played a pivotal role in steering the CBIRC through its formative years. The establishment of the CBIRC was accompanied by a broader initiative to enhance regulatory

[53] National Administration of Financial Regulation, 'Institution introduction', https://www.cbirc.gov.cn/cn/view/pages/jigougaikuang/jigougaikuang.html.

[54] State Council Institution Reform Plan, passed during the 2018 annual session of the National People's Congress.

capabilities and align China's financial regulatory framework with international standards. The CBIRC's primary mandate is to regulate and supervise the banking and insurance sectors to ensure their sound operation, mitigate risks, and safeguard the interests of stakeholders. Its regulatory scope encompasses a diverse array of financial institutions, including commercial banks, insurance companies, trust companies, and other entities engaged in banking and insurance-related activities. One of the CBIRC's central functions is to formulate and implement prudential regulations that govern the conduct of financial institutions under its jurisdiction. These regulations cover a spectrum of areas, including risk management, capital adequacy, corporate governance, and disclosure requirements. By setting and enforcing these standards, the CBIRC aims to foster a stable and resilient financial ecosystem that can withstand financial risks and economic challenges. Risk prevention and control represent key focal points for the CBIRC. The commission employs a risk-based regulatory approach, conducting regular assessments of financial institutions to identify and address potential vulnerabilities. The commission actively engages with international counterparts, participates in global regulatory forums, and strives to harmonize its regulatory framework with international best practices. Such efforts not only contribute to the development of a robust domestic financial system but also position China as a responsible and cooperative player in the global financial community. With the launched of NAFR in 2023, most of the CBIRC's functions and powers have been handed over to the new agency.

2.7 China Securities Regulatory Commission (CSRC)

The China Securities Regulatory Commission (CSRC) is the main regulator of China's capital markets and the securities industry. The Chinese modern securities markets have a relatively short history of forty years, with the Shanghai and Shenzhen stock exchanges established in 1990, and the latest addition, the Beijing Stock Exchange, launched in 2021.[55] China now possesses the world's second-largest capital market, trailing only the United States. It holds over 3,600 publicly listed companies, 156 million investors, and a network of more than 130 securities companies or stockbrokers.[56] The CSRC, established in 1992, has become an important and powerful

[55] Lerong Lu, 'Beijing Stock Exchange and Multi-Tier Capital Markets: How China Alters Share Listing and Trading Rules to Promote SME Finance?' (2022) 43 *Company Lawyer* 233–237, ISSN: 0144-1027 (with Ye, J.).

[56] *Xinhua*, 'From zero start, China now has the second largest capital market in the world' (8 October 2019), http://www.xinhuanet.com/fortune/2019-10/08/c_1210303693.htm, accessed 8 January 2020.

regulatory authority overseeing China's dynamic and rapidly growing securities markets that include stock markets, bond markets, future markets, and other securities-related activities. The formation of CSRC marked a critical step in the country's continuing financial reforms, showing the government's commitment to building a transparent, efficient, and investor-friendly marketplace for domestic and international investors. The CSRC, apart from its unique role in boosting economic growths and free-market reforms, aims to protect the integrity and stability of Chinese capital markets. The CSRC operates under the State Council's direct authority, forming a key part of China's financial regulatory framework. It is working as the market-based regulator as opposed to the NAFR which serves as the institution-based regulator. According to the *PRC Securities Law*, the securities regulatory body under the State Council (i.e. CSRC) is mandated to exercise centralized and unified supervision and administration over the country's securities markets; when deemed necessary, it has the authority to establish representative offices to carry out supervision and administration duties as authorized.[57] The head office of CSRC is located in Beijing, with the appointment of one chairman, four vice chairmen, and one secretary of the Disciplinary Inspection Commission.[58] In its central office, the CSRC comprises eighteen functional departments, one inspection division, and three centres. At the regional level, the commission has established thirty-six securities regulatory bureaus in provinces, autonomous regions, municipalities, and some special cities. Additionally, it operates the Shanghai Commissioner Office and Shenzhen Commissioner Office where the two main national stock exchanges are located.

The CSRC carries out a diverse range of duties in fulfilling its role as the securities regulator:[59] (1) study and formulate policies, development plans, and relevant laws and regulations for the securities and futures markets; (2) exercise vertical administration over domestic securities and futures regulatory institutions, ensuring unified supervision over the securities and futures markets; (3) supervise the issuance, listing, trading, custody, and settlement of various securities, including stocks, convertible bonds, and bonds of securities companies; (4) supervise securities market behaviours of listed companies and their shareholders in adherence to relevant laws and regulations; (5) monitor the listing, trading, and settlement of domestic

[57] Securities Law of the People's Republic of China 2020, Article 7.

[58] China Securities Regulatory Commission, 'About CSRC', http://www.csrc.gov.cn/csrc_en/c102023/common_zcnr.shtml.

[59] China Securities Regulatory Commission, 'About CSRC', http://www.csrc.gov.cn/csrc_en/c102023/common_zcnr.shtml.

contract-based futures, and oversee overseas futures businesses of domestic institutions; (6) supervise securities and futures exchanges, senior managerial personnel, and associations in the sector; (7) oversee securities and futures business institutions, investment fund management companies, depository and clearing corporations, and other related entities; (8) supervise the overseas issuance and listing of shares by domestic enterprises, as well as the listing of convertible bonds by companies listed overseas; (9) supervise the establishment of overseas securities and futures institutions by domestic entities and vice versa; (10) manage the communication of securities and futures information and handle statistics and information resources for the markets; (11) collaborate with relevant authorities in examining and approving the qualifications of accounting firms, asset evaluation institutions, lawyers, and law firms engaged in securities and futures intermediary businesses; (12) investigate and penalize activities that violate securities and futures laws and regulations; (13) administer foreign exchanges and international cooperation affairs in the securities and futures sector; and (14) the CSRC is also entrusted with any other duties assigned by the State Council.

The CSRC is tasked with enforcing the securities laws and regulations in China. Its primary functions encompass a broad range of regulatory activities, from rule-making to enforcement and market supervision. The CSRC oversees securities issuances, securities transactions, mergers and acquisitions, and the conduct of market participants to ensure fair and orderly market operation. Additionally, the CSRC is responsible for formulating and implementing regulations governing the practices and proper behaviours of listed companies, securities firms, and other entities within its jurisdiction. The CSRC holds the authority to issue guideline opinions, which, although not legally binding, serve as a reference for publicly traded corporations. Throughout its thirty years of history, the CSRC has played a vital role in steering the development of China's financial industry. The securities regulator has carried out a series of reforms to enhance market transparency, combat securities crimes, attract foreign investment, and bring Chinese domestic securities practices in line with international standards. As China seeks to integrate into international financial markets, the CSRC has made great efforts in opening up the stock exchanges to foreign investors, such as the launch of Shanghai–London Stock Connect and Shanghai–Hong Kong Stock Connect.[60] Such initiatives facilitate the direct access for international investors to join Chinese markets and allow international businesses

[60] Ningyao Ye and Lerong Lu, 'Building A Eurasian Capital Market: Understanding the Operating Mechanism and Legal Framework of Shanghai-London Stock Connect' (2020) 35 *Journal of International Banking Law and Regulation* 67–74.

to pursue a secondary listing in China. In the ever-changing landscape of the Chinese securities markets, the CSRC has been at the forefront of navigating possibilities and difficulties. Reflecting the government's high-level economic goals, its work goes beyond regulatory oversight to include the promotion of innovation and sustainable growth in capital markets. For instance, the latest Beijing Stock Exchange, regulated by the CSRC, is welcoming the listings of innovative SMEs in advanced manufacturing and modern service industries, with more relaxed listing standards regarding the market capitalization, dual class shares structure (DCSS), and variable interest entities (VIE).[61] In 2023, the CSRC was granted the power for auditing corporate bond issuances, taking over this role from the National Development and Reform Commission.

2.8 Conclusion

This chapter has discussed and analysed the overall regulatory objectives of financial regulation in China. First, the goal is to increase competition within the financial industry, enhancing capital allocation efficiency and aiding China's transition to a service-based economy. Second, a major focus is maintaining financial stability. Ensuring financial stability, and by extension broader economic and social stability, has always been a top priority for the Chinese government. Preventing and mitigating financial risks, particularly systemic ones, remain a constant regulatory priority. Third, the regulation aims to protect consumers' funds and other legitimate interests. With the world's largest population of financial consumers, China places significant emphasis on consumer protection. Fourth, financial regulation seeks to address significant financial risks in China, such as asset bubbles, debt issues, and capital flight.

The chapter has also assessed China's reform of regulatory agencies and their institutional frameworks. It introduces the historical evolution of Chinese regulators from the sector-based regulatory framework of 'one bank, three commissions' to the current system consisting of four agencies: the CFC, the People's Bank of China (PBoC), the NAFR, and the China Securities Regulatory Commission (CSRC). CFC is responsible for the overall supervision of the financial system, ensuring financial stability, and achieving strategic goals set by the CPC and the Chinese government. PBoC serves as

[61] Lerong Lu, 'Beijing Stock Exchange and Multi-Tier Capital Markets: How China Alters Share Listing and Trading Rules to Promote SME Finance?' (2022) 43 *Company Lawyer* 233–237, ISSN: 0144-1027 (with Ye, J.).

the central bank and monetary authority, responsible for making monetary policies and promoting economic growth. NAFR was officially established in 2023 as a central financial regulatory agency to enforce financial laws and regulations and supervise all parts of China's financial industry apart from the securities markets. NAFR is the main regulator for banking and insurance institutions. CSRC is the main regulator of China's capital markets and the securities industry. The CSRC supervises over 3,600 publicly listed companies and protects the interests of 156 million investors. This chapter lays the foundation for understanding China's financial regulatory framework and the ongoing efforts to enhance the efficiency, stability, and consumer protection within its financial industry.

Chapter 3
China's financial safety net

3.1 Introduction

Following the previous discussion on financial regulatory architecture, Chapter 3 considers China's financial safety net (FSN) as the important infrastructure of the country's financial industry. FSN plays a vital role in maintaining the systematic stability of financial industry. As China deepens its financial industry reform to attract more investment from private and international investors, the increased competition is likely to raise the possibility of bank runs and financial crises, which were previously uncommon in the socialist market economy. In light of this, the analysis in Chapter 3 focuses on China's latest financial regulatory reform and proposes the building of a well-functioning FSN. It argues for the necessity and urgency for China to introduce a modern FSN to accommodate the liberalization, innovation, and internationalization of its financial industry. It examines to what extent China's financial regulatory regime is capable of coping with potential financial crises and bank insolvency, which is a natural result of competition in a free-market economy. The discussion pays attention to whether consumer interests and financial stability could be safeguarded in the event of crises. Section 3.2 assesses the FSN's role in the financial industry and how it fits into the overall regulatory framework, explaining China's efforts in building the FSN to promote financial stability and consumer protection. The rest of the chapter considers three main pillars of an effective FSN: the deposit insurance system (Section 3.3), the lender of last resort (LOLR) (Section 3.4), and the bank insolvency regime (Section 3.5). The analysis draws on the experience of the US and other jurisdictions that have more established more mature financial regulatory regimes. Section 3.6 draws a conclusion to this chapter.

Towards Financial Superpower. Lerong Lu, Oxford University Press. © Lerong Lu (2025).
DOI: 10.1093/9780198948568.003.0003

3.2 Withstanding financial crisis: building a financial safety net for China

The strength and resilience of financial industry represent the core competitiveness of a nation, and financial safety constitutes an important component of national safety. It is important to enhance the prevention and resolution of systemic financial risks, safeguard national economic and financial security, and construct a robust FSN. The key focus of establishing an FSN lies in stabilizing market sentiment when financial institutions face runs, bankruptcies, or other risk events. This is achieved by protecting the interests of depositors (or investors), preventing risk spill-overs and contagion, reducing the likelihood of individual risks escalating into systemic risks. This, therefore, is likely to minimize the cost of fiscal rescues for the failing financial institutions. In China, preventing and resolving financial risks, especially preventing systemic financial risks, has been the eternal theme of the financial regulatory work.[1] Accordingly, China continues to deepen the financial system reforms and promote the construction of the FSN, with the aim to strengthen its capacity to better prevent and control systemic financial risks.

Banking institutions play a vital role in the economy as they receive deposits from the public and make loans to individuals, corporations, and anyone in need of funds. A robust and effective banking system supports the country's payment infrastructure, and improves investment, economic growth, and financial intermediation. Therefore, banks have been treated differently compared with other financial institutions, given their essential functions. Due to the maturity mismatch between their assets and debts, banks are subject to runs that could cause contagion and system risks. Throughout the world, banking crisis always happens on a massive scale, causing damaging and contagious effects. During the 2007–2008 financial crisis, large banking institutions went into crises, from the Lehman Brothers in the United States to the Royal Bank of Scotland in the United Kingdom. More recently in 2023, major banks like Credit Suisse and Silicon Valley also experienced severe liquidity crises.[2] Evidently, if developing countries like China continue their market-based financial reforms, the increased competition will likely cause the failure of some banks in the future. It calls for the financial regulators to establish crisis management mechanisms in advance.

[1] *People*, 'Preventing and defusing financial risks requires a good grasp of two relationships' (6 November 2023), http://theory.people.com.cn/n1/2023/1106/c40531-40110869.html.

[2] Stephen Morris, James Fontanella-Khan, and Arash Massoudi, 'How The Swiss "Trinity" Forced UBS To Save Credit Suisse', *The Financial Times* (20 March 2023), https://www.ft.com/content/3080d368-d5aa-4125-a210-714e37087017.

To reduce the potential economic and social damages caused by bank failures, it is important for the country to establish FSN, which is a framework that basically includes three pillars: deposit insurance scheme, LOLR, and bank insolvency regulation. In most economies, an FSN typically involves the work of the central bank acting as a provider of emergency liquidity assistance (which may also be responsible for the regulation and supervision of individual banks in some nations), the banking regulator, and the Ministry of Finance.[3] As the banking industry is under fierce competition with expanding risks, it has become a consensus that a robust, efficient, and viable FSN is highly desirable. The interaction among different participants of the FSN, including the regulator, lender-of-last-resort, and deposit insurer, is crucial for the overall backup mechanism and the protection of less sophisticated depositors.[4] Therefore, this interaction needs to be carefully designed.

The FSN plays a fundamental role in the financial system, offering protection for individuals and businesses during financial distress. It is designed to cushion against sudden economic downturns, ensuring economic stability, strengthening bank resilience, and protecting financial institutions from the worst impacts of financial crises. Moreover, the FSN can provide emergency liquidity to the economy, ensuring that financial institutions and businesses have access to the capital needed for operation and growth during urgent situations, thus contributing to the overall financial stability and safety of the country.[5] For these reasons, an integrated approach to the FSN is a major public concern in most countries. Special government policies need to be designed to limit bank failures and the potential panic they can cause. The FSN, which includes emergency liquidity injections from central banks, explicit deposit insurance, and special treatment of bank insolvency and regulations, functions as a government backstop. These measures are designed to limit banks' exposure to credit, market, and liquidity risks, as well as general insolvency risks within the nation's financial system.[6]

In 2023, Chinese President Xi Jinping emphasized the need to protect the new development paradigm with a new security framework, actively

[3] Andrew Campbell, 'Insolvent Banks and the Financial Sector Safety Net-Lessons from the Northern Rock Crisis' (2008) 20 *Singapore Academy of Law Journal* 316.

[4] Winston Keith Carr, 'Measures to Promote Effective Interrelationships Among Financial Safety Net Participants' (2006) 8 *Journal of Banking Regulation* 73.

[5] Kenneth Jones and Barry Kolatch, 'The Federal Safety Net, Banking Subsidies, and Implications for Financial Modernization' (1999) 12 *FDIC Banking Review* 1.

[6] Jeanne Gobat, 'Banks: At the Heart of the Matter', IMF, https://www.imf.org/en/Publications/fandd/issues/Series/Back-to-Basics/Banks.

shaping a favourable security environment for China.[7] Financial security is a vital component of national security and a crucial foundation for stable and healthy economic development. Safeguarding financial security is a strategic and fundamental task that impacts the overall development of China's economy and society. Since the 1990s, China's financial industry has achieved historic accomplishments, marked by orderly progress in financial reform and opening up, an increasing variety of financial products, enhanced inclusiveness of financial services, and strengthened financial regulation. However, effectively resolving major financial risks requires a continued focus on improving financial services, establishing a robust FSN, and maintaining the bottom line of preventing systemic financial risks. Overall, China's financial situation is favourable, and financial risks are manageable. Nevertheless, in the face of combined pressures from international and domestic economic downturns, China's financial development is confronted with numerous risks and challenges.

The long-term risk of a global economic slowdown is increasing after the COVID-19 pandemic, and the international monetary and financial environment is undergoing significant changes. In terms of currency and finance, consecutive significant interest rate hikes by the US Federal Reserve have led to a high-interest rate cycle in Europe, America, and some emerging economies. In 2023, the IMF estimated that 15% of low-income countries globally are facing a debt crisis and 45% are facing high debt vulnerability.[8] At the same time, the rapid tightening of monetary policy has triggered a series of 'black swan' events, such as the crises of Silicon Valley Bank and Credit Suisse, causing severe fluctuations in global financial markets.[9] Finance has become a tool in the geopolitical games, posing new challenges to global financial stability. The world economy and politics have been undergoing unprecedented changes, with a significant increase in factors of instability and uncertainty. As the public good, financial infrastructure is becoming increasingly politicized, significantly increasing the operational risks of the global economy and finance.

Currently, there are four aspects of financial risks and hazards in China's financial industry that merit close attention from the authorities and academics. First, the risks associated with the rapid growth of non-financial

[7] Jingxi Mo, 'Xi highlights key national security tasks', *China Daily* (31 May 2023), https://www.chinadaily.com.cn/a/202305/31/WS647654d7a3107584c3ac2f92.html.

[8] Kristalina Georgieva, 'The Time is Now: We Must Step Up Support for the Poorest Countries', *IMF Blog* (31 March 2023), https://www.imf.org/en/Blogs/Articles/2023/03/31/the-time-is-now-we-must-step-up-support-for-the-poorest-countries.

[9] George Steer, 'The inside story of Credit Suisse's collapse, by Credit Suisse' (2023) *Financial Times*, https://www.ft.com/content/857567b8-775c-496a-8578-c7b6419c9c96.

corporate and local government debt need to be monitored. Second, risks still exist in small and medium-sized financial institutions, with actual risks exceeding book values, difficulties in dealing with existing risks, and relatively concentrated regional risks. Third, the real estate industry is still in a transitional stage towards a new development model, and some real estate companies continue to face significant pressures for sustainable development. In the early 2020s, a number of leading property developers like Evergrande faced the debt crisis and became technically bankrupt, which has caused turmoil in the Chinese economy.[10] Finally, in the current situation, it is particularly important to focus on preventing the cross-contagion risks of credit risk, interest rate risk, and liquidity risk.

In April 2022, China issued a draft law on financial stability in an effort to fortify FSN net and reduce systemic financial risks.[11] The People's Bank of China (PBoC) and other pertinent agencies collaborated to create the draft, which clarifies the duties of the mechanism for coordinating national financial stability and growth. China will set up a comprehensive cross-agency structure for financial risk detection. At the same time, a financial stability protection fund will be set up to strengthen its capacity to handle significant financial concerns.[12] The fund, financed by financial institutions and financial infrastructure operators, aims to accumulate capital for the central government to address significant large-scale risks. It will be utilized when other sources of capital are insufficient to manage these risks.

China's efforts in strengthening the FSN are in line with the best international practices to ward off financial crisis. According to the PBoC, 98.9% of the assets in China's banking sector were deemed safe by the central bank's evaluation system by the end of 2021, which demonstrates the stability of financial institution operation.[13] In general, financial risks in China have been reduced and controlled at a manageable level. Risks associated with shadow banking have significantly diminished. As of the end of June 2022, 87% of asset management products had been converted to net worth products, which do not offer specific returns to investors.[14] With the

[10] Lerong Lu and Anat Keller, 'Is It China's Lehman Brothers Moment? Unveiling Evergrande Debt Crisis, Financial Risks, and Regulatory Implications' (2022) 16 *Law and Financial Markets Review* 133–144.

[11] PBoC, 'Financial Stability Law of the People's Republic of China (Draft)' (6 April 2022), http://www.pbc.gov.cn/goutongjiaoliu/113456/113469/4525742/index.html.

[12] *Reuters*, 'China issues draft financial stability law to prevent systemic risks' (6 April 2022), https://www.reuters.com/world/china/china-issues-draft-financial-stability-law-prevent-systemic-risks-2022-04-06/.

[13] Lanxu Zhou, 'New fund to strengthen financial safety net, smooth market slumps', *China Daily* (28 September 2022), http://www.chinadaily.com.cn/a/202209/28/WS63339dcaa310fd2b29e7a208.html.

[14] Ibid.

establishment of an effective FSN, China will expand financial institution reforms to enhance corporate governance, strengthen the regulatory foundation for financial stability, and mitigate risks among significant enterprise groups and financial institutions.

3.3 The deposit insurance system

As a vital component of the FSN, the deposit insurance system is designed to reduce or eliminate the potential risks that depositors face of losing their money when placing funds with a bank.[15] Due to its effectiveness in preventing bank runs and restoring depositor confidence, major jurisdictions have strengthened their deposit insurance schemes following several waves of financial crises. China, as the world's second-largest economy, has continuously debated the establishment of an explicit deposit insurance scheme since the 1990s. On 17 February 2015, the PRC Deposit Insurance Regulations (hereinafter referred to as the 'Regulation') were finally issued by the State Council, China's Cabinet, officially introducing the explicit deposit insurance programme.[16] This marks a significant step in improving China's financial infrastructure and FSN.

By emulating the practices of over 110 jurisdictions, the long-awaited Regulation aims to 'establish and regulate the deposit insurance system, protect the lawful rights and interests of depositors according to the law, timely prevent and eliminate financial risks, and maintain financial stability'.[17] The definitions of the participating institutions, the categories of the assured deposits, and the sum insured to the depositors are among the key components of the Regulation. According to Mr. Xiaochuan Zhou, the former governor of the PBoC, the establishment of the new deposit insurance scheme is considered a significant step forward for China in liberalizing interest rates and enabling bank resolution.[18] The newly established depository insurance fund is supposed to act as a safety cushion for the nation's 68 trillion-yuan deposits in household accounts. The following sections cover the historical development and underlying theory of deposit insurance, outline the structure of the

[15] Nicholas J Ketcha Jr, 'Deposit Insurance System Design and Considerations' (1999) 7 *BIS Policy Papers* 221.

[16] Chinese government, 'Bank deposit insurance program launched' (31 March 2015), http://english.www.gov.cn/premier/news/2015/03/31/content_281475080793833.htm.

[17] PRC Deposit Insurance Regulation 2015, Article 1.

[18] *The Wall Street Journal*, 'What's Behind China's Decision to Launch Deposit Insurance' (31 March 2015), https://www.wsj.com/articles/BL-CJB-26388.

Chinese deposit insurance scheme, and evaluate its potential impact on the financial industry.

3.3.1 The origin and latest developments of global deposit insurance schemes

A robust and sufficient depositor protection scheme plays a vital role in ensuring financial stability of the country. By eliminating the potential for a deposit run, the massive liquidity pressures that a stressed bank may face can be significantly mitigated. Therefore, the construction of a deposit insurance scheme helps maintain the stability and order in the bank industry when it comes to crisis management and resolution.[19] In the 1930s, the United States was the first country to launch a deposit insurance programme in response to the financial crisis and the Great Depression, aiming to provide economic stability and support the failing banking system.[20] The Federal Deposit Insurance Corporation (FDIC) was established in 1933 through the passage of the Glass–Steagall Act to protect depositors from potential bank insolvency triggered by the 1929 stock market crash. Initially, deposit coverage was set at $2,500 and later increased to $5,000.[21] From then on, deposit insurance has been introduced by an increasing number of nations around the globe. Since the Global Financial Crisis of 2007–2008, substantial efforts have been made worldwide to enhance the ability to respond to systemic financial crises, including the reform of deposit insurance schemes.

In the Eurozone, national Deposit Guarantee Schemes (DGS) provide depositors with protection by ensuring that deposits up to a specific level will always be reimbursed, even if the bank holding them fails. Initially, since 1994, the EU established a baseline of harmony across all European Economic Area (EEA) Member States for deposit guarantees, setting the coverage amount at €20,000 per account per credit institution.[22]After the Global Financial Crisis of 2007–2008, the level of deposit protection was revised to protect each eligible account up to €100,000 (or the equivalent amount in the local currency) regardless of the current level of financial resources

[19] Iris H-Y Chiu and Joanna Wilson, *Banking Law and Regulation* (Oxford University Press, 2019), p. 665.

[20] Federal Deposit Insurance Corporation, 'A Brief History of Deposit Insurance in the United States' (1998), https://www.fdic.gov/bank/historical/brief/brhist.pdf.

[21] Ibid.

[22] Atilla Arda and Mark Dobler, 'The Role for Deposit Insurance Funds in Dealing with Failing Banks in the European Banks' (2022) IMF Working Papers, https://www.imf.org/en/Publications/WP/Issues/2022/01/07/The-Role-for-Deposit-Insurance-Funds-in-Dealing-with-Failing-Banks-in-the-European-Union-511639.

available to any DGS.[23] In addition, DGS-protected deposits have also been given super preferential treatment in the hierarchy of bank creditors, which limits the impact of failures on DGS funding levels by making DGSs among the first-tier creditors paid out from the estate of the failed institution in the event of a bank failure. Starting in 2016, the European Banking Authority (EBA) has required Member States to increase their DGS funds to no less than 0.8% of the total deposits covered by them. To enhance transparency and facilitate policymaking in the area of deposit protection, the EBA has made this data publicly accessible on its website. The data consists of the amount of money available in the DGS funds ('available financial means') and the level of deposits protected by each DGS in each Member States ('covered deposits').[24]

In the United Kingdom, the institution providing deposit protection is the Financial Services Compensation Scheme (FSCS) which covers up to £85,000 per depositor per institution.[25] Overseen by the Prudential Regulation Authority (PRA) and the Financial Conduct Authority (FCA), the FSCS administers the UK DGS and is responsible for contacting depositors with eligible temporary high balances to verify their eligibility. FSCS aims to protect the UK customers who experience financial losses when firms authorized by the PRA are unable or likely to be unable to satisfy claims against them. The FSCS must also ensure that its responsibilities are discharged efficiently and effectively, so that public expenditure related to the UK financial services compensation scheme is minimized.[26]

3.3.2 China's implicit state guarantee for banking sector

While the majority of countries have established explicit deposit insurance scheme as a crucial financial infrastructure, China had been an outlier until the recent reform. Before the enactment of the Regulation, China had adopted the implicit deposit insurance system for years.

In contrast to explicit deposit insurance, implicit deposit protection lacks statutory rules regarding the eligibility of financial institution liabilities, the level of protection provided, or the form in which reimbursement will take

[23] European Banking Authority, 'Deposit Guarantee Schemes Data', https://www.eba.europa.eu/regulation-and-policy/recovery-and-resolution/deposit-guarantee-schemes-data.

[24] Directive 2014/49/EU of the European Parliament and of the Council of 16 April 2014 on Deposit Guarantee Schemes.

[25] *Bank of England*, 'Financial Services Compensation Scheme', https://www.bankofengland.co.uk/prudential-regulation/authorisations/financial-services-compensation-scheme.

[26] Financial Services and Markets Act 2000, Section 224ZA.

place.[27] This means all the deposits placed in China's domestic banks were fully backed by the state and the PBoC. State-owned commercial banks have maintained their dominant position in the Chinese banking sector, due to the active role of the Chinese government in banking and finance. During crisis times, government support such as bailouts or blanket guarantees are often granted to ensure financial and social stability, which hinders the competition in the Chinese banking industry. This explains why China does not need an explicit deposit insurance for a long time. The precedent of operating an implicit deposit insurance mechanism has been in place since the establishment of the domestic financial system in the late 1970s. As the financial industry grew increasingly diversified and complex, financial risks continued to mount, highlighting the inadequacy of regulators' abilities to deal with bank failures. Consequently, large-scale government bailouts were implemented in the late 1980s due to regulatory inertia surrounding the use of public funds to save banks.[28]

In 1998, the Chinese government established the first case of implicit deposit insurance during the bankruptcy of Hainan Development Bank (HDB), prompted by the real estate market collapse at that time.[29] After transferring all the debt obligations of HDB to another state-owned bank, the Industrial and Commercial Bank of China (ICBC), the PBoC bailed out all depositors, fearing that any shortage of a complete bailout would cause panic throughout the state's banking industry. However, the rescue packages are often funded by the government, meaning implicit deposit insurance schemes effectively transfer the full burden to the country's taxpayers. As a result, banks do not bear all the downside risk of their decisions, which can lead to a tendency for insured banks to use lower-cost insured deposits to take on riskier projects or investments than would be ideal. Besides causing moral hazard, government-funded rescue packages for failed banks may also impact market competition, particularly when the 'too big to fail' theory is applied.[30] Although all companies benefit from a safe and sound financial system, banks differ in their systemic importance. When a financial institution is so intertwined with the state's economy that its failure would be disastrous, the state is likely to bail out the bank to avoid a systemic economic collapse.[31]

[27] *IADI*, 'Glossary- Implicit Protection', https://www.iadi.org/en/core-principles-and-guidance/glossary/implicit-protection/.

[28] Yi Zhou, 'Establishing a Deposit Insurance System in China: A Long-Awaited Move toward Deepening Financial Reform' (2016) 16 *Chicago-Kent Journal of International & Comparative Law* 46.

[29] Sky Canaves, 'China Property Bubble, 1990s Style' (17 March 2010), *The Wall Street Journal*, https://www.wsj.com/articles/BL-CJB-7835.

[30] Reint Gropp and Jukka Vesala, 'Deposit Insurance, Moral Hazard and Market Monitoring' (February 2004) European Central Bank Working Paper Series No. 302, https://www.ecb.europa.eu/pub/pdf/scpwps/ecbwp302.pdf.

[31] Financial Stability Board, 'Evaluation of the effects of too-big-to-fail reforms—Consultation Report' (28 June 2020), https://www.fsb.org/wp-content/uploads/P280620-1.pdf.

This is highly likely to happen in the Chinese state-owned banks and such rescue would give those institutions a competitive advantage which is not good for the liberalization of the market reform.

Another example of the government's involvement in the banking sector can be seen in the rise of non-performing loan (NPL) problems in China. Despite the transition towards a market-based economy, state-owned commercial banks remained tightly controlled by the government. As a result, they were unable to grant credit on purely commercial grounds and were often instructed to finance the investment projects of state-owned enterprises (SOEs), even if the borrowers were unlikely to repay the debt. This led to an accumulation of NPLs on the banks' balance sheets, as these loans were frequently rolled over or evergreened.[32] Due to implicit guarantees provided by the government, Chinese banks were able to remain open despite their balance sheets being overwhelmed by NPLs. The NPL problem peaked during the 1980s and 1990s, even when the annual GDP growth was as high as 10%. The PBoC calculated that by the end of 1997, the NPL stock in China's banking sector totalled RMB 1.5 trillion, representing 25% of all bank loans and 20% of GDP.[33]

One of the biggest problems with China's implicit guarantee of deposits is the lack of transparency. It fails to specify the government's legal responsibilities regarding deposit compensation and bank liabilities, creating doubt among creditors and depositors. This discretionary approach to government bailouts meant that depositors were more likely to choose large state-owned commercial banks over smaller ones, as they were perceived to be more likely to receive government support. While the implicit guarantee scheme helped save sizable state-owned banks and provided stability during China's transitional economic period, it could not keep pace with the growth of the nation's banking industry.

3.3.3 The design of China's explicit deposit insurance scheme

With the rapid liberalization and expansion of China's banking industry, and the increasing entry of commercial banks, private banks, credit unions, and foreign-invested lenders into the domestic market, the Chinese government became aware of the side effects posed by its full backing of deposits. As a result, the Regulation signifies China's effort to transition from implicit to

[32] Shang-Jin Wei and Tao Wang, 'The Siamese Twins: Do State-Owned Banks Favor State-Owned Enterprises in China?' (1997) 8 *China Economic Review* 19.

[33] YK Mo, 'A review of recent bank reforming in China' (1999) BIS Working Paper, https://www.bis.org/publ/plcy07d.pdf.

explicit deposit insurance. Unlike implicit deposit insurance, explicit deposit insurance offers a better chance of maintaining financial stability during crises but only partially reimburses depositors in the event of bank failure. Typically, premiums collected from insured banks are used to build the fund, ensuring the government has the resources to promptly shut down a failing bank and bail out depositors, thereby preventing a single isolated financial failure from triggering nationwide bank runs.[34] Though China's current explicit deposit insurance scheme shares many objectives and features with those in other jurisdictions, its specifics differ in various aspects and need to be carefully designed to account for the country's unique characteristics. This section introduces the main features of China's deposit insurance scheme.

Membership

According to international common practice, compulsory membership is essential in an explicit deposit insurance programme and should be applied to all banks subject to prudential regulation and supervision.[35] The goal of making participation of the deposit insurance programme mandatory is to reduce discrimination and create a fair playing field for all relevant institutions. In light of the Chinese practice on the institutions' participation of the deposit insurance scheme, the Regulation indicates that all deposit-taking institutions in mainland China are included under the programme, including commercial banks, rural cooperative banks, and rural credit cooperatives.[36]

However, foreign bank branches and overseas Chinese banks' branches are not included under the programme, unless otherwise required by any applicable inter-governmental deposit insurance arrangement.[37] By December 2021, the combined deposits of China's Big Four state-owned banks surpassed 105 trillion yuan, and they continue to be key players in the domestic banking industry.[38] Given China's highly concentrated banking system, it is anticipated that opening membership to foreign bank branches will encourage overseas banks to establish operations in China. This move aims to reduce the dominance of state-owned commercial banks and pressure them to offer better services.

[34] Geoffrey P. Miller, 'Deposit Insurance for Economies in Transition' (1997) 2 *Yearbook of International Financial and Economic Book* 103.

[35] International Association of Deposit Insurers (IADI), 'IADI Core Principles for Effective Deposit Insurance System' (November 2014), Principle 7, https://www.iadi.org/en/assets/File/Core%20Principles/cprevised2014nov.pdf.

[36] PRC Deposit Insurance Regulation 2015, Article 2.

[37] Ibid.

[38] *Statista*, 'Total deposits of large state-owned commercial banks in China from 2014 to 2021', https://www.statista.com/statistics/1171187/china-total-deposits-of-large-state-owned-banks/.

Covered deposits

The scope of insured activities is another crucial aspect to consider in the explicit deposit insurance programme. On the one hand, it is important to limit the coverage to ensure that unnecessary activities are not included in the scheme. On the other hand, it is essential to avoid potential government involvement that could create distortions, skewing market decisions away from the most effective choices. To balance these considerations, the scope of the insured activities must be carefully determined.

The Regulation states that deposits held in both RMB and international currencies will be covered under the scheme, while deposits of senior managers within their own institutions as well as interbank deposits made by financial institutions are not insured under the explicit deposit insurance programme.[39] Other deposits may also be excluded from the scheme by the Deposit Insurance Fund Manager and it is unknown whether the structured deposits are protected. In terms of the sum insured, the Regulation indicates that the maximum protection for each individual depositors who save money in several institutions is RMB 500,000 per bank, including principal and interest; any deposits in excess of this ceiling will be exposed to the winding-up procedure of the insured institution.[40] In addition, according to the changes of the state economy, deposit structure and risk level, the PBoC can collaborate with other involved ministries under the State Council to adjust the maximum sum insured.

Following the payout of insured deposits, the fund management company would automatically subrogate insured depositors' creditor rights to pursue repayments from the insured institutions through the wind-up procedure. According to Xiaolong Huang, the deputy director-general of the bank's financial stability bureau, the insured deposit limit could cover 99.63% of depositors' total deposits. Depositors can expect to receive insurance reimbursement under the protection scheme within seven business days after the trigger event.[41] In addition, the funds for the insurance would be invested in high credit rating bonds, similar to government bonds or central bank notes, ensuring that the implementation of the deposit insurance scheme will not trigger 'deposit migration' in China.[42] With this level of coverage, China appears to fully protect the majority of its small depositors.

[39] PRC Deposit Insurance Regulation 2015, Article 4.

[40] PRC Deposit Insurance Regulation 2015, Article 5.

[41] Jiang Xueqing, 'Deposit insurance to improve competition' (December 2014) *China Daily*, https://www.chinadaily.com.cn/cndy/2014-12/01/content_19000665.htm.

[42] Ibid.

Management authority

The State Council has provisionally appointed the Financial Stability Bureau of the PBoC as the initial Deposit Insurance Fund Manager. The manager of the deposit insurance fund will set a deadline for deposit-taking institutions established before 1 May 2015, to make contributions to the scheme. Institutions established after that date have six months to contribute to the deposit insurance fund after acquiring a business licence that complies with the Fund Manager's requirements. The PBoC currently oversees the dedicated deposit insurance fund, which collects insurance premiums paid by banks. On 24 May 2019, the PBoC officially founded an independent entity, the Depository Insurance Fund Management Co., Ltd. (DIFMC), with registered capital of RMB 10 billion, to manage the deposit insurance fund. This move is part of efforts to align China's financial system with those of other jurisdictions.[43]

The establishment of the DIFMC is partly in response to the Baoshang Bank incident, which highlighted severe credit risk at the bank. Baoshang Bank's failure marked the first bankruptcy of a commercial bank in China in nearly twenty years. The China Construction Bank (CCB) has been entrusted by the PBoC and the China Banking and Insurance Regulatory Commission (CBIRC) to take control of the business operations of this Inner Mongolia-based small lender.[44] Although Baoshang Bank is a regional bank with an insignificant nationwide market share, it holds considerable assets, totalling more than RMB 500 billion.[45] Therefore, the central government took a major step by allowing Baoshang Bank to go bankrupt, a move previously resisted due to concerns about damaging confidence in the nation's banking system.

In the wake of the incident, it was revealed that only the bank's retail accounts were insured, while corporate and interbank deposits over RMB 50 million would face asset value reductions. This situation highlighted the assumption that all bank deposits were fail-proof due to the government's implicit guarantee. The Baoshang case demonstrates that Chinese authorities are willing to test the financial system's stability by authorizing principal

[43] Wu Yujian, Zhang Yuzhe, and Denise Jia, 'PBOC Sets Up Depository Insurance Fund Management Company', *Caixin* (30 May 2019), https://www.caixinglobal.com/2019-05-30/pboc-sets-up-deposit-insurance-fund-management-company-101421410.html.

[44] *Reuters*, 'Chinese regulator to take over Baoshang Bank due to credit risks' (24 May 2019), https://www.reuters.com/article/us-china-banks-regulator-baoshang-bank-idUSKCN1SU1DN.

[45] Samuel Shen and John Ruwitch, 'Baoshang failure takes a toll in China's interbank markets as contagion fears grow', *Reuters* (21 June 2019), https://www.reuters.com/article/us-china-markets-baoshang-idUSKCN1TM11T.

haircuts for sizable deposits. In the long term, this is a healthy step towards liberalizing China's capital markets by allowing more defaults. It encourages the market to more accurately assess risks and incentivizes companies to improve corporate governance. However, the risks involved must not be overlooked, especially given the uncertainties brought by external factors such as the pandemic or the trade war.

Ex-ante funding mechanism

Since China has established a stand-alone fund for the deposit insurance scheme, monies need to be available whenever needed, so premiums must be charged based on realistic assumptions, considering potential losses and other costs. The Regulation confirms an ex-ante funding mechanism for the deposit insurance fund, which includes the following sources: insurance premiums paid by institutional policyholders; property distributed in the liquidation of institutional policyholders; proceeds gained from the use of the deposit insurance fund by the deposit insurance fund management institution; and other legal income.[46]

In terms of the insurance premiums, according to a working paper by the International Association of Deposit Insurers (IADI), flat-rate premium system is widely adopted by most deposit insurance programmes due to the simplicity in design, implementation, and administration.[47] However, flat-rate premium systems do not account for the various degrees of risk that different banks can present. Thus, a single flat-rate premium might be viewed as unjust, since all insured banks pay the same fees regardless of the level of risk they pose to the deposit insurance fund. To avoid the side effect of single flat-rate premium mechanism, under China's scheme, the premium rate consists of standard rates (flat charge) and risk-based differential rates which are dependent on the business management and risk profile of the insured bank.[48]

According to the PBoC, the initially fixed rate has been set between 0.01% and 0.02%, substantially lower than those assed in other jurisdictions.[49] It is

[46] PRC Deposit Insurance Regulation 2015, Article 6.

[47] IADA, 'Evaluation of Differential Premium Systems for Deposit Insurance' (2020), https://www.iadi.org/en/assets/File/Papers/Approved%20Research%20-%20Discussion%20Papers/DPS_Paper_final_16June2020_Final.pdf.

[48] PRC Deposit Insurance Regulation 2015, Article 9.

[49] In Asian jurisdictions like Hong Kong, Taiwan, and Singapore, they have adopted the risk-adjusted basis rates, with premiums ranging from 0.02% to 0.48%. China Mainland requires the lowest premiums compared with these regions. Susan Desai, 'A Regional Comparison of China's New Deposit Insurance System' (2016) *FED Bank of San Francisco Pacific Exchange Blog*, https://www.frbsf.org/banking/asia-program/pacific-exchange-blog/regional-comparison-chinas-new-deposit-insurance-system/.

likely to take a decade to build up the funds necessary to cover the deposits of even the smallest bank with such low premium rate. Therefore, it is likely that the government would provide funding for the agency's starting operations.[50] However, although this rate may be lower than the international average, it is reasonable to set a lower fixed rate when considering additional risk-based premiums. In practice, determining the appropriate ratio for this risk assessment premium is challenging, involving judgements based on imperfect information about potential losses of individual institutions. So far, the PBoC has not provided any further details or regulations regarding the calculation of risk-based premiums. The assessment of risk-based premiums is further complicated by the need to consider additional factors, such as the economic costs related to premium volatility, which may be necessary to consistently maintain a certain reserve ratio. These factors suggest that flexibility in selecting an appropriate premium ratio and determining the best implementation methods may result in a better balance of the pertinent goals.[51]

3.3.4 Impacts of China's explicit deposit insurance

Since 1978, China has made significant progress in transitioning from a centrally planned economy to a market-based economy. Despite notable developments in the banking industry, the sector still faces long-standing structural issues. In recent years, the State Council and the PBoC have aimed to implement small-scale market changes in the banking industry, such as deregulating deposit interest rates. There is concern that increased competition for deposit interest rates may cause depositors to transfer their money from small and medium-sized depository institutions to state-owned commercial banks.[52] The PBoC believes that an explicit deposit insurance scheme, designed to compensate depositors in the event of a bank collapse, could mitigate the risks associated with growing interest rate competition for small and medium-sized banks.[53]

[50] *The Economist*, 'A premium for risk: A scheme to protect savers exposes Chinese banks to useful uncertainty' (4 December 2014), https://www.economist.com/finance-and-economics/2014/12/04/a-premium-for-risk.

[51] Luc Laeven, 'Pricing of Deposit Insurance' (July 2002) World Bank Policy Research Working Paper 2871, https://documents1.worldbank.org/curated/en/917821468739467603/106506322_20041117162012/additional/multi0page.pdf.

[52] YK Mo, 'A review of recent bank reforming in China' (1999) BIS Working Paper, https://www.bis.org/publ/plcy07d.pdf.

[53] *Bloomberg*, 'China Drafts Bank Deposit Insurance in Move to Free Rates' (30 November 2014), https://www.bloomberg.com/news/articles/2014-11-30/china-drafts-deposit-insurance-in-move-to-free-interest-rates#xj4y7vzkg.

However, introducing a reliable explicit deposit insurance scheme in a country with a high national savings rate like China is easier said than done. While the global average savings rate is 23.47%, China stands out with one of the highest rates in the world, at 45.7% in 2021.[54] Therefore, it may be challenging to persuade depositors that deposits in city or rural commercial banks are just as safe as those in major state-owned commercial banks, even with an explicit deposit insurance scheme in place. For example, if the explicit deposit insurance fund had been launched in 2003, it would have taken ten years and cost RMB 1.1 trillion to create a fund with a coverage target of 1.35% of all deposits (the same target as the Federal Reserve in the United States). As a result, the return on assets (ROA) of the domestic banking sector would have decreased by 14%, from 1.35% to 0.97%. While the fund would have been robust enough to cover the failure of certain larger city commercial banks, it would still be far from sufficient to cover a bank the size of China Minsheng Bank, whose deposits make up 2% of the country's total, let alone the failure of the Big Four, which account for 12.2% of all deposits in the banking system.[55]

From its historical origins, the deposit insurance system was introduced to ensure the stability of the financial system. As mentioned before, the United States was the first nation to formally adopt deposit insurance to protect depositors from losses caused by insolvent banks. The 1929 stock market crash and the Great Depression of the 1930s led to the near-complete collapse of the nation's commercial banking system, causing people to stop depositing money in these institutions. This loss of deposits crippled the banks' ability to support the financial expansion of businesses and industry, which was essential for economic recovery.[56] Therefore, in an effort to regain depositors' confidence and spur economic growth, the FDIC was established to provide deposit insurance for commercial banks. As a result, the deposit insurance has proved to be a great success in prevention of panics and large-scale deposit destruction at that time.

Similar to the United States, the introduction of an explicit deposit insurance system in China plays a crucial role in ensuring financial stability. Establishing a deposit insurance system will provide a market-based mechanism for the orderly exit of commercial banks from competition, optimizing

[54] World Bank, 'Gross domestic savings (% of GDP)-China', https://data.worldbank.org/indicator/NY.GDS.TOTL.ZS.

[55] Ryan Rutkowski, 'Too big to fail: Deposit Insurance and Chinese State Banks' (2013) Peterson Institute for International Economics, https://www.piie.com/blogs/china-economic-watch/too-big-fail-deposit-insurance-and-chinese-state-banks.

[56] Thad Grundy Jr., 'Practical Aspects of the Deposit Insurance System' (1988) 44 *Business Lawyer* 169.

the banking structure by distinguishing winners and losers based on market choices. In the long run, this will improve the competitiveness of banks, enhance the overall level and risk resistance of the banking sector, and contribute to the nation's financial stability. In practice, it is recommended to introduce a grace period at the initial stage of the deposit insurance program, during which only mergers and acquisitions would be used to handle failed banks. This approach creates a situation where banks can fail without causing public loss, stabilizing depositor confidence and weeding out banks with poor financial health. For the disposal of insolvent banks, setting up a bridge bank would help cushion the impact on the banking sector. The primary objectives of a bridge bank are to maintain core services and continuity of operations essential for financial stability. Under such circumstances, all insured deposits can be transferred to the bridge bank, contributing to its viability and preserving financial stability. This would minimize the disruption to the financial system that might otherwise occur if those functions were subject to wind-up and liquidation procedures.

3.4 The lender of last resort

The Global Financial Crisis of 2007–2008 highlighted the importance of central banks' emergency liquidity support, known as the lender of last resort (LOLR), for financial institutions and posed challenges regarding the execution of these operations. Despite extensive literature on the subject, central banks' practices and procedures vary.[57] The LOLR is the second pillar of one country's FSN. It is one of the most contentious functions of a central bank. On the one hand, the primary role of a central bank is to provide financial institutions with emergency liquidity support. This is supported by their ability to generate liquid assets in the form of reserves, their central role in the payment system, and their goal of macroeconomic stabilization. On the other hand, the LOLR role is extremely risky, as it may lead to widespread moral hazard, expose the central bank to significant financial risks, and blur the line between monetary and fiscal policy. Additionally, providing liquidity support to specific institutions can be highly controversial and may damage the recipient's reputation.

The financial crisis served as a reminder of how crucial the LOLR is in restoring financial stability. However, more important issues have been

[57] Dietrich Domanski and Vladyslav Sushko, 'Rethinking the lender of last resort' (2014) BIS Papers No. 79, https://www.bis.org/publ/bppdf/bispap79.htm.

raised regarding the construction of the LOLR frameworks and the implementation of the LOLR regulations. How can the LOLR function be maximized while minimizing the risks for the central bank? What are the conditions for central banks to provide emergency liquidity to individual institutions? Should central banks be vague about the terms and conditions of liquidity support in public, or is there a rationale for clearly stated LOLR regulations that are publicized in advance as a component of a larger framework for financial stability? This section discusses these issues with a view to examining the best international practices and highlighting several challenges regarding LOLR policies, in order to shed light on the Chinese practice in this field.

3.4.1 Historical development of the lender of last resort theory

A central bank may need to provide the banking sector with liquidity in a variety of situations. If the market has an *ex-ante* shortage of reserve money, central banks need to use open-market operations to insert reserve money into the financial markets; they also use open-market operations to facilitate the payment function, such as intra-day loans or a credit standing facility. Furthermore, central banks can also react to the increased demand for overall reserve currency, foreign currency or liquid assets as a result of a market shock when regular market functioning is disturbed, as well as the peculiar demands of a bank or a group of banks.[58] LOLR support is the last one of these, which is granted at the central bank's discretion to prevent ripple effects that could threaten the stability within the nation's financial system.

Central Bank's role of LOLR is a monetary authority that can calm a brewing banking panic and the ensuing scramble for liquidity by assuring the market in good time that the central bank will supply whatever powerful capital is needed to meet the demand. In a banking panic, the general public makes all attempts to convert their deposits into liquidity, and commercial banks try to respond by boosting their reserve holdings in relation to deposit obligations. In a fractional reserve banking system, a banking panic can happen when a significant bank failure or series failures trigger bank runs that spread like wildfire and endanger the viability of otherwise sound financial

[58] Mark Dobler, Simon Gray, Diarmuid Murphy, and Bozena Radzewicz-Bak, 'The Lender of Last Resort after the Global Financial Crisis' (2016) IMF Working Paper, https://www.imf.org/external/pubs/ft/wp/2016/wp1610.pdf.

institutions. In a more contemporary setting, a LOLR must deal with liquidity shocks before they have an impact on the financial system.[59]

The phrase 'lender of last resort' first appeared in the United Kingdom at the end of the eighteenth century when Sir Francis Baring described the function of the Bank of England as a 'dernier resort'.[60] Henry Thornton was one of the main proponents of the concept of LOLR, urged the Bank of England to calm a panic by freely lending to the money market on the basis of reliable collateral.[61] Later in 1873, Walter Bagehot developed the concept into the Bagehot's rule as following: (1) In the face of a liquidity crisis (internal drain), the bank should lend freely and discount all the sound collateral; (2) in the face of an external drain (an outflow of the bank's reserves), the bank should charge a high rate (above market); (3) in the face of both an internal and external rate, the bank should lend freely at a high rate (often referred to as a 'penalty rate'); (4) prevent illiquid but solvent bank from failing; (5) the policy should be clearly expressed in advance.[62] In the late nineteenth century, the Bank of England at that time avoided dealing with specific banks directly in its LOLR operations. Instead, it gave the market access to liquidity anonymously. The discount houses were contacted by the commercial banks to rediscount their paper, and the discount houses in turn approached the Bank of England for accommodation. Thus, the anchor for the financial system was the Bank's discount rate or known as 'Bank rate'.[63]

In the United States, the development of LOLR is considerably different from that of the United Kingdom. Before the Federal Reserve System was established, clearing houses in major cities of the United States operated as a quasi-LOLR by issuing loan certificates in the absence of a central bank, which serves as an emergency form of currency at that time.[64] Due to strident calls for reform of the banking system, the Federal Reserve Act passed in 1933, but the act kept silent on how the Fed should serve as a LOLR.

[59] George G. Kaufman, 'Lender of Last Resort: A Contemporary Perspective' (1991) 5 *Journal of Financial Service Research* 95.

[60] Paul Kosmetatos, 'Last Resort Lending Before Henry Thornton? The Bank of England's Role in Containing the 1763 and 1772-1773 British Credit Crises' (2018) 23 *European Review of Economic History* 299.

[61] Thomas M. Humphrey, 'Lender of Last Resort: The Concept in History' (1989) 75 *FRB Richmond Economic Review* 8.

[62] Michael D. Bordo, 'Rules for a lender of last resort: An historical perspective' (2014) 49 *Journal of Economic Dynamics & Control* 126.

[63] Mike Anson, David Bholat, Miao Kang, and Ryland Thomas, 'The Bank of England as lender of last resort: New historical evidence from daily transactional data' (2017) Bank of England Staff Working Paper No. 691, https://www.bankofengland.co.uk/working-paper/2017/the-bank-of-england-as-lender-of-last-resort-new-historical-evidence-from-daily-transactional-data.

[64] Gary Gorton, 'Clearing Houses and the Origin of Central Banking in the United States' (1985) 45 *The Journal of Economic History* 277.

The drafters believed that they had designed a foolproof system that would stop panics before they started. However, the Fed clearly failed to respond correctly during the Great Depression in the 1930s and did not serve as LOLR as they were supposed to do.[65]

The Global Financial Crisis of 2007–2008 rekindled interest in central banks' LOLR role, particularly in its design and operating modalities. Originating in the shadow banking system, the subprime mortgage crisis soon spread to universal banks and the entire financial system. The Fed needed to address the long-standing stigma problem as well as the challenges posed by the burgeoning shadow banking industry.[66] Since Walter Bagehot advocated the theory in the nineteenth century, it has been widely held that the Central Bank should lend freely to financial institutions and at a high interest rate in exchange for solid collateral as considered in normal times, with the presumption that a bank without sufficient collateral is bankrupt.[67] Indeed, contrary to what happened during the Great Depression when the Fed manifestly fell short of its LOLR obligations, the Fed's measures during the Global Financial Crisis of 2007–2008 did help to calm the financial panic. However, some policies the Fed adopted may lead to future issues. For instance, during the Global Financial Crisis of 2007–2008, the Fed provided credit directly to the markets and businesses which it determined to be in the greatest need of liquidity. This credit policy is opposed to that of the Bank of England, which provides credit in an anonymous manner through open-market operations or through the frosted glass window of the Bank of England.[68]

Furthermore, the market's decision to favour targeted lending over imperial liquidity provision has left the Fed vulnerable to the temptation to politicize the institution it chooses to lend to. Overall, there was criticism that the actions the Fed took during the Global Financial Crisis of 2007–2008 have eroded the central bank's independence and have weakened its credibility in pursuing the goals of macro stability and LOLR.[69] Last but not least, the Fed has not adhered to Bagehot's rule to explicitly state the LOLR policy in advance. Instead, the Fed's rescue strategy during the crisis has been primarily

[65] Ben S. Bernanke, *The Federal Reserve and the Financial Crisis* (Princeton University Press, 2013), p. 23.

[66] Ibid., p. 64.

[67] Michael D. Bordo, 'Rules for a Lender of Last Resort: An Historical Perspective' (2014) 49 *Journal of Economic Dynamics & Control* 126.

[68] Anna J. Schwartz, 'Origins of the Financial Crisis of 2008' (2009) 29 *The Cato Journal* 19.

[69] William Nelson, 'Lessons from lender of last resort during the crisis: The Federal Reserve experience' (2014) BIS Papers No. 79, https://www.bis.org/publ/bppdf/bispap79d.pdf.

ad hoc and discretionary.[70] It seems that its decision to save Bear Stearns and AIG while letting Lehman Brothers fail was contradictory and confused the market.[71]

In general, it has been widely accepted that it is unfair to protect banks from the repercussions of their actions, regardless of the net social benefit, especially at a time when there is a great deal of suffering caused in part by the banks' behaviour. Such inequity is worsened by lending to new counterparties, because it inevitably draws lines in the process of credit allocation by selecting winners and losers. In addition, the effects of the LOLR's unpopularity extend beyond the disdain of the central bank. The public backlash also jeopardizes the independence and efficiency of the central bank. For instance, stricter disclosure requirements for all the loans made by the Fed have been made due to the public backlash, which in fact, conflict with the goal to lessen the institution's stigma attached to approach the discount window as a source of credit.[72] Due to the Fed's credit allocation decisions and its credit risk, the range of lending alternatives was expanded by risk-sharing agreements with fiscal authority. However, collaborating with the Treasury on loan facilities altered the nature of the relationship between the central bank and the fiscal authority, putting the independence of the central bank in jeopardy further.

In terms of the qualifications to have access to the discount window, the US practice could not provide efficient experience in this regard. While depository institutions regularly have access to the discount window in the United States, other entities with banking-like functions, such as broker-dealer and money funds, do not.[73]As part of the Monetary Control Act of 1980, reserve requirements have been expanded to all depository institutions. Even those non-Fed member banks have access to the discount window. Given that the reserve requirements are less onerous as a result of the payment of interests on payments, it is unclear why other bank-like entities do not have access to the discount window in the United States. In general, the US experience during the crisis shows confusing implications for who should normally have access to the discount window.[74]

[70] Allan H. Meltzer, 'Regulatory Reform and the Federal Reserve' (2009), the US Senate Committee on Banking, https://www.banking.senate.gov/imo/media/doc/MeltzerTestimony72309.pdf.

[71] Michael D. Bordo, 'Rules for a Lender of Last Resort: A Historical Perspective' (2014) 49 *Journal of Economic Dynamics & Control* 126.

[72] Marc Labonte, 'Federal Reserve: Oversight and Disclosure Issues' (2017) Congressional Research Service, https://sgp.fas.org/crs/misc/R42079.pdf.

[73] Elizabeth Klee, 'The First Line of Defense: The Discount Window during the Early Stages of the Financial Crisis' (2021) 17 *International Journal of Central Banking* 143.

[74] William Nelson, 'Lessons from lender of last resort during the crisis: the Federal Reserve experience' (2014) BIS Papers No 79, https://www.bis.org/publ/bppdf/bispap79d.pdf.

3.4.2 Analysis of China's LOLR practice

Under Chinese law, central bank acting as LOLR is an integral part of the nation's FSN. The PBoC may, as required by the implementation of monetary policy, determine the amount, maturity, interest rate, and form of a loan to a commercial bank.[75] The maximum maturity of the loan shall not exceed one year. In 1999, the PBoC promulgated the Emergency Loan Measures, detailing the prerequisites for acquiring emergency loans, their use, maturity, and interest rates.[76] This marked a significant breakthrough in the construction of China's FSN. In practice, the PBoC has been able to assist troubled financial institutions through various means, including bailouts, mergers and acquisitions, debt restructuring, takeovers, liquidation, and closure.

Although the assistance of the PBoC has taken a variety of forms, from direct capital injection to debt-to-equity swaps, the PBoC and the Chinese government are always the last resort to pay the debts of financial institutions in China. The practice of such a LOLR mechanism has undoubtedly contributed to moral hazard of financial institutions and their dependency on the central bank in the Chinese financial market. This is because the LOLR mechanism of the PBoC does not operate in accordance with its theoretical basis, i.e. the assistance of the PBoC does not have the independence and ambiguity which it should have when deciding whether to provide emergency liquidity. The PBoC does not make a substantive distinction between liquidity and insolvency issues during the rescue of financial institutions. Instead, the authority always provides support to financial institutions through various disguised means, and there is no need to indicate that any rescue operation would ultimately be borne by taxpayers.

For instance, in 1998, the Ministry of Finance in China issued a special treasury bond to raise RMB 270 billion more than double the amount expected by the market, to help recapitalize the state-owned insolvent banks.[77] The magnitude of the offering enabled the banks to achieve the minimum capital-adequacy ratio of 8% stipulated by the Basel Committee. Later in 1999, the PRC government established four asset management corporations (AMC) to address the NPL issue in the banking system. The AMCs were expected to acquire and sell the 'Big Four' state commercial bank's bad debts over the course of ten years, but the contribution of these AMCs have made

[75] Law of the People's Republic of China on the People's Bank of China, Article 28.

[76] PBoC, 'Interim Measures for the Administration of Emergency Loans of the People's Bank of China', Yinfa [1999] No. 407, http://www.pbc.gov.cn/zhengcehuobisi/125207/125213/125437/125815/2835315/index.html.

[77] *South China Morning Post*, 'China bonds to bail out banks' (2 March 1998), https://www.scmp.com/article/231741/china-bonds-bail-out-banks.

in solving the NPL problem is rather little, acquiring less than half of the Big Four's NPLs in the first two years.[78] The Ministry of Finance provided initial equity capital injection of RMB 40 billion for purchasing the NPLs and the four AMCs acquired NPLs amounting RMB 1.4 trillion from 1999 to 2000. By the end of 2006, the AMCs have stopped NPL activities after transferring roughly RMB 136.3 billion to the Ministry of Finance and PBoC.[79]

In addition, the PBoC's practice of LOLR is also contrary to the principles of market economy to some extent. The market economy is supposed to provide a level playing field for all the parties under the rule of law, which advocates fair competition under equal opportunities. However, the PBoC's LOLR mechanism clearly breaks the fair market principles. The PBoC's bailout or disguised direct capital injection to the state-owned commercial banks has undoubtedly resulted in unfair competition between state-owned commercial banks and non-state-owned commercial banks. Such LOLR mechanism performed by the PBoC will distort market incentives and further hinder the development of prudent banking industry.

3.4.3 Policy implications for improving China's LOLR

This section discusses some policy implications for improving China's LOLR, such as reconciling transparency and ambiguity, pricing the LOLR, and assessing systemic importance.

Reconcile transparency and ambiguity

The design of the LOLR mechanism should involve a judicious balancing of transparency and ambiguity. Keeping ambiguity at times can facilitate for the central bank to function in private. In the context of central bank's LOLR function, an optimal approach has been described by the BIS as 'Constructive Ambiguity', meaning that the conditions and operational arrangement of the central bank are not fully disclosed.[80] Under this theory, the PBoC should blur the conditions under which it will rescue the individual institution, as well as the terms and conditions at which it will employ the LOLR operation, with the aim of minimizing the moral hazard and to hold the maximum autonomy in deciding whether or not to undertake a bailout during

[78] Guonan Ma and Ben S C Fung, 'China's asset management corporations' (2002) BIS Working Papers No. 115, https://www.bis.org/publ/work115.pdf.

[79] Lily S. Engbith, 'China: 1999 Asset Management Corporations' (2021) 3 *Journal of Financial Crises* 485.

[80] Mark Dobler, Simon Gray, Diarmuid Murphy, and Bozena Radzewicz-Bak, 'The Lender of Last Resort after the Global Financial Crisis' (2016) IMF Working Paper, https://www.imf.org/external/pubs/ft/wp/2016/wp1610.pdf.

the financial crisis. Ambiguity is relevant to increased expected variance in results, so risk-averse institutions will take more precautions than they would if they were certain that the authorities would come to their rescue. As a result, there should be less chance of high-risk bank investment and less expectation of bank failures.

There is a claim that the provision of LOLR support from the central bank is the most effective application of the FSN because it is not visible to the public.[81] On this view, the health of a banking system depends in part on the public confidence of the system, and such confidence could decline if the public knows that a rescue has been mounted which indicates that the bank was already in trouble. Indeed, optimal policy depends on acquiring comprehensive information, but banking information, such as the liquidity adequacy and prospective viability, has the characteristic of being inherently imperfect and difficult to assess. Therefore, it is necessary for the PBoC to use discretion to decide the level of assistance required in order to reduce the risk of unjustifiable bank failures and bank runs.

However, in deciding whether to provide liquidity to support a bank, there is a chance that a bank which is in need of support does not receive liquidity support from the central bank, while the one which should not be supported does. It is obvious that there is a need for a system which would reduce the likelihood of such errors. Therefore, transparency also has justification in contributing to a rule-based system. Advocates of rules tend to favour transparency on the grounds that it could benefit the credibility of authority is also important, because transparency offers a precise benchmark against which to assess, *ex post*, deviations from a rule.[82] It would be challenging to evaluate whether the decision of the authority was appropriate if the regulation was unclear.

In summary, it may lead to moral hazard if the terms and conditions of financial details are clear in advance, but the degree of public belief placed on the execution of the rule is also important to the credibility of the authority. Therefore, it is suggested to reconcile the approaches of transparency and ambiguity, by matching 'ex-ante' ambiguity with stringent 'ex post' transparency. 'Ex-ante' ambiguity means blurring the terms and conditions of the central bank's LOLR mechanism in advance, which is designed to curtail moral hazard. 'Ex post' transparency means the central bank's financial support to individual institution being explained to the public to make sure the

[81] Charles Enoch, Peter Stella, and May Khamis, 'Transparency and Ambiguity in Central Bank Safety Net Operations' (1997) IMF Working Papers, https://www.imf.org/external/pubs/ft/wp/wp97138.pdf.

[82] Finn E. Kydland and Edward C. Prescott, 'Rules Rather than Discretion: The Inconsistency of Optimal Plans' (1977) 85 *Journal of Political Economy* 473.

policy is coherent and fair to all the parties in system crisis.[83] The operation of the PBoC's LOLR operation should therefore involve a judicious mixture of the transparency and ambiguity, so as to minimize the moral hazard problem while maintaining the credibility of the PBoC at the same time.

The pricing of LOLR

In terms of the cost to approach the LOLR operation of the central banks, the pricing mechanism can vary considerably. For instance, the European Central Bank applies a fixed spread to the Central Bank's overnight lending facility, regardless of market conditions; while in Hong Kong, the Monetary Authority bases its rate on its policy rates plus a spread taking the current market conditions into account.[84] The practice of the Bank of England adopts a flexible rate depending on the circumstances and the credibility of the individual institutions.[85]

To receive emergency liquidity assistance from the PBoC, banks must be solvent even if they are illiquid. This means that, although they may not be able to pay out all their depositors in the short term, they are still able to pay them back in the long run. A bank can become illiquid while remaining solvent because its funds might be tied up in longer-term loans it has given to its customers.[86] Therefore, the emergency liquidity assistance from the central banks comes at a price. However, the rate to charge individual institutions is somehow difficult to set. On the one hand, the rate should be high enough to deter the use of LOLR rescue and curtail moral hazard, while not that high to exacerbate the liquidity problem of the institutions.[87] Normal practice would be central banks accept collateral of lesser quality for emergency liquidity assistance loans compared to non-emergency funding, and as such, they apply a haircut to the collateral and charge banks a higher interest rate to compensate for the

[83] Examples of the 'ex-post' transparency and accountability include Congressional investigations into management of the Savings and Loan crisis in the United States, and the Parliamentary Committee investigations into bank collapses in the United Kingdom. See Charles Enoch, Peter Stella, and May Khamis, 'Transparency and Ambiguity in Central Bank Safety Net Operations' (1997) IMF Working Papers, https://www.imf.org/external/pubs/ft/wp/wp97138.pdf.

[84] Hong Kong Monetary Authority, 'Policy Statement On The Role Of The Hong Kong Monetary Authority As Lender Of Last Resort', Quarterly Bulletin 8/1999, https://www.hkma.gov.hk/media/eng/publication-and-research/quarterly-bulletin/qb9908/fa04.pdf.

[85] Michael Anson, David Bholat, Miao Kang, and Ryland Thomas, 'The Bank of England as Lender of Last Resort: New Historical Evidence from Daily Transactional Data' (2017) Bank of England Working Paper No. 691, https://www.bankofengland.co.uk/-/media/boe/files/working-paper/2017/the-bank-of-england-as-lender-of-last-resort-a-new-historical-evidence-from-daily-transactional-data.pdf.

[86] *European Central Bank*, 'What is a lender of last resort?' (2019), https://www.ecb.europa.eu/ecb/educational/explainers/tell-me-more/html/what-is-a-lender-of-last-resort.en.html.

[87] Andrew Hauser, 'Lender of last resort operations during the financial crisis: Seven practical lessons from the United Kingdom' (2014) BIS Working Paper No.79, https://www.bis.org/publ/bppdf/bispap79e.pdf.

increased risk. Considering that China is still at a nascent stage for implement the LOLR mechanism, a 'reduction approach' in this context would be easier to operate in practice, i.e. the PBoC to charge a high rate at the beginning of the LOLR operation to deter insolvent banks from approaching the LOLR, and gradually lower the rate for those solvent but illiquid institutions with long-term needs. At the same time, to provide stricter scrutiny over those long-term lending to make sure adequate collateral has been provided.[88]

The assessment of systemic importance

In considering whether to provide emergency liquidity assistance to individual banks, the PBoC should take into account the suggestion by the IMF to develop its own standards for gauging systemic importance, which take into account the unique characteristics of each institution as well as the financial and economic environment of the state.[89]According to the IMF, the assessment should be on a series of factors, such as: (1) The size of the individual institution, which can be determined by examining the market share of deposits and lending held by that institution; its participation in the interbank market; and its role in the payment system, including volume and global reach; (2) the complexity of the operation of LOLR, which could increase the danger of an uncontrolled resolution and sudden issues; and (3) linkages with the financial system, which could raise the possibility of contagion in the event of failure.

It is important for the PBoC to establish its own assessment framework and collect information that allow it to rapidly evaluate the systemic importance of any financial institution, especially during the crisis times. If a system test is applied, this would enable the PBoC to swiftly carry out a systemic impact assessment and make a timely determination of whether or not an institution could receive emergency liquidity assistance through the operation of LOLR mechanism. It should also be noticed that some indicators, such as the market share of specific products, could be objectively quantified, while other relevant indicators are more subjective. For example, it may not be immediately apparent how an institution's failure would impact the provision of credit, asset prices and the real economy.[90]

[88] Charles Enoch, Peter Stella, and May Khamis, 'Transparency and Ambiguity in Central Bank Safety Net Operations' (1997) IMF Working Papers, https://www.imf.org/external/pubs/ft/wp/wp97138.pdf.

[89] Mark Dobler, Simon Gray, Diarmuid Murphy, and Bozena Radzewicz-Bak, 'The Lender of Last Resort after the Global Financial Crisis' (2016) IMF Working Paper, https://www.imf.org/external/pubs/ft/wp/2016/wp1610.pdf.

[90] Ibid.

3.4.4 Outstanding challenges of LOLR mechanism

As discussed, central banks' assistance in LOLR is selective, limited only to banks experiencing short-term liquidity shortages rather than insolvency. Therefore, central banks often find themselves in a dilemma in practice. Due to factors such as information asymmetry, central banks are often caught in a bind: on the one hand, if banks know they will receive support from the central bank during a liquidity crisis, they may relax their risk management and neglect the importance of prudent operation. This moral hazard can lead to undesired loopholes in the banking safety net. On the other hand, if the central bank abandons problem institutions facing liquidity crises, it cannot prevent the spread of panic. Market participants, due to information asymmetry, may exhibit the phenomenon of 'herd behaviour', with everyone eager to escape risk, ultimately exacerbating the risk and causing no one to be spared. Therefore, from this perspective, central banks often find themselves in a relatively passive position when deciding when and how to apply the LOLR operation. In fact, considering the aforementioned policy implications, the legal foundation of this LOLR mechanism is weak, because the whole LOLR mechanism is not legally mandated but rather discretionary by the central bank, which is precisely the crux of the problem. When performing this function, central banks not only have to face the challenge of identifying whether problem banks are facing liquidity risk or insolvency risk, but also the issue of moral hazard after providing assistance. Therefore, regardless of the outcome, central banks find themselves trapped in a vicious circle of solving old problems while encountering new ones.

There is no doubt that the LOLR system has played an effective role in the FSN since its implementation, in practice, the operation of theory must undergo two considerations. The first is the issue of the limited availability of resources at the disposal of the central bank. Several waves of financial crises in recent decades have demonstrated that the resources available to central banks are ultimately limited. Therefore, the LOLR operation must be applied cautiously. A study of the banking industry in 24 industrialized countries revealed that out of 104 bank crisis cases worldwide, 73 were rescued, with only 2 instances where central banks individually saved troubled banks.[91]Other problematic banks were rescued through the combined provision of funds from central banks, commercial banks, deposit insurance programmes, and governments.[92] These cases indicate that the

[91] Charles Goodhart and Dirk Schoenmaker, 'Should the Functions of Monetary Policy and Banking Supervision Be Separated?' (1995) 47 *Oxford Economic Papers* 539.

[92] Ibid.

assistance capacity of central banks alone is extremely limited. The second consideration arises from the challenge posed by the 'too big to fail' theory of banking institutions. If certain financial institutions are of significant size and face not just temporary liquidity issues but insolvency, central banks, considering the potential collapse of the entire financial system, may intervene and provide unnecessary guarantees and loans. The traditional LOLR mechanism undoubtedly increases the moral hazard generated by these large banks, thereby weakening the disciplinary role of the market and increasing the accumulation of risks. The market firmly believes that receiving assistance will lead to excessive risk-taking.

From this perspective, although it is beneficial for financial stability when the central bank intervenes to provide emergency assistance to problem institutions and eliminate systemic risks, the outcome often leads to the central bank facing new problems while attempting to resolve existing ones. Therefore, when formulating emergency assistance measures, the central bank should focus on how to scientifically design institutions to minimize moral hazards. In order to ensure the policy objective of a stable financial system, the principle of 'letting the losers exit' must be established in operating the LOLR mechanism, which means that market forces should be allowed to play a role in resolving failures.

3.5 The bank insolvency regime

The bank insolvency regime is the third pillar of a country's FSN. The Global Financial Crisis of 2007–2008 prompted a re-examination of bank insolvency from both national and supranational perspectives. The crisis highlighted the importance of having a legal framework in place to appropriately manage distressed banks during difficult times. As a result of the shortcomings exposed by the global financial crisis, reforming the bank insolvency regime has become a priority for governments worldwide. This chapter focuses on the features of the legal and regulatory framework that China could establish to more effectively address bank insolvency issues.

3.5.1 Different frameworks in the bank insolvency proceedings

It is not an easy endeavour to reach a commonly accepted definition of bank insolvency, because there does not exist a harmonized standard of this issue and the trigger points for the bank insolvency proceedings.[93] Furthermore, it is difficult for the policymaker to decide in making the rules of bank insolvency, whether it should be more favourable to debtor or it should be pro-creditor, as the field of insolvency regulations is deeply linked with other commercial laws and regulations.

In general, there are two types of legal regimes regarding the bank insolvency proceedings, *lex generalis* and *lex specialis.* The former refers to the framework where banks are subject to the general corporate insolvency laws, while the latter indicates that banks are applied to a special insolvency regime.[94] According to the IMF and the World Bank, in recent years, a consensus is emerging in many jurisdictions as to the necessity to establish a special regime within the nation, in which the conditions of bank insolvency are regulated by a law which differs from the general corporate insolvency law and principles. Although invariably takes place in courts, insolvency proceedings under a special regime for banks could be either court-based or administrative in nature.[95]

Indeed, since the general corporate insolvency rules are primarily focused on private interests and aim to ensure the maximum and equitable realization of assets of all creditors, they are not sufficient enough to work in a bank crisis situation. In the event of corporate insolvency, bank assets would need to be liquidated in order to meet all the liabilities, which is difficult inherently. A considerable decline in value could result from the liquidation of bank assets since the bank loans may not have reached their maturity and may not have a ready an appropriate market value yet.[96] However, in a nationwide systemic banking crisis, the interest of domestic financial stability may conflict with, or to be more specific, trump the private interest of individual creditors. This is due to the extreme importance role of the banks, which provide vital financial services such as processing payments and offering liquidity, and the insolvency of the bank could bring chaotic and costly disruption to the domestic financial system.

In China, however, banks are still subject simply to the normal corporate insolvency laws and regulations without specific solvency regimes designed for banks. Therefore, a special resolution process overseen and directed by

[93] Rosa Lastra and Andrew Campbell, 'Definition of Bank Insolvency and Types of Bank Insolvency Proceedings' in Rosa Lastra (ed.), *Cross-Border Bank Insolvency* (Oxford University Press, 2011), p. 27.

[94] Rosa Lastra, 'Northern Rock, UK Bank Insolvency and Cross-Border Bank Insolvency' (2008) 9 *Journal of Banking Regulation* 165.

[95] IMF, 'An Overview of the Legal, Institutional, and Regulatory Framework for Bank Insolvency' (2009), https://www.imf.org/en/Publications/Policy-Papers/Issues/2016/12/31/An-Overview-of-the-Legal-Institutional-and-Regulatory-Framework-for-Bank-Insolvency-PP4327.

[96] Iris H-Y Chiu and Joanna Wilson, *Banking Law and Regulation* (Oxford University Press, 2019), p. 603.

the regulator is necessary to better meet the demands of financial stability and protect critical customer continuities in China.

3.5.2 Example of the Lex Specialis in bank insolvency

A series of financial crises worldwide has clearly demonstrated the need for a special framework to deal with insolvent banks as part of the overall FSN, due to the unique characteristics of banks. As the IMF suggested, a bank failure can produce a much wider spectrum of negative consequences than the failure of a non-financial enterprise.[97]

The United Kingdom is an example of this situation where the need for a *lex specialis* in dealing with systemic bank insolvency has been realized against the Northern Rock Crisis episode. Northern Rock is a UK publicly listed building society. Within thirty years, it had grown from an amalgamation of small regional building companies into a leading competitor in the UK household lending market. It had demutualized and rose to the top of FTSE 100, the exclusive club for the elite UK quoted companies, and in the process had become the fourth-largest bank in the United Kingdom by share of lending.[98] However, Northern Rock crisis led to one of the most enduring images of the financial crisis in the United Kingdom, with a long line of panicked customers queueing to withdraw cash in September 2007. The collapse of Northern Rock was due to its reliant on short-term financing from the wholesale markets and securities issuances, rather than on retail deposits to fund mortgages.[99] Given the unusual distortion to the wholesale markets, temporary special funding may seem to be inevitable, which was the issue that the FSN and LOLR facilities were originally designed to handle. However, they did not provide confidence to depositors and investors during the Northern Rock crisis episode. This lack of confidence made the UK policymaker realize there is a lack of appropriate framework in dealing with the crisis-stricken banks. The way that the UK government has handled the Northern Rock has indicated a strong official desire to preserve the company at almost any cost. Apart from direct cash injection by the government of over £40 billion, Northern Rock and other banks also benefited from the

[97] IMF, 'An Overview of the Legal, Institutional, and Regulatory Framework for Bank Insolvency' (2009), https://www.imf.org/en/Publications/Policy-Papers/Issues/2016/12/31/An-Overview-of-the-Legal-Institutional-and-Regulatory-Framework-for-Bank-Insolvency-PP4327.

[98] Dominic O' Connell, 'The collapse of Northern Rock: Ten years on', *BBC* (12 September 2017), https://www.bbc.co.uk/news/business-41229513.

[99] Emma Dunkley, 'Ten years after Northern Rock: Has UK banking changed?', *Financial Times* (12 September 2017), https://www.ft.com/content/d05c3ea4-97bf-11e7-a652-cde3f882dd7b.

government assistance in attempting to segregate their toxic assets into new legal companies.[100]

In 2008, the Banking Act 2009 was passed by the UK House of Parliament, providing a special resolution regime for resolving banks. The UK practice has a widespread influence, leading to a degree of global harmonization in the framework for bank crisis management and resolution. Similarly, the failure of the US investment bank Lehman Brothers also highlights the problems in relying on corporate insolvency laws to resolve a failed bank. Soon after the UK Banking Act 2009, the US Dodd–Frank Act 2010 was passed, giving the FDIC extensive rights in resolving and liquidating banks as conservator, with a set of special insolvency regime for banks. For instance, with regard to the distribution of the banks' assets and liabilities, the FDIC has the authority to make other banks accountable for the losses of a failed bank under its shared supervision (e.g. within the same bank holding company). In addition, the FDIC has broad jurisdiction to revoke agreements made by insolvent bank before it entered conservatorship or receivership if such arrangement would facilitate the efficient management of the bank's operations.[101]

3.5.3 Policy implications for China

Up till now, the PRC Enterprise Bankruptcy Law 2006, which took effect on 1 June 2007, is the most significant piece of legislation governing the insolvency system in mainland China. Although there has been a strong call for legislation on bank insolvency, the liquidation and resolution of bank is still subject to the general corporate insolvency regime. As has been illustrated by the practice of other jurisdictions during several waves of the global financial crisis, a bank insolvency framework is crucial for the safety and soundness of the financial system at large, from the integrity of the payment systems to the public confidence in the domestic banking system.

China is edging closer to enacting a financial stability law which would fix the scattered set of rules currently used to handle the financial risks and provide a legal basis for the prevention and resolution of major financial risks.[102] On 6 April 2022, the PBoC published the Financial Stability Law of the People's Republic of China (Draft), which contains important provisions on the

[100] Roman Tomasic, 'Creating a Template for Banking Insolvency Law Reform after the Collapse of Northern Rock' in Paul Omar (ed.), *International Insolvency Law* (Routledge, 2013).

[101] Iris H-Y Chiu and Joanna Wilson, *Banking Law and Regulation* (Oxford University Press, 2019), p. 605.

[102] OuYang Shi Jia and Zhou Lan Xu, 'Draft law on financial stability targets risks', *China Daily* (29 December 2022), https://www.chinadaily.com.cn/a/202212/29/WS63acedfaa31057c47eba6bff.html.

bankruptcy and restructuring of financial institutions. The draft law introduces a series of resolutions, including overall transfer of assets and liabilities, establishment of bridge banks and special purpose vehicles, and suspension or termination of netting, in accordance with the principle of international market-based rule of law.[103] From such legal system arrangements, it seems that the legal conditions are ready to promote bankruptcy and reorganization within banking and financial institutions in China.

The specificity of the objectives that support a *lex specialis* in China's banking system is based on the uniqueness of banks, given their functions as intermediaries for payments, deposit takes, and credit providers; the risk contagion in the event of bank failures, due to their special vulnerability under a fractional reserve system, where a bank will never be able to honour the convertibility guarantee; and the public interest associated with sound banking and the efficient operation of the financial system.[104]

Over the past few decades, China has continued its efforts at banking reform. However, the absence of legal basis, inadequate transparency and government intervention constitute main problems in banking insolvency proceedings. It is imperative to make further improvements in each of these areas. First, as mentioned above, a special legislation for banking insolvency is strongly recommended in China, in order to provide detailed information for bank closures. Without a consistent way guided by legislation, the authorities may occasionally decide on a case-by-case basis regarding the closure and liquidation of banks, and such *ad hoc* approach may invariably not always transparent enough for all participants in the financial markets.[105] Second, the bank restructuring and liquidation policies in China needs to be more transparent. In practice, the dividing line between illiquidity and insolvency of banks is not always easy to draw. The competent authorities may not always declare an economically insolvent bank legally insolvent; alternatively, they may offer financial assistance. Therefore, it is helpful if a set of fundamental indicators to be published by individual banks for analysing the economy and liquidity condition of each institution. In addition, the independence of the PBoC in the proceeding of bank insolvency and liquidation has long been a problem in China. Typically, local governments have a large influence on the decision regarding the liquidation or closure of the local bank. In order to safeguard local interest, local governments would even impede the closure

[103] PBoC, 'Financial Stability Law of the People's Republic of China (Draft)' (6 April 2022), Article 30, http://www.pbc.gov.cn/goutongjiaoliu/113456/113469/4525742/index.html.

[104] Rosa Lastra and Andrew Campbell, 'Definition of Bank Insolvency and Types of Bank Insolvency Proceedings' in Rosa Lastra (ed.), *Cross-Border Bank Insolvency* (Oxford University Press, 2011), p. 39

[105] Zhu Jun, 'Closure of financial institutions in China' (1999) BIS Working Paper, https://www.bis.org/publ/plcy07u.pdf.

or liquidation process, which makes the PBoC even harder to adhere to the market principles.[106] In this regard, to reduce governments' intervention in the field of bank insolvency should also be emphasized, stepping forward to a more independent central bank in China.

In the past decade, bank insolvency law has evolved into a field of its own, intersecting with and affecting branches of law as well as core values in those branches. Despite its incomplete state in China, it has proved to be a source of constant fascination and intellectual curiosity for those in the banking industry and academia. It is certain to remain so in the foreseeable future.[107]

3.5.4 How three pillars of FSN work together effectively?

Bank crisis management comprises a series of responses that function as the FSN, aimed at dealing with crisis situations that may threaten the stability of the financial market and the continuation of bank activities.[108] Typically, the FSN framework contains three pillars: first, an explicit deposit insurance scheme; second, the central bank's role as the LOLR; and third, bank insolvency regulation. The cooperation and coordination mechanism among these three pillars of the FSN is as important as the improvement of detailed mechanisms to achieve effective financial regulation.

Establishing an FSN framework is essential for quickly restoring and maintaining public confidence in the banking and financial system, which is the primary goal of the entire crisis management process. Furthermore, to facilitate globally consistent approaches and international coordination, China must establish an independent resolution framework with comparable key authorities. This will allow crisis management processes to be framed within similar institutional frameworks globally. The relationship among the three pillars is especially important in the context of financial crisis management, where the framework combines ex-ante rules and explicit procedures. Relevant crisis management authorities, including the PRC Finance Ministry, the PBoC, and the National Financial Regulatory Administration (NFRA), should coordinate with each other, specify each department's obligations, and outline the procedures to be followed in managing a crisis.

The FSN is closely intertwined with the country's macroprudential regulation. Macroprudential policy seeks to address systemic financial risks both

[106] Ibid.

[107] Matthias Haentjens and Bob Wessels, 'Three Paradigm Shifts in Recent Bank Insolvency Law' (2016) 7 *Journal of International Banking Law and Regulation* 396.

[108] Rosa M. Lastra and Geoffrey Wood, 'Bank Insolvency in the Context of Crisis Management' in Rosa Lastra (ed.), *Cross-Border Bank Insolvency* (Oxford University Press, 2011), p. 1.

broadly and in a countercyclical manner. Specifically, it aims to enhance the financial system's resilience to withstand shocks through the timely setting and release of buffers, avert the accumulation of systemic risks, and restrain structural vulnerabilities arising from financial system interconnections. Therefore, macroprudential regulation is an important complement to the FSN, as it helps mitigate the risks that the safety net is designed to protect against. Currently, the PBoC is leading a joint conference on financial regulation and coordination, which includes the banking regulator (NFRA), the China Securities Regulatory Commission (CSRC), and the State Administration of Foreign Exchange (SAFE) as participants.[109] Therefore, China may be approaching an end to the uncertainty and ambiguity surrounding the management and resolution of bank crises, supported by international convergence in establishing an FSN. China will expand its financial institution reforms to further strengthen the regulatory framework for financial stability and mitigate risks among key enterprise groups and financial institutions.[110]

3.6 Conclusion

After years of persistent efforts, China's construction of an FSN has yielded positive results, effectively guarding against systemic financial risks. Significant progress has been made towards the reform goals of preventing and resolving major financial risks to better safeguard China's national economic and financial security. This involves continuously improving the pillars of the traditional FSN, including the deposit insurance scheme, the LOLR, and a special bank insolvency regime. This chapter provides a detailed analysis of the best international practices for these three pillars and their application in China. It also highlights ways to enhance the effectiveness of the FSN by improving cooperation and coordination among these pillars. Additionally, strengthening macroprudential regulation plays an important role in creating a more robust and effective FSN. A well-functioning FSN, together with the institutional reform of Chinese financial regulators, will contribute to the effective regulation of China's financial industry.

[109] The People's Bank of China, 'Macroprudential goals, implementation and cross-border communication' (2017) BIS Paper No. 94, https://www.bis.org/publ/bppdf/bispap94h.pdf.

[110] Lanxu Zhou, 'New fund to strengthen financial safety net, smooth market slumps', *China Daily* (28 September 2022), http://www.chinadaily.com.cn/a/202209/28/WS63339dcaa310fd2b29e7a208.html.

Chapter 4
China's banking industry

4.1 Introduction

The size and strength of financial institutions, especially banks, is a key metric in assessing financial superpowers. When we talk about the big names in any country's financial industries, we are likely to first think about their well-known banks, such as the HSBC from the United Kingdom, JPMorgan Chase from the United States, MUFG Bank from Japan, BNP Paribas from France, Banco Santander from Spain, and UBS from Switzerland, and HDFC Bank from India. Banks play an essential role in modern economies by taking deposits from the public and then lending funds to individuals, corporations, governments, and other organizations that need financing. Through banks' credit intermediation function, the quantity of currency in circulation is multiplied. In many countries in continental Europe (e.g. France, Germany, and Italy) and Japan, a majority of financial resources have been allocated through banks in contrast to direct capital markets financing that plays a secondary role in such countries. In countries like the United States and the United Kingdom, banking institutions and capital markets tend to play an equally important role in matching the supply and demand of funds in the economy. The division between financial institutions-based financing and financial markets-based financing varies across the globe. The banking industry has been the cornerstone of any financial industry, so we first examine China's banking industry before discussing the country's capital markets and Fintech sectors in the latter chapters.

There is no doubt that China's banking industry is the largest in the world if we consider the total amount of banking assets in the country. In 2022, Chinese banks together hold financial assets worth $47 trillion.[1] It is larger than that of any G7 countries, including the US banking sector (with $30 trillion asset as the world's second-largest banking industry) and the UK banking sector (with $16.88 trillion asset as the largest in Europe). If we look at the

[1] Statista, 'Total assets of the banking sector in select countries worldwide 2022, by country', https://www.statista.com/statistics/875144/banking-sector-assets-worldwide-by-country/.

Towards Financial Superpower. Lerong Lu, Oxford University Press. © Lerong Lu (2025).
DOI: 10.1093/9780198948568.003.0004

size of individual banks, Chinese banks are also incomparable. Among the world's top 100 banks valued by total assets, China has 20 of the largest banks, compared with 11 from the United States, 8 from Japan, 6 from the United Kingdom, 6 from France, 6 from South Korea, 5 from Australia, and 4 from Germany.[2] Each of the 'big four' bank—the Industrial and Commercial Bank of China (ICBC), the China Construction Bank (CCB), the Agricultural Bank of China (ABC), and the Bank of China (BOC)—holds assets worth over $4 trillion, making top five banks globally. In contrast, the largest US bank, JPMorgan Chase, possesses assets worth $3.7 trillion, while the largest UK bank, HSBC, has $2.9 trillion on its balance sheet.[3] Not only are Chinese banks the biggest financial institutions on our planet, but they are also the most profitable corporations in the world. For example, the ICBC posted a net profit of CNY360 billion ($50 billion) in 2022, with an increase of 3.1% from the previous year.[4]

This chapter focuses on China's gigantic banking sector and analyses its practice and regulation. The discussions cover most segments of China's banking industry, including central banking, commercial banking, and shadow banking.[5] Section 4.2 considers the practice of the People's Bank of China (PBoC) as the Chinese central bank and its monetary policy tools like the required reserve ratio (RRR), relending and rediscounting, open market operation (OMO), and other innovative monetary policy instruments. Central banking is discussed first because it sets the macroeconomic environment where commercial banks and other financial institutions operate. Section 4.3 discusses the practice and status quo of Chinese commercial banks. It covers the main players in the banking arena like the large national banks (the big four and joint-equity commercial banks), the regional banks (various urban and rural commercial banks), as well as the new players such as the private banks, digital banks, and foreign-equity banks. It then assesses the regulatory regime for China's banking industry, including the capital requirement, prudential regulation, consumer protection, and interest rate mechanism

[2] S&P Global, 'The world's 100 largest banks, 2023', https://www.spglobal.com/marketintelligence/en/news-insights/research/the-world-s-100-largest-banks-2023.

[3] Ibid.

[4] *People Finance*, 'ICBC: 2022 net profit exceeded 360 billion yuan with growth rate of 3.1%' (31 March 2023), http://finance.people.com.cn/n1/2023/0331/c1004-32655126.html.

[5] The discussion in this chapter will not cover three policy banks in China: China Development Bank, The Export-Import Bank of China, and Agricultural Development Bank of China. Policy banks are specialized, non-profit financial institutions created by the Chinese government to execute its economic policies and manage financial operations within designated sectors. This approach differentiates policy banks from commercial banks as the former handles clearly defined policy-related activities. These banks primarily secure their funds through the issuance of financial bonds or loans from the central bank, and typically do not accept deposits from the public.

(e.g. the Loan Prime Rate or LPR). Section 4.4 demystifies the trillion-dollar-worth shadow banking system in China that consists of various banking-like activities operating outside of the regulated sector, such as private lending, P2P lending, wealth management, and trust lending. Shadow banking helps capital-starved private entrepreneurs raise finance and provides investment opportunities for ordinary residents. Section 4.5 draws a conclusion for the chapter.

4.2 Central banking: devising effective monetary policy tools

The PBoC has been the monetary authority and central bank since the foundation of the People's Republic of China in 1949.[6] It is an extremely powerful agency in the Chinese economy since it used to operate commercial banking businesses directly during the plan economy period. The PBoC also assumed most regulatory functions for overseeing Chinese banks, insurance, and securities industries, before relevant power had been delegated to other specialized agencies established in the 1990s and the 2000s. At present, the PBoC's role is mostly aligned with other major central banks like the US Federal Reserve System, the Bank of England, the European Central Bank, the Bank of Japan, and the Reserve Bank of India. Nonetheless, the PBoC is mandated with the task to promote economic developments and to support the important economic strategies in China.[7] Given the PBoC's important role in the macroeconomic management in the socialist market economy, it is worth examining its major monetary policies tools, both new and old. This section considers the traditional monetary policy tools such as the RRR, relending and rediscounting, OMO, as well as some innovative monetary policy tools.

4.2.1 Required reserve ratio

The PBoC employs a monetary policy tool known as the deposit required reserve ratio (RRR) to regulate the amount of funds that financial institutions must deposit in the central bank's reserve.[8] It refers to the percentage of

[6] For the history and functions of PBoC, see Section 2.5 'The People's Bank of China (PBoC)' of Chapter 2.

[7] The PBoC's objective of monetary policy is to maintain the stability of the value of the currency and thereby promote economic growth. See the Law of the People's Republic of China on The People's Bank of China, Article 3.

[8] PBoC, 'People's Bank of China decides to raise reserve requirements ratio' (23 August 2023), http://www.pbc.gov.cn/english/130721/2830889/index.html.

the PBoC's required deposit to the bank's total deposit. After depositing the reserve, commercial banks are not able to use the funds freely like lending out or investing in financial markets. RRR ensures that banks could meet the demand from their customers to withdraw funds and other fund-clearing needs, working as a cushion against any unexpected withdrawals of funding that are likely to cause bank runs. In practice, central banks or monetary authorities, by adjusting the RRR, could affect the credit expansion capacity of financial institutions, thereby indirectly controlling the money supply. For instance, if the PBoC increases the RRR, Chinese banks will have to set aside a larger chunk of their deposits and thus have a lower amount of funds to lend. This will decrease the money supply in the economy, which might slow down the overheated economy and control inflation. On the contrary, if the PBoC lowers the RRR, Chinese banks will have more funds at hand to lend. This will increase the supply of money in the economy and potentially lower the costs of borrowing. It is likely to boost the economic growth and raise inflation. Therefore, RRR is a key monetary instrument in influencing the country's money supply and credit conditions.

Drawing lessons from the international practices, the PBoC adjusts the RRR to manage liquidity in the banking industry, stabilize prices, and support economic growth. The RRR serves as a vital policy lever, allowing the central bank to strike a balance between fostering economic activities and preventing excessive financial risks and banking crises. Nonetheless, the application of the RRR also reflects China's unique economic landscape and policy objectives. Given the diverse structure of China's banking system, which includes a mix of state-owned commercial banks and other banking institutions backed by private or foreign capital, the PBoC tailors its RRR policies to address the specific needs and operating challenges of these institutions, depending on their sizes and deposit bases. As of the 19 September 2023, the deposit reserve rate for large financial institutions is 10.50%, while the rate for small and medium-sized financial institutions is 7.50%.[9] The differentiated rates are hugely beneficial for the world's largest banking sector. Figure 4.1 shows the historical RRR level in China from 2007 to 2023. As the Chinese government continues its efforts to balance economic expansion with risk mitigation, the RRR remains a dynamic and adaptive tool within the broader framework of the country's monetary policies.

There are several advantages of using RRR as the monetary policy tool. First, the effect of adjusting RRR is strong compared with other policy

[9] PBoC, 'Required reserves', http://www.pbc.gov.cn/en/3688229/3688335/3730270/index.html.

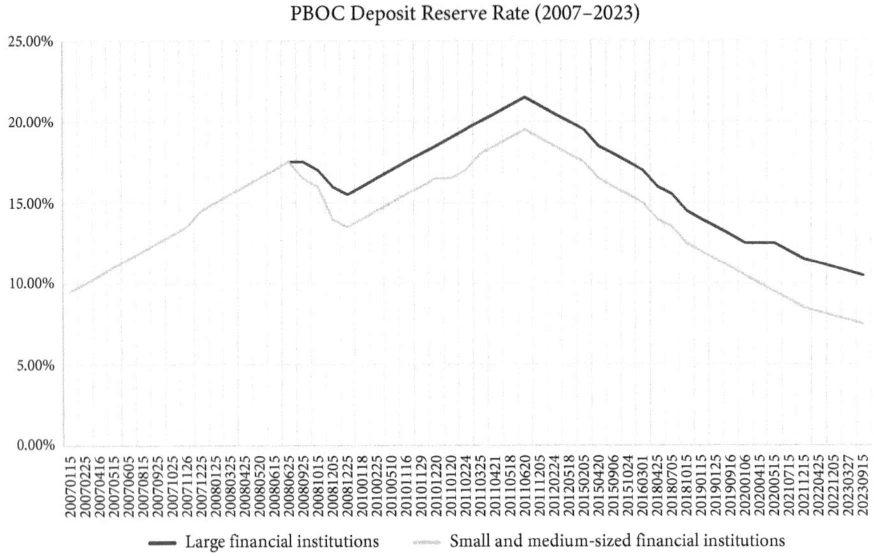

Figure 4.1 The People's Bank of China deposit reserve rate (2007–2023)
Source: The People's Bank of China.

instruments. The increase in deposit reserves can quickly freeze excess liquidity on the market. On the contrary, the reduction of the reserve ratio can rapidly release liquidity to the economy. Second, the adjusting of RRR is at the full discretion of PBoC, since the central bank has absolute control over the deposit reserve ratio and could exercise its power at any time when it sees fit. Third, as the policy intention of PBoC is strong, modifying the RRR is likely to have a very quick effect when it directly affects market expectations. However, there are also certain limitations to the use of RRR. For example, adjusting the RRR could bring a great shock to the economy within a short period of time, since the policy tool is directly linked to the change of currency multiplier, thus affecting the volume of money supply. In practice, the policy impact is likely to be different for different banks as each institution has dissimilar liquidity structure. The adjustment of RRR could do great harm to banks that are short of liquidity, as they are prone to a liquidity crisis. Moreover, the adjustment of RRR will interfere with the operation plans of commercial banks and increase the difficulty of liquidity risk management. Raising the RRR will essentially act as a tax rise on banks, pushing up the cost of capital. It indirectly raises the cost of borrowing in the society, affecting most households and businesses.

4.2.2 Relending and rediscounting

Relending and rediscounting are two important financial mechanisms utilized by the PBoC as part of its monetary policy toolkits. Relending (or reloan) and rediscounting are often used together by the PBoC which frequently issues a combined quota of relending and rediscounting for commercial banks.[10] For instance, in June 2023, the PBoC expanded the relending and rediscount quota by CNY200 billion, resulting in the outstanding relending loans and balance of rediscount nationwide totalling CNY2.6 trillion.[11] In terms of relending, the PBoC provides direct credit for other financial institutions, such as policy banks, commercial banks, and other lending institutions. It aims to support specific economic sectors so as to achieve wider macroeconomic objectives. The relending facility involves the PBoC making direct loans to financial institutions, which, in turn, lend to targeted sectors, such as agriculture sectors, small businesses, green projects, or other areas in the economy that attract policy priority. Rediscounting facility, in contrast, belongs to indirect lending. It involves the PBoC purchasing unexpired bills of exchange or other short-term credit instruments from Chinese commercial banks and other eligible financial institutions. The short-term debt instruments will be bought by the central bank at a discount to their face value. Rediscounting enables commercial banks to convert the illiquid or less liquid assets into cash. This action, therefore, immediately increases the liquidity position of banks and affects the general credit condition in the country. Through conducting the rediscounting operation, the PBoC provides a liquidity lifeline to commercial banks, thereby supporting their ability to create extra credits.

Relending and rediscounting instruments play an important and indispensable role in the China's implementation of effective monetary policies. They have some obvious advantages. The tools of relending and rediscounting offer flexibility in fine-tuning monetary conditions, contributing to a more elastic currency.[12] They allow the PBoC to respond swiftly and accurately to the evolving economic circumstances and to fulfil the evolving

[10] PBoC, 'The PBoC increased reloan and rediscount quota by 300 billion yuan this year to support the financing of small and micro businesses and private enterprises' (23 October 2018), http://www.pbc.gov.cn/english/130721/3650283/index.html.

[11] The State Council of China, 'China's central bank steps up financial support to agriculture, small firms' (30 June 2023), https://english.www.gov.cn/news/202306/30/content_WS649ed7c4c6d0868f4e8dd642.html.

[12] Scott Freeman, 'Rediscounting Under Aggregate Risk' (1999) 43 *Journal of Monetary Economics* 197–216.

policy objectives. The central bank could direct funds to specific sectors they deem vital for economic development, ensuring the efficient functioning of credit markets. Moreover, relending and rediscounting relate to the fulfilment of the central bank's role as the lender of last resort (LOLR) when commercial banks in short of liquidity have nowhere else to borrow funds. Such tools are of great importance for maintaining China's financial stability. However, there are certain limitations of the PBoC's relending and rediscounting instruments. For instance, despite providing such credit facilities, the PBoC cannot compel commercial banks to utilize them. Banks, as commercial organizations, could freely choose to take up the credit instruments or not. Thus, it might have limited policy effects on influencing the supply of credit in the economy, compared with the direct adjustment of RRR. Also, as the central bank plays the role of LOLR, it is likely to increase the moral hazard faced by commercial banks since bankers could always expect the salvation from the central banks so will take excessive risks in their business operations.

4.2.3 Open market operation

Open market operations (OMOs) are a popular monetary policy tool used by global central banks, such as the US Federal Reserve, the European Central Bank, and the PBOC, to influence the availability of credit and steer interest rates.[13] It denotes the process by which a central bank purchases or sells securities in the public financial markets with the aim of regulating the monetary supply. Through the OMOs, central banks can infuse or withdraw liquidity from the overall economy. The use of OMOs also sends a signal about the central banks' stance on monetary policy. Purchasing securities injects capital into the economy, which in turn reduces interest rates, increases the availability of funds, and stimulates economic growth. Conversely, selling securities withdraws capital, which elevates interest rates, escalates borrowing costs, and slows down economic activity. The PBoC has a number of OMO tools, such as transaction in cash, repurchase agreement (repo), reverse repurchase agreement (reverse repo), central bank bills swap (CBS), and short-term liquidity operations (SLO).[14] Quantitative easing (QE) is a monetary tool akin to OMO, as it involves the central bank purchasing a large volume of financial assets in the markets, such as the long-term government

[13] Federal Reserve Board, 'Open market operations', https://www.federalreserve.gov/monetarypolicy/openmarket.htm.

[14] PBoC, 'Open market operations', http://www.pbc.gov.cn/en/3688229/3688335/3730267/index.html.

bonds, to stimulate the economic activities by increasing the money supply and lowering interest rate.[15]

There are some preconditions for central banks to carry out effective OMOs. First of all, the central bank must have sufficient power and financial strength (or capital reserve) to intervene in the entire financial market. Second, there should exist a developed and well-functioning financial market. For OMOs to be successful, the range of tradable securities needs to be substantial, the rationality of market participants must be high, and the policy transmission mechanism should be well-established. Moreover, OMOs must be complemented by other monetary policy tools to make them effective in practice. In terms of China, it has one of the largest financial markets in the world as thousands of shares, bonds, and other financial instruments are being traded publicly.[16] Also, the PBoC is a very powerful institution with the legislative mandate to conduct various monetary policy tools.[17] It is well capitalized with a total asset worth CNY45.69 trillion.[18] All these conditions enable the PBoC to conduct OMOs in a timely and efficient manner to regulate the supply of money in China.

We could observe some advantages of using OMOs compared with other monetary policy tools. For example, the PBoC takes the initiative to buy and sell securities in the public financial market with absolute autonomy. It could inject or withdraw an exact amount of liquidity from the economy. However, we should bear in mind that the policy objective of OMOs is to regulate the supply of money, but not to make a profit like other market participants. In addition, OMOs are considered to have strong flexibility. The PBoC is able to carry out regular and continuous operations, and the number of transactions can be as large or small. It is safe to say that OMOs are the most important monetary policy tool of the central bank to be used on a daily basis. OMOs come with a moderate effect, which causes limited market volatility.

Nonetheless, the utilization of OMOs has a notification function that tends to suggest the attitudes and stance of the central bank, having far-reaching influence in the financial industry and overall economy. Some research indicates that adjustments to the PBoC's target rate within OMOs are highly effective in adjusting the short-term treasury rates.[19] OMOs are likely to

[15] Bank of England, 'Quantitative easing', https://www.bankofengland.co.uk/monetary-policy/quantitative-easing.

[16] For discussion of capital markets in China, see Chapter 4.

[17] The Law of the People's Republic of China on the People's Bank of China, Article 23.

[18] PBoC, 'Balance sheet of monetary authority' (January 2024), http://www.pbc.gov.cn/diaochatongjisi/resource/cms/2024/01/2024011616021539705.htm.

[19] Zheng Qiao and Yangshu Liu, 'Open Market Operation Effectiveness in China' (2017) 53 *Emerging Markets Finance and Trade* 1706–1719.

directly affect the bank interest rate, inflation level, and employment rate. Rather than using alternative monetary policy tools to adjust lending volume, OMOs enable the PBoC to mitigate price inflation or deflation and alter the credit cost. This empowers the central bank to moderate the fluctuations of the economic cycle and alleviate financial turbulence. The PBoC, during the downturns, reduces the borrowing costs to boost commercial activities and economic expansion. In contrast, during the period of rapid economic expansion, the PBoC could escalate the borrowing costs to curb speculative behaviours and deflate possible economic bubbles. Finally, OMOs have the functionality to influence employment levels. By injecting liquidity and reducing interest rates, the PBoC can facilitate the creation of new businesses and the hiring of staff, leading to a rise in job numbers, or vice versa.

4.2.4 Innovative monetary policy tools

The PBoC has been using a range of monetary tools, some of which are more innovative and newly created. This section discusses the new-type monetary policy instruments that had been created during the 2010s and 2020s.

Standing Lending Facility (SLF): The PBoC invented the SLF in 2013, as a liquidity adjustment tool, to meet the short-term liquidity needs of financial institutions.[20] Acting as the upper limit of the interest rate corridor, the SLF operation aids in maintaining the stability of money-market interest rates. The common operational period of SLF is overnight, seven days, and one month. For example, in January 2024, the PBoC conducted SLF transactions totalling CNY2.812 billion.[21] This comprised CNY112 million in overnight operations, CNY1 billion in seven-day operations, and CNY1.7 billion in one-month operations. SLF is a new monetary policy tool of the central bank, mainly issued to policy banks and national commercial banks, which is equivalent to banks pledging their high-quality bonds and credit assets to the central bank to borrow money. There are some special characteristics of SLF. SLF will be initiated by financial institutions (instead of the central bank), which can apply for standing lending facilities according to their own liquidity needs. The PBoC will extend loans to the financial

[20] PBoC, 'Standing lending facility', http://www.pbc.gov.cn/en/3688229/3688335/3730279/index.html.

[21] PBoC, 'SLF operations in January 2024', http://www.pbc.gov.cn/en/3688229/3688335/3730279/5238313/index.html.

institutions upon request, and the loan amount is limited by the pooled collateral provided. SLF is a one-to-one transaction between the central bank and financial institutions, which is highly targeted. The counterparty coverage of the SLF is fairly wide, usually covering depository financial institutions. The primary function of the SLF is to enhance the efficacy of monetary policy implementation, mitigate liquidity risks within the banking system, and strengthen the effectiveness of money-market interest rate regulation. In practice, many global central banks have adopted monetary policy tools similar to SLF, such as the US Federal Reserve's discount window lending,[22] the European Central Bank's Marginal Lending Facility,[23] and the Bank of Japan's Complementary Lending Facility.[24]

Influenced by increased uncertainty of the international economic and financial situation and the fluctuation of various factors affecting liquidity, the volatility of short-term liquidity supply and demand of our country's banking system has increased in recent years. Especially when multiple factors stack up to each other or market expectations change, it is possible that the gap between short-term fund supply and demand in the market is difficult to be solved in a timely manner through the money-market financing. It not only increases the difficulty of liquidity management of financial institutions, but also is not conducive to the central bank to adjust the total liquidity. In order to improve the effect of monetary regulation, it is necessary to further innovate and improve the liquidity supply and regulation mechanism, constantly improve the ability to cope with short-term liquidity fluctuations and provide necessary liquidity guarantee for maintaining the normal operation of the financial system. When the market liquidity gap is relatively serious at some specific time (such as before the Spring Festival), and the direction of monetary policy has not fully turned to easing, then SLF can save the emergency. Therefore, compared with conventional monetary policies such as lowering the reserve ratio and interest rate, SLF can effectively control liquidity according to market conditions.

Medium-term Lending Facility (MLF): MLF was established in September 2014, usually for three to twelve months.[25] The operational period for MLF is longer than that of SLF. Its operation is more policy-oriented, as

[22] The Federal Reserve, 'Discount window lending', https://www.federalreserve.gov/regreform/discount-window.htm.

[23] European Central Bank, 'Standing facilities', https://www.ecb.europa.eu/mopo/implement/sf/html/index.en.html.

[24] Bank of Japan, 'Complementary lending facility', https://www.boj.or.jp/en/mopo/measures/mkt_ope/len_a/index.htm.

[25] PBoC, 'Medium-term lending facility', http://www.pbc.gov.cn/en/3688229/3688335/3730282/index.html.

MLF is often used to support agriculture, rural enterprises, and small and micro enterprises. MLF targets commercial banks and policy banks that meet the requirements of macroprudential regulation. MLF can be carried out through bidding. The central bank will conduct regular MLF operations on a monthly basis, and might renew the issued lending facilities near the maturity date with renewed interest rates. In February 2024, the PBoC carried out MLF operations worth RMB 500 billion to meet financial institutions' liquidity demands.[26] These were one-year loans at an interest rate of 2.50%, the same as the previous month, with the outstanding MLFs reaching RMB 7.292 trillion at the month's end. The specific mode of MLF operation is that financial institutions will provide high-quality bonds such as treasury bonds, central bank bills, policy financial bonds, and high-grade credit bonds as qualified collaterals, and then the central bank provides credit funds to such institutions. MLF influences the medium-term financing cost of financial institutions and supports relevant institutions to provide low-cost loans for their borrowers, with the purpose of indirectly reducing social financing costs.

Pledged Supplementary Lending (PSL): PSL was created by the PBoC in April 2014 as an original monetary policy instrument. PSL provides a new channel for the central bank to adjust the monetary base. The PSL interest rate, which is the rate at which policy and commercial banks secure financing from the central bank by pledging assets, steers the medium- to long-term interest rates. Since the end of 2013, the central bank has established an effective interest rate corridor for short-term rates through the SLF, with the PSL designated to guide mid- to long-term rates. PSL operations are conducted in the form of pledge, and qualified collateral includes high-grade bond assets and high-quality credit assets. In January 2024, the PBoC's net issuance of PSL to the China Development Bank, Export-Import Bank of China, and Agricultural Development Bank of China amounted to RMB 150 billion; the total outstanding PSLs were RMB 3.4022 trillion.[27] In the practice of central banking, the PSL is a monetary policy tool very similar to relending. Relending is an unsecured credit loan, although the market tends to attach a financial stability connotation to relending, meaning that an institution will be relent only if it goes wrong (i.e. when the financial institutions face some liquidity or insolvency issues). During the 2010s, the PBoC had been gradually replacing the relending tool with PSL, but relending is still in the central bank's policy tool basket despite being used less frequently now.

[26] PBoC, 'MLF operations in February 2024', http://www.pbc.gov.cn/en/3688229/3688335/3730282/5260695/index.html.

[27] PBoC, 'PSL operations in January 2024', http://www.pbc.gov.cn/en/3688229/3688335/3730285/5238337/index.html.

The main function of PSL is to support the development of key areas and social undertakings in the national economy and to provide large-scale financing with a longer term to financial institutions, most of which are policy banks in practice. In China, there is a significant amount of credit issuance, such as infrastructure construction and people's livelihood projects expenditure, which are often government-guaranteed to some extent but exhibit poor profitability.[28] If commercial banks were to set their own prices solely based on market interest rates and adopt a completely commercial pricing approach, the higher cost of credit would fail to meet the demand for such financing. The central bank's PSL mechanism aims at guiding investment in these sectors by providing commercial banks with a portion of low-cost funds that aligns with the medium to long-term policy interest rate level. This measure can effectively contribute to reducing the overall cost of social financing.

Other structural monetary policy instruments: Apart from the above monetary policy tools, the PBoC has launched a series of new monetary policy instruments targeting special economic areas to fulfil certain policy objectives. For example, the PBoC has made lending facilities for supporting environment protection and green energy development, such as the carbon emission reduction facility (CERF).[29] Following State Council executive meeting decisions, the PBoC, in collaboration with the National Development and Reform Commission (NDRC) and the Ministry of Ecology and Environment (MEE), initiated the CERF in November 2021. The CERF serves twenty-one nationally licensed financial institutions, and selects foreign-funded and local banks, offering specialized support in clean energy, energy efficiency, environmental protection, and carbon reduction technologies. The PBoC supplies these lenders with funds at a low cost, amounting to 60% of the principal of the loans issued under the CERF. The PBoC also has other lending facilities for the clean and efficient use of coal (2021–2023), for the sci-tech innovation enterprises (2022), for the inclusive elderly care services (2022–2024), for the troubled property developers (2023), and for expanding rental housing supply (2023–2024). All of these special lending facilities help the PBoC play a proactive role in supporting the sustainable economic growth in China, complementing its main function as the monetary authority.

[28] China's policymakers prioritize people's livelihood projects that aim to enhance the well-being of the underprivileged and poor by providing job and business opportunities, improving housing conditions, and offering other forms of support. The PSL operations often provide support for the revitalization of shantytowns, the implementation of affordable housing projects, the development of agriculture, and the promotion of small and micro enterprises.

[29] PBoC, 'Introduction to structural monetary policy instruments (by the end of September 2023)', http://www.pbc.gov.cn/en/3688229/3688335/4738114/5241680/index.html.

4.3 Commercial banking: the key players and regulatory issues

China's commercial banking industry is large and diverse. At present, the major players in China's banking industry include the 'big four', which refers to the four largest state-owned banks in China, a dozen national joint-equity commercial banks, and hundreds of city commercial banks, rural commercial banks, and credit cooperatives. Compared to their Western rivals, Chinese banks have remained intact from the Global Financial Crisis of 2007–2008, and some of them have become the most valuable and profitable banks in the world. Most Chinese banks have certain government background as the state plays a multiple role in the industry as the shareholder, the regulator, and the player. This section introduces the composition of China's banking industry, including the large national banks, the regional banks, and the new entrants such as private banks and Fintech-empowered digital banks. It then discusses the key regulatory issues for the banking sector, such as the benchmark interest rate, the capital requirement, and the consumer protection regulation.

4.3.1 Large national banks

China has eighteen large banks operating in most provinces, including six 'large state-owned commercial banks' (or big six) and twelve 'joint-equity commercial banks'. Together the eighteen banks take up around 60% of total banking assets in the country, representing the major players in the banking industry.[30] The big six refers to the largest Chinese commercial banks directly controlled by the state through either the Ministry of Finance or the Central Huijin Investment Ltd which is the investment vehicle of China's central government. Headquartered in Beijing, Central Huijin was founded in December 2003 with the mandate to fulfil the state's role as an investor in major state-owned financial institutions.[31] However, Central Huijin refrains from intervening in the routine business activities of the entities it invests in. The big six includes the ICBC, the CCB, the ABC, the BOC, the Bank of Communications (BOCOM), and the Postal Savings Bank of China (PSBC). They are the tier-one players in China's banking industry that are concerned with

[30] NFRA, 'Total banking assets, total liabilities 2023 (Quarterly)' (21 February 2024), https://www.cbirc.gov.cn/cn/view/pages/ItemDetail.html?docId=1109300&itemId=954.

[31] Central Huijin Investment Ltd, 'About us', http://www.huijin-inv.cn/huijineng/About_Us/index.shtml.

Table 4.1 Large state-owned commercial banks in China

Banks' name	Year of establishment	Headquarter	Total assets (RMB, as of December 2022)
Bank of Communications	1908	Shanghai	13.0 trillion
Bank of China	1912	Beijing	28.9 trillion
China Construction Bank	1954	Beijing	34.6 trillion
Agricultural Bank of China	1979	Beijing	33.9 trillion
Industrial and Commercial Bank of China	1984	Beijing	39.6 trillion
Postal Savings Bank of China	2006	Beijing	14.1 trillion

Source: The 2023 financial reports of ICBC, CCB, ABC, BOC, BOCOM, and PSBC.

the financial stability in the country and internationally. Table 4.1 displays the big six's basic information such as their year of establishment, headquarter, and total assets.

In the media, it is more common to use the term 'big four' to call the ICBC, CCB, ABC, and BOC, as they have been the top lenders in China for many decades before the recent rise of BOCOM and PSBC.[32] In April 1987, the BOCOM officially opened for business and has become the first national state-owned joint-stock commercial bank in China. Now in the eyes of China's financial regulator, the BOCOM, due to its enormous size and financial strength, is being treated in the same way as the big four rather than other twelve joint-stock commercial banks. The PSBC is a relatively new bank, as it was established on 20 March 2007. It is a state-owned commercial bank built on the basis of China's previous postal savings management system. The PSBC inherited the postal finance business operated by the former State Post Bureau and China Post Group Corporation along with their banking assets and liabilities. Given the extensive network of China's post office system and its massive banking clients, the PSBC immediately became the fifth-largest bank in China after its formation. Therefore, the PSBC receives the same regulatory treatment as the largest commercial banks in China.

[32] See, for example, Cheng Leng and Edward White, 'China's biggest four banks feel property pinch from failing loans', *The Financial Times* (7 September 2022), https://www.ft.com/content/2f0eb985-ac20-4b09-8955-3be8925f1a12.

Although China holds over 3,900 deposit-taking institutions, the country's banking assets are relatively concentrated in the hands of a few largest institutions. At the end of 2023, the big six accounted for RMB 176.8 trillion or 42.4% of the total banking assets in China, which increased 13.1% from one year before.[33] In the banking industry, the size of a bank's assets is often perceived as an important indication of its strength and market position. Therefore, the leading market position of big six had made them hard to challenge by other Chinese banks for a long time. However, we also observe the rapid rise of some joint-stock commercial banks or city commercial banks that quickly expanded business operation across the country. Also, the rise of Alipay, WeChat Pay, and other Fintech platforms has diverted a lot of financial assets to new digital platforms, posing a threat to the big banks. The increased competition has forced the big four, or the big six, to improve the business efficiency and customer experience if they want to maintain their market status in the future.

During the 2000s and 2010s, the big six had all become a public company by listing their shares on the stock exchanges in Shanghai and Hong Kong. By inviting domestic and foreign investors to become their shareholders, the big six actively choose to receive more public scrutiny over its financial situation and business operation. This helps with the improvement of such banks' corporate governance standards, contributing to the building of modern financial institutions. For example, the British bank HSBC holds 19.03% of shares in the BOCOM as the second-largest shareholder, just next to China's Ministry of Finance that owns 23.88% in the BOCOM.[34] The Bank of America used to own 9.9% of stakes in the CCB as its strategic investor when the CCB went for the IPO in 2005.[35] Nonetheless, the government still have strong influence over the operation of the largest Chinese banks, since the state is their majority shareholder. The State Council has over 60% ownership in each of the big four. In reality, the central government appoints the Chairmen and CEOs of these banks, granting them the authority of vice-ministerial rank, which tends to cast them more as government officials than as traditional banking executives. Moreover, senior officials in the PBoC (central bank) and the National Financial Regulatory Administration (NFRA) (financial regulator) often have work experience in the big four,

[33] NFRA, 'Total banking assets, total liabilities 2023 (Quarterly)' (21 February 2024), https://www.cbirc.gov.cn/cn/view/pages/ItemDetail.html?docId=1109300&itemId=954.

[34] Bank of Communications, 'Shareholding info' (30 August 2023), https://www.bankcomm.com/BankCommSite/shtml/jyjr/en/2600223/2600238/2600348/list.shtml.

[35] Fiona Law, Prudence Ho, and Shayndi Raice, 'Bank of America Exits China Bank Stake', *The Wall Street Journal* (3 September 2013), https://www.wsj.com/articles/SB100014241278873244324045t79052401692576092.

or vice versa. The close relationship between the big four and the Chinese government has been a complicated issue for China's banking industry as it might hinder competition and reduce the efficiency of allocating financial resources.

Judging from the international standard, the big six are also the largest lenders in the world, as all of them rank as the top twenty-five global banks in terms of total assets.[36] The majority of their businesses is still taking place in China but they have established an international network with branches and offices located in most international financial centres. For instance, the BOC has been providing comprehensive financial services for its customers through its global network across the Chinese mainland, Hong Kong, Macau, Taiwan, and thirty-one overseas countries and regions.[37] By the end of 2018, ICBC had established 426 branches across 47 countries and regions, creating a global service network that spans Asia, Africa, Latin America, Europe, North America, and Australia.[38] They are international banking corporations providing financial services for Chinese and foreign citizens, corporations, and governments. It is a symbol of China's rise as an emerging financial superpower on the global stage.

Next to the big six, there are twelve joint-equity commercial banks, including China Merchants Bank (established in 1987, headquartered in Shenzhen), China CITIC Bank (1987, Beijing), Ping An Bank (1987, Shenzhen), Evergrowing Bank (1987, Yantai), China Guangfa Bank (1988, Guangzhou), Industrial Bank (1988, Fuzhou), China Everbright Bank (1992, Beijing), Hua Xia Bank (1992, Beijing), Shanghai Pudong Development Bank (1992, Shanghai), China Minsheng Bank (1996, Beijing), China Zheshang Bank (2004, Hangzhou), and China Bohai Bank (2005, Tianjin). Joint-equity commercial banks are significant lending institutions with operations across the country and most of them are publicly listed companies. They tend to be smaller than the big six in scale, but they typically exhibit stronger asset quality and profitability. The twelve banks in total own assets worth RMB 70.9 trillion or 17.0% of the national banking assets.[39] Like the big six, they are the mainstay of China's banking industry. The top eighteen banks (the big six plus the twelve joint-equity commercial banks) hold 60% of the market

[36] Relbank, 'World's largest banks by assets 2019' (20 October 2019), https://www.relbanks.com/worlds-top-banks/top-world-banks-by-assets-2019.

[37] Bank of China, 'Bank of China global network' (2011), https://pic.bankofchina.com/bocappd/report/201104/P020110427561564499932.pdf.

[38] ICBC, 'Overseas branches', https://big5.icbc.com.cn/en/column/1438058479532523524.html.

[39] NFRA, 'Total banking assets, total liabilities 2023 (Quarterly)' (21 February 2024), https://www.cbirc.gov.cn/cn/view/pages/ItemDetail.html?docId=1109300&itemId=954.

share in the country, while the remaining over 3,000 regional banks account for only 40%.

Joint-equity commercial banks possess significant governmental ties since most of them were originally established by local authorities. For instance, the Department of Finance in Fujian Province has been the largest shareholder of the Industrial Bank. Shanghai International Group, which is controlled by the Shanghai municipal government, has been the largest shareholder of Shanghai Pudong Development Bank. The notable outlier among national banks is China Minsheng Bank, founded in 1996 by private investors. Up until recently, it stood as the sole entirely privately owned bank in China. The big six and other national banks have traditionally been considered as more policy-oriented commercial banks due to significant political influence and state involvement. They are able to make substantial profits, benefiting from the quasi-monopolistic position and preferential policy support. In 2022, the ICBC posted the annual net profit of RMB 360.48 billion ($52.46 billion), making it one of the most profitable corporations in the world.[40]

4.3.2 Smaller regional banks

Apart from the eighteen national banks, China has thousands of smaller regional banks that operate within the boundaries of cities, counties, villages, and towns. There are 125 city commercial banks in the country that collectively hold assets worth RMB 55.2 trillion, representing 13.2% of the country's banking assets.[41] City commercial banks operate in the banking sector within specific geographical regions. Most of them are local banks, although some successful ones have developed into larger banks with branches in other cities or even outside the province where they originally come from. For instance, the Bank of Jiangsu's branch network not only covers all counties in Jiangsu Province but also includes 530 business outlets and over 16,000 employees in major Chinese regions such as the Yangtze River Delta, Pearl River Delta, and Bohai Rim.[42] It is fairly easy to spot a city commercial bank in China, since most of them have their city (or province in some cases) in the names, such as Beijing Bank, Shanghai Bank, Ningbo Bank, Nanjing Bank, Hangzhou Bank, Harbin Bank, and Xiamen International Bank.

[40] Xinhua, 'ICBC profit expands in 2022' (2 April 2023), https://english.news.cn/20230402/836f4f2c288e4b22b0cb0acc3cc20856/c.html.

[41] NFRA, 'Total banking assets, total liabilities 2023 (Quarterly)' (21 February 2024), https://www.cbirc.gov.cn/cn/view/pages/ItemDetail.html?docId=1109300&itemId=954.

[42] Bank of Jiangsu, 'About us', https://www.jsbchina.cn/EN/aboutus/aau/11040.html.

City commercial banks have been built upon urban credit cooperatives most of which were established in 1980s and 1990s. Such banks were founded to serve the local economy by providing loans for local small and medium-sized enterprises and offering saving accounts to local residents. Similar to the big four that are backed by the central government, city commercial banks have strong ties to the local governments that provided funding for these homegrown banking businesses. City commercial banks are mostly owned by the local governments or state-owned enterprises as the key shareholders. Their level of development depends on the local economic situation, government support, and overall business environment.

Due to geographical limitations of city commercial banks, their average asset size is much smaller than the large national banks. They are generally small or medium-sized banking institutions that play a fundamental role in the regional economy. However, there has been an increasing divergence in the asset size of city commercial banks. The ten largest city commercial banks each hold assets exceeding RMB 1 trillion on their balance sheets, whereas the smallest city commercial banks have assets ranging from only RMB 10–20 billion. The larger players in this category already have the strength and potential to compete with national banks. At the same time, the smaller players struggle to capture market share due to intense competition with other local and national banks. Moreover, the asset scale of city commercial banks in economically developed regions, such as large cities or those in the East coastal area, is likely to be larger. For example, city banks in Beijing, Shanghai, and Jiangsu province are among the top five in this category, which is inseparable from the strong local economic activities and their cities having the status as important financial centres in China. In contrast, the asset scale of city banks in less developed areas is relatively small. This suggests that the development of city commercial banks is closely related to the economic environment of the cities in which they are located.

Beginning in 2005, various city commercial banks have broadened their shareholder base by welcoming both domestic and international private firms to acquire minority stakes, engaging in mergers and acquisitions, and establishing cross-shareholding arrangements. Additionally, over thirty city commercial banks, including Beijing Bank, Shengjing Bank, and Changsha Bank, have gone public with their shares listed on the Chinese stock exchanges, and have become large financial institutions with substantial deposit bases. During the 2010s, there has been a noticeable trend of city commercial banks expanding their operations beyond their original regions. They frequently act as the primary shareholders and key investors in rural financial institutions including village and township banks. In practice, some urban commercial banks have an ambiguous market positioning, as they are inclined towards poaching customers and businesses from larger banks. However, their corporate governance is relatively immature, their business strategies are limited in scope, and their product innovation capabilities are not strong enough. These banks find themselves in a challenging position, sandwiched between the monopoly of large state-owned banks above them and competition from thousands of rural banks below them, as well as foreign bank rivals. As for the future of city commercial banks with a smaller asset scale, it is not without opportunities for their survival and further development in China's banking industry. They can offer more differentiated banking services by focusing more on personalized banking and risk management, working closely with local governments, and even considering cross-border expansion into other cities and provinces. With the right strategy, even small city banks can find their footing in a competitive market.

In addition to city commercial banks, China has over 3,000 rural financial institutions, including 1,604 rural commercial banks, 513 rural credit cooperatives, 23 rural cooperative banks, and 1,640 village banks.[43] Rural commercial banks are the most mature business model of rural financial institutions in China. They are local commercial banks that primarily serve local farmers, agriculture, and rural economic development. Some examples are Shenzhen Rural Commercial Bank, Suzhou Rural Commercial Bank, and Wuhan Rural Commercial Bank. Rural commercial banks need to adopt the form of joint-stock limited companies, and most of them had been upgraded from former rural credit cooperatives. They may, according to the needs of business development, set up branches, sub-branches, branch offices, and savings offices within their jurisdiction. In most cases, they are not allowed to operate business or set up branches outside their based region, limiting their further growth into large banking corporations.

Rural commercial banks denote the majority of Chinese banks in terms of number, but most rural financial institutions are very small in terms of size. Over 3,000 rural banks collectively hold RMB 54.6 trillion on their balance sheets, which accounts for only 13.1% of China's banking assets.[44] Despite their large number, rural banks have a similar total asset value to the 125 city commercial banks, which control 13.2% of China's banking assets, as previously discussed. Nonetheless, a small number of rural banks have grown successfully to sizable banking institutions. For example, Dongguan Rural

[43] PBoC, 'China financial stability report 2023', pp. 17–18, http://www.pbc.gov.cn/jinrongwendingju/146766/146772/5177895/2023122217072818365.pdf.

[44] NFRA, 'Total banking assets, total liabilities 2023 (Quarterly)' (21 February 2024), https://www.cbirc.gov.cn/cn/view/pages/ItemDetail.html?docId=1109300&itemId=954.

Commercial Bank was established in 1952 as rural credit cooperative union and underwent corporate modernization during the 2000s, before listing its shares on the Hong Kong Stock Exchange in 2021.[45] As of June 2023, the banking group's total assets reached RMB 686.212 billion, with the deposit balance of RMB 485.89 billion and the total loan balances of RMB 355.06 billion.[46]

4.3.3 New private banks

Most Chinese banks have the government background, as the state plays a key role in the banking industry as the owner, regulator, and strategic setter. This phenomenon is widely observed in both the large national banks and smaller regional banks in the country. However, during the 2010s, China launched a pilot reform to allow qualified private investors to establish new banks. So far, there have been nineteen private banks established between 2014 and 2024, as the latest addition to the state-dominated banking industry. We call them private banks or privately owned banks, as their founders and major investors are private individuals or corporations, in contrast to state-owned banks and state-backed banks. The emergence of private banks sector signals the diversification of the country's banking business and the increasing competition in the market. Moreover, a lot of new private banks have adopted a different business model by embracing the digital technologies or Fintech to operate banking businesses, giving them a competitive edge in the crowded sector. In most cases, private banks target small and medium-sized enterprises and ordinary consumers as their primary customers, meaning that they play a more supplementary role in China's financial industry.

The story of private banks began in 2013 when the Chinese government and the communist party of China (CCP) launched a series of financial reforms. In November 2013, during the third plenary session of CCP's eighteenth central committee meeting, it resolved to strengthen social and economic reforms, which included permitting qualified private capital to establish new banks as part of a broader dozen-point reform agenda.[47] In 2014, the Chinese government initiated a pilot project that led to the formation of five new completely private investor-owned banks in Shanghai, Tianjin, Zhejiang, and Guangdong. Before 2014, the only privately owned bank

[45] Dongguan Rural Commercial Bank, 'About us', https://www.drcbank.com/drcbank_news/gywx60/bxjj/index.html.

[46] Ibid.

[47] Tom Mitchell, 'Xi's four-point plan gives reason for optimism', *The Financial Times* (15 November 2013), http://www.ft.com/intl/cms/s/0/4469ec2c-4e06-11e3-8fa5-00144feabdc0.html.

in China had been the Minsheng Banking Corporation. In the government working report 2015, the then Chinese Premier, Mr. Li Keqiang, restated the government's determination to move ahead with financial reforms by allowing qualified private investors to set up small and medium-sized banks and other financial institutions without a quota being imposed.[48] It shows the government's decision to bring more competition to China's banking industry which benefits Chinese citizens and corporations they will have access to better banking services.

Thanks to the policy of liberalizing banking industry in early 2010s, China has seen the establishment and rapid rise of some private banks since 2015. There were the first group of private banks which obtained a licence from the banking regulator and opened for business in 2015, including WeBank, Zhejiang E-Commerce Bank (MYBank), Kincheng Bank of Tianjin, Shanghai Huarui Bank, and Wenzhou Minshang Bank. The latest private bank that started operation is the Wuxi Xishang Bank (since 2020). From Table 4.2, we could see that China has nineteen private banks with a total asset value of RMB 1.94 trillion at the end of 2023. There are five private banks that have passed the scale of having over RMB 100 billion worth of assets, namely, WeBank, MYBank, Jiangsu Merchants Bank, Wuhan Zhongbang Bank, and Sichuan Xinwang Bank. Unlike the mainstream banks that target larger corporations and high-net-worth individuals that could bring more revenues and profits, the private banks tend to focus more on the long-tail customers such as ordinary individual customers and small or micro enterprises. Long-tail customers represent a very large quantity in the industry but have relatively low financial assets, which have been overlooked by big banks for a long time. However, with the help of AI, big data, cloud, and other Fintech, private banks could now easily reach such customers and have a better understanding of their specific demands. Fintech offers a low-cost and intelligent solution to provide small clients with bespoke and diversified financial products, helping many private banks grow quickly and seize market shares from established rivals.

WeBank is an example of private banks that have utilized Fintech to become a successful digital bank within ten years of establishment. In January 2015, WeBank, a joint venture launched by Tencent, China's internet giant holding a 30% stake, received significant media attention.[49] WeBank has a registered capital of RMB 3 billion yuan and it was named after Tencent's star mobile app product WeChat. WeBank is a full bank without physical

[48] Li Keqiang, 'Government Work Report 2015', National People's Congress (5 March 2015).
[49] Gabriel Wildau, 'China's first online-only lender launched', *The Financial Times* (6 January 2015), p. 16.

Table 4.2 Overview of China's private banks ranked by assets

Rank	Bank name	Year of establishment	Headquarter	Asset scale (at the end of 2023, RMB bn)
1	WeBank	2015	Shenzhen, Guangdong	535.58
2	Zhejiang E-Commerce Bank (MYBank)	2015	Hangzhou, Zhejiang	452.13
3	Jiangsu Su Merchants Bank (SMB)	2017	Nanjing, Jiangsu	116.65
4	Wuhan Zhongbang Bank (Z-Bank)	2017	Wuhan, Hubei	114.48
5	Sichuan Xinwang Bank (XWBank)	2016	Chengdu, Sichuan	102.93
6	Kincheng Bank of Tianjin (KCB)	2015	Tianjin	73.47
7	Beijing Zhongguancun Bank (ZGCB)	2017	Beijing	72.71
8	Chongqing Fumin Bank	2016	Chongqing	60.42
9	Hunan Sanxiang Bank (BOS)	2016	Changsha, Hunan	58.93
10	Blue Ocean Bank	2017	Weihai, Shandong	52.77
11	Jilin Yillion Bank	2017	Changchun, Jilin	51.78
12	Shanghai Huarui Bank (SHRB)	2015	Shanghai	49.27
13	Wenzhou Minshang Bank (MSBank)	2015	Wenzhou, Zhejiang	43.30
14	Meizhou Hakka Bank	2017	Meizhou, Guangdong	39.38
15	Wuxi Xishang Bank	2020	Wuxi, Jiangsu	36.97
16	Fujian OneBank Company	2017	Fuzhou, Fujian	33.37
17	NewUp Bank of Liaoning	2017	Shenyang, Liaoning	29.58
18	Anhui Xin'an Bank	2017	Hefei, Anhui	19.29
19	Jiangxi Yumin Bank	2019	Nanchang, Jiangxi	17.67 (2022)

Source: The 2023 financial reports of nineteen commercial banks.

branches or outlets. Customers are able to access banking services through their websites or mobile apps. WeBank primarily focuses on internet users, including individual consumers and small to micro businesses that do not qualify for traditional bank loans. As of December 2023, WeBank served 400 million individual customers and 4.5 million business customers.[50] The operation of WeBank and other digital banks heavily depends on the latest information technologies, such as face recognition and big data, enabling the lender to conduct credit rating and identity verification online. The key products of WeBank include WeiLiDai (unsecured credit products, offering individuals instant microcredit on demand) and WeiYeDai (online unsecured credit products for businesses, providing corporate working capital financing solutions). In October 2019, WeBank collaborated with Shenzhen University and set up the WeBank Institute of FinTech that offers undergraduate and postgraduate education in the emerging areas such as bachelor's degree in Fintech and master's degree in AI (smart finance).[51]

Most of pilot private banks have been expanding their businesses so far, and they filled the market gap by providing online deposit and loan services. However, their development is not without challenges. First of all, most private banks began their business in the late 2010s, with the latest Xishang Bank starting in 2020. We have not seen any new banking licences granted to private investors from 2021 to 2024, which might suggest the tighter regulatory environment during the pandemic and the subsequent economic downturn. By their size, all the new private banks remain small or medium-sized financial institutions as they operate in a highly competitive sector. China has thousands of banking institutions ranging from the big six to rural commercial banks. It is not easy for private banks to capture more market share, especially when they do not have close ties to the state as most other Chinese banks do. Even the two most successful private banks, WeBank and MYBank, together hold around RMB 1 trillion asset, which is only the size of a top city commercial bank and less than 8% of the assets owned by the BOCOM (the smallest within the big six). As China's banking industry is already mature, having more banking assets simply means larger profits and more stable business model.

Moreover, private banks are also facing new competition from outside the traditional banking industry, particularly from Fintech platforms offering more convenient and bespoke services with attractive returns. This shift has drawn billions of yuan away from bank deposits. For example, Yuebao

[50] WeBank's Official Website, www.webank.com.
[51] Shenzhen University WeBank Institute of FinTech (SWIFT), https://swift.szu.edu.cn/en/.

('leftover treasure'), an online investment product based on money-market funds, has become a popular alternative to bank deposits in China.[52] Given that WeBank is backed by Tencent (a leading BigTech corporation in Asia) and MYBank is a subsidiary of Ant Group (the Fintech platform launched by Alibaba, the largest e-commerce company), operating a banking business remains a difficult task for new players, most of which do not have the enormous customer base and technological resources that Tencent and Alibaba possess.

4.3.4 Effective regulation of commercial banks

The main regulatory body in China's banking industry is the National Administration of Financial Regulation (NAFR) which took over the supervision of commercial banks from the China Banking and Insurance Regulatory Commission (CBIRC) in May 2023. The PBoC as the central bank is responsible for setting the benchmark interest rate and fulfilling certain regulatory functions alongside the NAFR. Moreover, the financial safety net has been a vital element of one country's banking regulatory regime, as it deals with bank crisis and insolvency and contributes to financial stability and depositor protection. This section focuses on some specific issues for the effective regulation of Chinese commercial banks which have not been discussed before in Chapter 2 when we examine the overall financial regulation in China. The following sections consider the benchmark interest rate, capital requirements, and data regulation and information technology.

Benchmark interest rate and LPR

The PBoC used to mandate a set of benchmark lending and deposit rates that all banks in the country were required to strictly follow. This ensured the profits of Chinese commercial banks, as the margin between deposit and lending rates directly translated into earnings (simply multiply the interest rate margin by the total loan amount). The more deposit and loan assets a bank has, the more money it can make. This mechanism is extremely beneficial for large banks that hold trillions of yuan in assets, such as the big four. To promote a more competitive and market-based banking industry, the Chinese regulators initiated the reform of liberalizing banking interest rates

[52] Simon Rabinovitch, 'Treasure piles up for Alibaba as depositors desert China's banks', *The Financial Times* (20 December 2013), https://www.ft.com/content/58dfd7ce-63d8-11e3-98e2-00144feabdc0.

from 2004 to 2015.[53] The reform has provided commercial banks with greater flexibility in setting their product rates. Consequently, an increasing number of banks, particularly newly established private lenders, can now offer high deposit rates to attract savers while using low lending rates to attract borrowers.

The PBoC has been replacing the officially guided benchmark loan rate with the market-based LPR mechanism. On 25 October 2013, the PBoC officially announced the implementation of the centralized quotation and release mechanism for LPR.[54] There is no doubt that the LPR furthers the interest rate liberalization process as it guides the pricing of credit market products. The LPR, which stands for the interest rate calculated and published by the National Interbank Funding Centre (NIFC) authorized by the PBoC, is determined based on the loan interest rate executed by each quotation bank for its top-tier (prime) customers. In practice, LPR is formed by adding or deducting points to the OMO interest rate. Each commercial bank, based on the LPR, can adjust their actual loan interest rates taking into account factors such as borrowers' credit status, collateral, loan term, and the way how interest is being calculated (e.g. fixed or floating).

The LPR quotation bank currently consists of twenty commercial banks in China, and the quotations should be submitted to the NIFC on the twentieth of each month (postponed in the case of public holidays) before 9 o'clock.[55] These quotations are based on the OMO interest rate, primarily referring to the MLF interest rate. The NIFC calculates the loan market's quoted interest rate by taking an arithmetic average after excluding the highest and lowest quotations. Currently, there are two maturity varieties included in LPR: one year and over five years. Since August 2019, the PBoC has been publishing the LPR on a monthly basis, meaning that LPR has become the default interest rate mechanism for loan markets in China. The pricing of most bank loans, including residential mortgages, is based on the LPR and determined by the commercial banks. China has said goodbye to the old time when the PBoC dictated the interest rate for banks and successfully completed the interest rate liberalization reform. According to the PBoC and NIFC, as of 20 May 2024, the one-year LPR is 3.45% and the over-five-year LPR is 3.95%.[56]

[53] For the PBoC's gradual process of liberalizing retail bank deposit and lending interest rates, see Lerong Lu, *Private Lending in China: Practice, Law and Regulation of Shadow Banking and Alternative Finance* (Routledge, 2019), pp. 155–156.

[54] Chinese Government, 'Loan prime rate centralised quotation and release mechanism officially launched' (25 October 2013), https://www.gov.cn/jrzg/2013-10/25/content_2515184.htm.

[55] PBoC, 'LPR', http://www.pbc.gov.cn/en/3688229/3688335/3883798/index.html.

[56] PBoC, 'Announcement on loan prime rate (20 May 2024)', http://www.pbc.gov.cn/en/3688229/3688335/3883798/5357018/index.html.

Capital requirements and prudential regulation

Bank capital plays an important role in the operation of commercial banks in terms of defending individual banks' risks and systemic risks. The main international standard for bank capital regulation is the Basel III accord.[57] It is a set of global banking regulations, developed by the Bank for International Settlements (BIS), that aims to promote stability within the international financial system. Basel III was introduced after the Global Financial Crisis of 2007–2008 to enhance banks' resilience to financial stress and to improve their transparency and disclosure practices. The key principles of Basel III include the minimum capital requirements, countercyclical measures, leverage ratio, and liquidity requirements. As a member of the Basel Committee on Banking Supervision, China has been actively bringing its banking regulation in line with the latest international standards, in particular, the capital rules and risk exposure.

In November 2023, the NFRA issued the latest Rules on Capital Management of Commercial Banks ('Capital Rules') that came into effect on 1 January 2024.[58] As China's implementation of Basel III, the Capital Rules have made substantial changes to the previous capital regulation in the following areas: building a differentiated bank capital regulatory system, revising the standards for calculating banks' risk-weighted assets (RWAs), ensuring the applicability and prudence of risk weights, strengthening supervisory oversight and optimizing stress testing, and improving information disclosure standards.[59] The NFRA is overseeing the implementation of the Capital Rules by commercial banks, using capital requirements to steer banking resource allocation. The Capital Rules are likely to help Chinese banks optimize their asset composition, so they could provide better support for the businesses and real economy.

The Capital Rules have established a differentiated capital regulatory system based on the scale of banks' assets and cross-border operation, and all commercial banks in China are divided into three tiers (see Table 4.3).[60] Tier 1 commercial banks are those with a large asset scale of over RMB 500 billion or those having substantial cross-border transactions. They are subject to the stringent capital requirements that are consistent with the international standards in Basel III. For example, commercial banks' core tier 1

[57] BIS, 'Basel III: International regulatory framework for banks' (December 2017), https://www.bis.org/bcbs/basel3.htm.

[58] NFRA, 'Rules on Capital Management of Commercial Banks', NFRA 2023 No. 4 Order (26 October 2023).

[59] NFRA, 'NFRA issues the rules on capital management of commercial banks' (1 November 2023), https://www.cbirc.gov.cn/en/view/pages/ItemDetail.html?docId=1142371.

[60] NFRA, 'Rules on Capital Management of Commercial Banks', NFRA 2023 No. 4 Order (26 October 2023), Article 6.

Table 4.3 The classification of Chinese commercial banks for capital regulation

Bank classification	Standards
Tier 1 Commercial Bank	1. The total asset balance, which includes off-balance sheet assets and is calculated after the adjustment of consolidated financial statements, exceeds RMB 500 billion (inclusive); and/or 2. The balance of overseas creditors' claims and debts exceeds RMB 30 billion (inclusive) and constitutes more than 10% (inclusive) of the total asset balance.
Tier 2 Commercial Bank	1. The total asset balance, which includes off-balance sheet assets and is calculated after the adjustment of consolidated financial statements, exceeds RMB 10 billion (inclusive), and they do not fall within the classification of Tier 1 Commercial Ban; and/or 2. The total asset balance, which includes off-balance sheet assets and is calculated after the adjustment of consolidated financial statements, is less than RMB 10 billion, and they have any positive balance (over 0) of overseas creditors' claims and debts.
Tier 3 Commercial Bank	The total asset balance, which includes off-balance sheet assets and is calculated after the adjustment of consolidated financial statements, is less than RMB 10 billion, and they do not have any positive balance (0) of overseas creditors' claims and debts.

Source: National Financial Regulatory Administration.

capital adequacy ratio should be no less than 5%, their tier 1 capital adequacy ratio should be no less than 6%, and their capital adequacy ratio should be no less than 8%.[61] In addition to the minimum capital rules, commercial banks should allocate reserve capital, with the current rate being 2.5% of RWAs, as well as the countercyclical capital that will be determined by the PBoC and NFRA.[62] Moreover, systemically important banks (both domestic and international) should allocate additional capital on top of the above-mentioned capital categories.[63] Tier 2 commercial banks are those with smaller scale and fewer cross-border operations, where relatively simplified capital regulatory rules are applied. Tier 3 commercial banks consist of even smaller banks without cross-border operations, with further simplified capital measurement requirements, as their businesses focus on county-level banking services and microfinance. Differentiated capital regulation does

[61] Ibid., Article 26.
[62] Ibid., Article 27.
[63] Ibid., Article 28.

not lower the capital requirements; instead, it aims to stimulate the financial activities of small and medium-sized banks while maintaining the overall stability of China's banking industry and reducing compliance costs for smaller banks.

The new Capital Rules were formulated according to the three pillars under Basel III: Pillar 1 addresses capital and liquidity adequacy with minimum requirements, Pillar 2 sets supervisory monitoring and review standards, and Pillar 3 enhances market discipline through mandated public disclosures. The measurement of RWAs is based on the perceived riskiness of a bank's assets. The riskier the asset according to the classification metrics set by regulators, the higher its risk rating and the more capital required. The latest weighting method for RWAs focuses on optimizing risk exposure classification standards by adding risk drivers and refining risk weights. Further, the Capital Rules fully considered the economic reality and recent developments of the Chinese economy, such as the property market crisis and the failure of major property developers like Evergrande in early 2020s.[64] In the case of real estate exposures, residential mortgage loans are assigned multiple risk weights based on the property type, source of repayment, and loan-to-value ratio (LTV).[65] The CRA calculating criteria will be more sensitive to the risks linked to mortgage loans. It is perceived as the regulatory response addressing the mounting financial risks resulting from the overheated property market for two decades (2000–2020). In contrast, the new rules have reduced risk weightings for loans associated with the real economy. Certain types of business loans and local governments' general bonds, primarily funding public welfare projects, will receive lower risk weightings than before.

Digital bank regulation

Another regulatory concern involves novel online-only banks like WeBank and MYBank. Unlike traditional institutions, these banks operate on a unique business model that leverages the latest information technologies, such as AI, big data, and cloud computing, which may pose specific regulatory challenges relating to users' data protection and identity verification. The Chinese banking regulator is considering the data governance and information technology risks when rating commercial banks' risk level for the supervisory purpose.[66]

[64] Lerong Lu and Anat Keller, 'Is It China's Lehman Brothers Moment? Unveiling Evergrande Debt Crisis, Financial Risks, and Regulatory Implications' (2022) 16 *Law and Financial Markets Review* 133–144.

[65] NFRA, 'Rules on Capital Management of Commercial Banks', NFRA 2023 No. 4 Order (26 October 2023), Article 71.

[66] CBIRC, 'Notice from the China Banking and Insurance Regulatory Commission on Issuing the Measures for Commercial Bank Supervision Ratings', CBIRC 2021 No. 39, Article 6(1).

Since digital banks do not have physical branches, account opening and all transactions, including borrowing loans, are conducted online. Therefore, verifying users' identities for new accounts, logging in, and any online transactions could present regulatory problems. In practice, digital banks have developed sophisticated facial recognition systems for identity verification, allowing them to accurately recognize users online by examining their images and videos against the personal data held by commercial banks and public authorities.

However, the collection of massive amounts of information might lead to the leakage and misuse of customer data. In some recent cases, private banks have been fined by the central bank or financial regulator for non-compliance. For example, in 2021, the PBoC Chengdu Branch imposed a fine of RMB 6.3 million on Sichuan Xinwang Bank for its transactions with unidentified customers and multiple failures to fulfil the obligations of customer identification, to keep customer identity information and transaction records as required, and to submit large transaction reports or suspicious transaction reports in accordance with regulations.[67] As an increasing number of commercial banks are heavily reliant on internet platforms to take deposits and make loans, violations of rules regarding customer identity, data protection, and transaction reporting have become common areas that trigger regulatory actions.

4.4 Shadow banking: popularity, crisis, and regulation

Outside the regulated banking industry, China has a gigantic shadow banking sector that is less formal and almost unregulated. In 2007, economist Paul McCulley first proposed the concept of shadow banking, defining it as 'the whole alphabet soup of levered up non-bank investment conduits, vehicles and structures'.[68] In the United States, the growth of shadow banking was facilitated by regulatory and legal changes that favoured three key institutions: money-market mutual funds (MMMFs), which attracted retail deposits from traditional banks; securitization, which allowed traditional banks to move assets off their balance sheets; and repurchase agreements (repos), which enabled the use of securitized bonds as money.[69] In China,

[67] China Economy Net, 'Xinwang Bank was fined 6.3 million yuan: transactions with unidentified customers' (26 July 2021), http://www.ce.cn/cysc/newmain/yc/jsxw/202107/26/t20210726_36751717.shtml.

[68] Paul McCulley, 'Teton Reflections' (September 2007), PIMCO Global Central Bank Focus, p. 2.

[69] Gary B. Gorton and Andrew Metrick, 'Regulating the Shadow Banking System', Brookings Papers on Economic Activity (Fall 2010), p. 261.

the concept of shadow banking is not entirely the same as it is in the United States and Europe. The shadow banking system in China encompasses quasi-banking activities outside the traditional banking sector, such as trust lending, entrusted lending, and private lending.[70] This section will use private lending—moneylending agreements between business borrowers and debt investors without bank involvement—as an example to illustrate the causes, risks, and regulatory solutions of Chinese shadow banking.

4.4.1 What contributes to the rise of shadow banking sector

The formation and popularity of the Chinese shadow banking sector have two root causes. First, the financing demands from China's private sector cannot always be met by the state-dominated banking industry. The challenge of securing financing for SMEs is a significant and widespread issue, faced by entrepreneurs in both developed and emerging economies. Despite their significant contributions to global economic growth and recovery following the 2007–2008 financial crisis and the COVID-19 pandemic, SMEs have received insufficient credit from formal financial institutions. In practice, SMEs rely more heavily on domestic bank lending compared to large corporations, as their financing options beyond bank loans are limited. In the EU, around 99% of all non-financial companies are SMEs, creating 58% of value added and 66% of total jobs; however, after the Global Financial Crisis of 2007–2008, new bank lending to these SMEs in the eurozone fell by 35%.[71] According to a Federal Reserve's report in 2022, although small businesses play a crucial role in the US economy, they frequently face challenges in obtaining credit, as lending to small businesses is typically viewed as riskier and more expensive compared to lending to larger firms.[72]

In China, the financial situation of SMEs is even worse than their American and European counterparts. Despite generating nearly 60% of the GDP and creating 80% of the total jobs, Chinese SMEs receive only 20% of the total bank loans.[73] This is because China's banking sector is dominated by state-owned lenders who are sometimes reluctant to lend to private businesses.

[70] For the detailed discussion of Chinese shadow banking, see Lerong Lu, *Private Lending in China*, pp. 32–38.

[71] *The Economist*, 'Financing Europe's small firms: Don't bank on the banks' (16 August 2014), http://www.economist.com/news/finance-and-economics/21612251-small-businesses-seek-alternatives-banks-leave-them-lurch-dont-bank.

[72] The Federal Reserve, 'Availability of credit to small businesses' (October 2022), https://www.federalreserve.gov/publications/2022-october-availability-of-credit-to-small-businesses.htm.

[73] Emma Dong and Simon Rabinovitch, 'China's lending laboratory', *The Financial Times* (23 May 2012), http://www.ft.com/intl/cms/s/0/90e7f67a-a41b-11e1-a701-00144feabdc0.html.

Although the government mandates that a small portion of bank credit be allocated to small firms, most state-owned banks tend to prioritize lending to other well-connected state-owned enterprises (SOEs). As a result, Chinese SMEs, rejected by mainstream banks, are forced to borrow from shadow banks and private lenders to fund their operations. Credit Suisse reports that the total value of outstanding loans in China's informal lending market is RMB 4 trillion.[74] The private lending industry is regarded as an important component of the Chinese shadow banking system.

Second, Chinese citizens and corporations have accumulated large capital after four decades of fast economic growth (1980s–2010s). Chinese investors are seeking profitable investment opportunities, and the accumulation of private wealth in China provides ample funding for the burgeoning moneylending industry. For a long time, Chinese individual investors have had limited investment options because of underdeveloped capital markets. Chinese residents are renowned for their high savings rate, which typically stands at 40%, the highest in the world.[75] Chinese investors with substantial savings have been seeking new investment opportunities that offer higher returns. In the 2000s and early 2010s, private lending, which can generate significant interest, became a popular investment alternative for them. Moreover, a growing number of industrialists who were formerly exporters or manufacturers sought to diversify their businesses, with many investing in the money lending sector. Even some state-owned groups with substantial cash reserves attempted to participate in moneylending by extending loans to cash-strapped enterprises to achieve higher profits.[76] The demand for capital from cash-strapped entrepreneurs and the supply of money from wealthy savers and capitalists have fuelled the growth of China's trillion-yuan shadow banking system.

4.4.2 Shadow banking crisis

China's shadow banking system provided mutual benefits for both SMEs and their investors. Following the market-oriented reforms initiated in 1978, the country experienced remarkable economic growth, largely propelled by

[74] Credit Suisse, 'China: Shadow banking—Road to heightened risks', Securities Research & Analytics (February 2013).

[75] *The Economist*, 'China's economy: Coming down to earth' (18 April 2015), http://www.economist.com/news/briefing/21648567-chinese-growth-losing-altitude-will-it-be-soft-or-hard-landing-coming-down-earth.

[76] Shen Wei, 'Shadow Banking System in China—Origin, Uniqueness and Governmental Response' (2013) 28 *Journal of International Banking Law and Regulation* 20–26.

the rapid expansion of the private sector, as demonstrated by an average annual GDP growth rate of 9.8% until 2012.[77] As a result, by utilizing private finance, many entrepreneurs were able to secure sufficient capital for their businesses and consequently benefited from the rapid growth of the Chinese economy. The substantial profits generated from prosperous businesses easily offset the high cost of borrowing private loans. At the same time, lenders enjoyed significantly higher returns on their investments compared to bank savings. According to *The Economist*, a businessman from Wenzhou, a renowned commercial city in East China, described the prevalent underground financing situation by stating that 100,000 people in Wenzhou can raise RMB 1 billion within forty-eight hours.[78]

After the Global Financial Crisis of 2007–2008 and the more recent COVID-19 pandemic, the economic growth has slowed down significantly when the debt problem in China is exposed. The export-based economic system suffered due to weakened demand from the rest of the world. The IMF projects that China's economy will grow by 5% in 2024 and 4.5% in 2025.[79] The current economic growth is much slower than ten years ago when double-digit growth was the norm. In addition to declining export businesses, China's decade-long property market boom, which accounts for approximately 20% of its economic growth, recently came to a halt as the housing market faced a significant correction. Evergrande, one of the largest property developers in China, has total liabilities exceeding $300 billion.[80] In late 2021, Evergrande failed to meet interest payments on its bonds to international investors. The crash in property markets has a negative impact on the Chinese economy, as the total housing market value to GDP ratio in China stood at 414%, much higher than the figures in the United States (148%) and the United Kingdom (339%).[81] As a result of worsened economic conditions, defaults in the private lending market increased as many entrepreneurs could not repay the excessive interest charged by moneylenders and faced insolvency due to a lack of cash flow.

[77] *People's Daily*, '35 years, Chinese economy keep rising' (21 November 2013), p. 4.

[78] *The Economist*, 'Entrepreneurship in China: Let a million flowers bloom' (10 March 2011), https://www.economist.com/briefing/2011/03/10/let-a-million-flowers-bloom.

[79] IMF, 'IMF staff completes 2024 Article IV Mission to the People's Republic of China' (May 28, 2024), https://www.imf.org/en/News/Articles/2024/05/28/pr24184-china-imf-staff-completes-2024-art-iv-mission.

[80] Lerong Lu and Anat Keller, 'Is It China's Lehman Brothers Moment? Unveiling Evergrande Debt Crisis, Financial Risks, and Regulatory Implications' (2022) 16 *Law and Financial Markets Review* 133–144.

[81] Hung-Gay Fung, Alan Guoming Huang, Qingfeng Wilson Liu, and Maggie Xiaoqin Shen, 'The Development of the Real Estate Industry in China' (2006) 39 *The Chinese Economy* 84–102.

Since 2011, China has experienced a wave of lending credit crunches and corporate insolvencies across the country. Wenzhou was the first Chinese city to experience a significant financial crisis triggered by its shadow banking system. Many local entrepreneurs attempted to flee the city to avoid their debts, and one-fifth of Wenzhou's 360,000 private businesses ceased operations and became insolvent.[82] The list of fugitive bosses includes several high-profile entrepreneurs, such as Mr. Hu Fulin, chairman of the Zhejiang Centre Group, a leading eyewear company.[83] Between August 2011 and May 2012, the municipal court system in Wenzhou handled 22,000 civil cases related to private lending disputes, with a combined monetary value of approximately RMB 21 billion.[84] Following the lending crunch in Wenzhou, the rest of China also experienced a shadow banking crisis characterized by waves of defaults, failed businesses, and absconded bosses. For example, Mr. Ding Hui, the former chairman and CEO of Fujian Nuoqi Co Ltd, a well-known Chinese clothing manufacturer listed on the Hong Kong stock exchange, suddenly disappeared in July 2014.[85] This led to a more than 50% slump in the company's share price over three consecutive days. Mr. Ding's disappearance was due to his debt of nearly RMB 1.5 billion yuan owed to private lenders, which he had used to fund the expansion of his clothing stores in the pre-IPO period.

Shortly after the outbreak of default cases, the private lending crisis swept across China, often referred to by the media as 'China's subprime crisis'.[86] The widespread financial crisis had a catastrophic impact on relevant stakeholders and the financial stability. As business borrowers failed to meet their debt obligations, moneylenders and investors incurred significant financial losses. Because the private lending market operates outside China's financial regulatory system, private debt investments do not receive official protection. Accordingly, the only legitimate way for debt investors to claim back their money is to file a civil lawsuit against borrowers. Such legal claims are based on the creditor–debtor contractual relationship. Following the crisis, a surge of private lending-related civil cases overwhelmed China's court system. In 2014, Chinese courts heard 1.02 million private lending cases, making

[82] *BBC News*, 'Fears surface over Chinese debt amid lending practices' (6 October 2011), http://www.bbc.co.uk/news/business-15194663.

[83] *The Economist*, 'China's economy: Hitting the kerb' (22 October 2011), http://www.economist.com/node/21533412.

[84] *China Economic Weekly*, 'Before and after the Wenzhou Private Financing Regulation' (9 December 2013), p. 58.

[85] *Xinhua*, 'Nuoqi's share slumping reason: chairman Ding Hui missing' (26 July 2014), http://news.xinhuanet.com/fortune/2014-07/26/c_126799805.htm.

[86] Austin Ramzy, 'A credit crisis in China's most enterprising city is making the country nervous', *Time* (28 November 2011), http://content.time.com/time/magazine/article/0,9171,2099675,00.html.

private financing the second largest category of civil litigation in the country, surpassed only by marriage and family cases.[87] According to Beijing High Court, from 2019 to 2023, the proportion of private lending disputes under review was around 7% of total civil cases, reaching its peak at 8.52% in 2021.[88]

4.4.3 Shadow banking regulation

Chinese authorities began to recognize the severe systemic risk posed by the shadow banking system, worth trillions of yuan, and the significant financial pressures faced by millions of privately owned businesses. This realization prompted the government, the judiciary, and financial regulators to commit to implementing reforms. The regulation of private lending consists of PRC Civil Code on loan agreements, the judicial interpretations, the interest rate regulations, and certain criminal offences.[89]

PRC Civil Code on loan agreements

A loan contract is a moneylending agreement between a borrower and one or more moneylenders, documenting mutual promises concerning the terms and conditions of the loan. Despite the substantial sums involved in private lending, these activities fundamentally represent a contractual relationship between a creditor and a debtor. Therefore, lending parties have to comply with provisions under the PRC Civil Code's Chapter XII Loan Contracts.[90] A valid private lending agreement, like any other contracts, comprises basic elements including offer, acceptance, and consideration (interests). Nonetheless, the common issues regulated by the general principles of contract law are not discussed here, while the attention is focused on specific provisions governing loan agreements. The PRC Civil Code lies down basic requirements

[87] *Xinhua*, 'Private lending disputes became China's second largest civil litigation type; The Supreme Court issued new judicial interpretation' (6 August 2015), http://news.xinhuanet.com/legal/2015-08/06/c_1116171913.htm.

[88] China Court, 'The Beijing High Court held a press conference on the retrial and review of private lending disputes' (26 December 2023), https://www.chinacourt.org/chat/chat/2023/12/id/53196.shtml.

[89] This section only discusses the legislations and financial regulations about private lending at national level. In practice, the local governments and financial regulatory authorities have made some specific rules for local private financing activities. For instance, Wenzhou City has required certain private financing transactions to be registered with the authority and compiled data about private financing transactions. They publish the so-called Wenzhou index (Wenzhou private financing comprehensive annualized interest rate index).

[90] The PRC Civil Code was adopted at the Third Session of the Thirteenth National People's Congress on 28 May 2020, and came into effect on 1 January 2021. It replaced all previous legislation in the field of civil laws in China, including contract laws. Prior to the Civil Code, private lending agreements were regulated by the PRC Contract Law of 1999 (specifically, Chapter 12 on 'loan contracts').

for formalities and contents of a lending agreement, legal rights and obligations of lending parties, and situations that lead to a breach and relevant remedies.

The following section summarizes relevant provisions (Articles 667–680) under the PRC Civil Code:

- Definition of Loan Contract: A 'loan contract' means the agreement whereby a borrower borrows funds from a lender, and repays the loan with interests when it falls due.[91]
- Form Requirement and Main Clauses: A loan contract shall be made in written form, except for lending agreements between natural persons. A loan contract shall contain essential clauses including the loan's type, currency, purpose of use, amount of money, interest rate, term time, and method of repayment.[92]
- Borrower's Obligation to Disclose Financial Information: When making a loan contract, the borrower, as requested by the lender, shall provide truthful information regarding its business activities and financial conditions relevant to money lending.[93]
- Prohibition of Deducting Interests in Advance: The interest of a loan shall not be deducted from the principal prior to lending. If the interest is deducted in advance, the loan shall be repaid according to the actual amount of money received by the borrower, so shall the interest rate be calculated.[94] In practice, a lot of moneylenders try to deduct interests from the principal, before they transfer the money to borrowers. Two reasons can explain for it. First, some moneylenders charge interests which exceed the official restriction set by the state. In order to get around the restriction, they choose to deduct the excessive part of interests from the principal in advance. Second, some moneylenders do this to reduce the risk of lending by realizing interest incomes at first. Clearly, this unfair lending practice prejudices the interest of borrowers who in most cases are in a vulnerable position and have no choice but to accept all conditions.
- Liability for Breach of Contract: If the lender fails to offer the right amount of loan at the agreed time, which leads to the borrower's losses, it shall be liable to compensate such losses; if the borrower due to its

[91] PRC Civil Code 2021, Article 667.
[92] PRC Civil Code 2021, Article 668.
[93] PRC Civil Code 2021, Article 669.
[94] PRC Civil Code 2021, Article 670.

fault fails to collect the loan at the agreed time, it still has the obligation to pay interests.[95]

- Lender's Right to Inspect Loan Performance: The lender is entitled to inspect and supervise how the borrower uses the loan. The borrower shall provide financial statements to the lender at regular intervals as stated in the contract.[96]
- Remedy for Violating the Use of Loan: Where the borrower does not use the loan for the prescribed purpose, the lender can stop issuing the loan, recall the loan prior to its due date, or terminate the contract.[97]
- Interest Payment: The borrower shall pay the interests at the prescribed time according to the contract.[98] Where the time of interest payment is not agreed or the agreement is unclear, nor can it be determined in accordance with Article 510 of the PRC Civil Code (which is about the remedy for unclear contract clauses): if the loan term is less than one year, the interest shall be paid together with the principal at the end of the contract; if the loan term is one year or longer, the interest shall be paid at the end of each annual period, and where the remaining period is less than one year, the interest shall be paid together with the principal at the end of the contract.
- Principal Repayment: The borrower shall repay the principal at the prescribed time.[99] Where the time of repayment is not agreed or the agreement is unclear, nor can it be determined in accordance with Article 510 of the PRC Civil Code, the borrower can repay the loan at any time; and the lender can demand the loan repayment at any time, provided a reasonable notice period is given to the borrower.
- Overdue Interest: Where the borrower fails to repay the loan at the prescribed time, it shall pay an overdue interest in accordance with the contract or relevant regulations of the state.[100] Failing to pay the loan constitutes a breach of contract, so the legislation enables lenders to charge overdue interest as financial compensations.
- Early Repayment: Where the borrower prepays the loan early, unless otherwise agreed by the parties, the interests shall be calculated based on the actual period of borrowing.[101] A debtor is allowed to pay

[95] PRC Civil Code 2021, Article 671.
[96] PRC Civil Code 2021, Article 672.
[97] PRC Civil Code 2021, Article 673.
[98] PRC Civil Code 2021, Article 674.
[99] PRC Civil Code 2021, Article 675.
[100] PRC Civil Code 2021, Article 676.
[101] PRC Civil Code 2021, Article 677.

off debts earlier than the original term, and the Law protects the debtor's rights by asking it to pay interests based on the real time of borrowing.

- Loan Extension: The borrower can ask the lender for an extension of the loan term before its maturity date; upon the lender's consent the loan term may be extended.[102]
- Time of Taking Effect for Loans Between Natural Persons: A loan contract between natural persons becomes effective at the time when the lender provides the loan.[103] It means that the action of drafting and signing the loan contract does not guarantee its effectiveness, unless the lender provides the money for the borrower. However, if the lending contract involves a legal person as one of its contracting parties, the loan agreement will take effect when it is signed.
- Interest Rate for Loans: Usurious loans are prohibited, and the interest rate for lending shall not violate the relevant regulations of the State (which will be discussed later).[104] Where there is no agreement on payment of interest in the loan contract, the loan shall be deemed as bearing no interest. Where the agreement on the payment of interest in a loan contract is unclear, if the parties are unable to reach a supplementary agreement, the interest shall be determined by taking account of the practices of the local area or between the parties such as the method of transaction, course of dealing, the market interest rate, and the like. Where the loan is between nature persons, the loan shall be deemed as bearing no interest.

Judicial interpretations on private loans

In addition to the PRC Civil Code, there are several judicial interpretations issued by the Supreme Court regarding private lending contracts. These interpretations hold the status of law and are binding on all court decisions in the country. They provide additional rules for the parties involved in a private lending agreement to follow. In 2015, the Supreme Court published a judicial interpretation entitled 'The Provisions of the Supreme People's Court on Several Issues Concerning the Application of Law in the Trials of Private Lending Cases', widely known as 'Provision 18'.[105] The interpretation was revised twice in 2020 following the adoption of new civil code and the recent

[102] PRC Civil Code 2021, Article 678.
[103] PRC Civil Code 2021, Article 679.
[104] PRC Civil Code 2021, Article 680.
[105] Supreme People's Court, 'The Provisions of The Supreme People's Court on Several Issues Concerning the Application of Law in The Trials of Private Lending Cases' (2015, FASHI No.18).

judicial practices in hearing private lending-related civil disputes from 2015 to 2020.[106]

According to the judicial interpretation, private lending refers to moneylending activities among natural persons, legal persons, and other organizations; however, it does not apply to lending disputes involving financial institutions and their branches that have obtained licence from financial regulators to engage in loan-making business.[107] The Civil Code outlines general circumstances that render a contract invalid, such as when one party uses fraudulent or coercive methods to finalize the contract or if the contract involves a malicious conspiracy that harms the interests of the nation, a collective, or a third party. In addition, the judicial interpretation stipulates the following circumstances where a court will consider a private lending contract as invalid:

- When the lender borrows a loan from financial institutions at first, and then relend the money to the borrower at a higher rate;
- When the lender borrows a loan from other enterprises or raises funds from its own employees or illegally takes deposits from the public, and then relend the money to the borrower for the purpose of making profits;
- When the lender is not possessing a licence to make loans, they lend money to unspecific borrowers in the society for the purpose of making profits;
- When the lender knows or should have known in advance that the borrower takes the loan for criminal activities, but still provides the loan;
- When the contract violates laws, administrative regulations, and other mandatory rules; or
- When the contract violates the public order or good morals.[108]

In the past, the validity of a private lending contract largely depended on the identities of the lending parties. For a long time, Chinese authorities recognized the legitimacy of moneylending agreements only between two individuals (natural persons) and remained very sceptical about loan contracts involving non-financial enterprises. It is because the primary concern of the authority was to combat illegal financial practice, in particular, some enterprises that make loans and take deposits without a banking license.

[106] Supreme People's Court, 'The Provisions of The Supreme People's Court on Several Issues Concerning the Application of Law in The Trials of Private Lending Cases' (2020, FASHI No.17).
[107] Ibid., Article 1.
[108] Ibid., Article 13.

Therefore, in the judicial practice, a private financing contract between two non-financial enterprises would be deemed null and void by a Chinese court which would ask the borrower to return the principal to the lender. However, the latest judicial interpretation has seen a big shift in the official attitude towards private lending between two non-financial enterprises. It states that 'a private lending agreement entered by legal persons and other organisations, for the purpose of production and business operation, will be held valid by a court, provided that it does not have circumstances under the Articles 146, 153, and 154 of PRC Civil Code and the Article 13 of this regulation.'[109] Clearly, it legalizes private financing activities between two companies or other business organizations without requiring a bank as an intermediary. This allows Chinese businesses in need of funds to borrow directly from other corporate and individual investors, which can, to some extent, alleviate the financing difficulties faced by entrepreneurs.

Interest rate regulation

In 1991, China implemented a strict set of interest rate regulations for private lending contracts, which was referred to as the 'four-time red line'. The four-time red line (1991 regulation) means that the interest rate of private lending shall not exceed four times of the interest rate of a bank loan of the same kind.[110] Any lending practices crossing this line might be declared as usuries, and as a result, lenders could be subject to heavy administrative or criminal sanctions. For example, if the interest rate of a one-year bank loan is 5% (which depends on the benchmark rate set by the PBoC), the corresponding interest rate cap for a one-year private loan will be 20%.

In 2015, the four-time red line was officially abolished and replaced by new regulations under the Provision 18:

- If the annualized interest rate of a private loan does not exceed 24%, it will be held valid by a court;[111]
- If the annualized interest rate exceeds 36%, the excessive part of interests will be deemed invalid by a court, which shall be returned to the borrower upon request;[112] and

[109] Ibid., Article 10.

[110] Supreme People's Court, 'Some Opinions Concerning the Hearing of Private Lending Cases by People's Courts' (1991, FAMINFA No.21), Article 6.

[111] Supreme People's Court, 'The Provisions of The Supreme People's Court on Several Issues Concerning the Application of Law in The Trials of Private Lending Cases' (2015, FASHI No.18), Article 26.

[112] Ibid.

- If the annualized interest rate is more than 24% but less than 36%, a court will make judgments depending on the specific circumstances.[113] Where the borrower has already paid the interests to the lender, the court will not compel the lender to return the excessive part of interests. Nor will the court support the lender's claim for the borrower to pay interests over 24% when the interests are unpaid.

The 2015 regulation has adopted a three-level approach. Any claims of interests under 24% will be fully supported by a court, while any claims over 36% will be declared null and void. The tricky part is the interests between 24% and 36%, which will be treated as *naturalis obligatio* by a court, namely, a legal obligation which is unenforceable. Compared with the old four-time red line, the new regulation gave more autonomy to lending parties regarding the interest rate, which indicates the less interventionist approach of the authority. It is consistent with the country's general policies in terms of interest rate liberalization for both banking and non-banking sectors.

The 2020 regulation has further reformed the interest rate regulation for private loans, bring it in line with the banking regulation, in particular, the recent introduction of LPR for banking loans. The courts will support claims for private loans with interest unless the interest rate exceeds four times the one-year LPR.[114] It abandoned the three-level approach in 2015 regulation and works more similarly to the original 1991 regulation despite replacing the old calculating standard (the PBoC loan benchmark rate) with the new LPR. For instance, if the one-year LPR is 3.85% (May 2024), the relevant upper limit for private loans will be 15.4%, which is much lower than the fixed standard (24%) set in the Regulation 2015. As China entered the low-interest rate period after the introduction of LPR, the current interest rate level for private loans is expected to be going down. It is beneficial for business borrowers as the financing costs are reduced.

Illegal moneylending offences

Lending parties and their legal advisers should be cautious of certain illegal lending and borrowing practices that may constitute criminal offences under the PRC Criminal Law. For example, the offence of 'illegal absorbing public deposits' punishes anyone (an individual or the person in charge of an organization) who, without a financial licence, illegally takes deposits from the

[113] Ibid., Article 31.

[114] Supreme People's Court, 'The Provisions of The Supreme People's Court on Several Issues Concerning the Application of Law in The Trials of Private Lending Cases' (2020, FASHI No.17), Article 25.

public or does so in a disguised form, leading to the disruption of financial stability.[115] The offender is subject to criminal detention or imprisonment up to three years, or/and a fine. Where the amount of deposits is relatively large or other serious circumstances exist, the offender could face a sentence of up to ten years, plus a fine. The purpose of this law is to penalize individuals and corporations that conduct deposit-taking businesses without a formal licence from NFRA. The major distinction between private financing and illegal deposit-taking depends on whether the borrower approaches potential investors in a public way or not. If the borrower solicits funds from a large number of unspecific people, such as making advertisements in newspapers, billboards, websites, text messages, and social networking, it will constitute the offence. Therefore, entrepreneurs seeking to borrow funds from private investors should avoid public advertising, as private lending must be conducted in a private manner.

Moreover, borrowers need to be cautious about the offence of 'fraudulent fundraising', as many Chinese entrepreneurs have been imprisoned for this crime over the past few years.[116] Whoever, for the purpose of illegal possession raises funds by fraudulent methods, if the amount involved is relatively large, will face criminal detention or a fix-term sentence from three to seven years, plus a fine; if the amount involved is enormous or other serious circumstances exist, it will face sentence over seven years or life imprisonment, plus a fine. In practice, if the borrower genuinely intends to use the money to finance their business venture, the relevant lending agreement will not constitute a criminal offence, even if the borrower defaults in the future. Conversely, if the borrower intends to illegally possess the money when borrowing the funds, it will be considered fraud. However, it remains a challenging task for Chinese judges to determine the borrower's true intention when borrowing money. Consequently, in many cases, they presume that borrowers who owe large sums to several investors are fraudsters if they fail to repay loans on time. The offence of 'fraudulent fundraising' has raised significant controversy due to its vagueness. In a well-known criminal case in Zhejiang, Ms. Wu Ying, a young multi-millionaire in Zhejiang Province, was sentenced to death for defrauding RMB 770 million from eleven people by promising unreasonably high interest rates.[117] This case triggered a public debate in China, as many people, including legal experts, did not consider Wu a criminal, arguing that her actions amounted to no more than informal

[115] PRC Criminal Law 2024 (12th Amendment), Article 176.
[116] PRC Criminal Law 2024 (12th Amendment), Article 192.
[117] *R v. Wu Ying* (2009) ZJJH.

financing or private lending without banks.[118] Finally, the Supreme Court ordered a retrial for the case, and Wu's life was spared.

4.5 Conclusion

This chapter has provided a comprehensive analysis of China's banking industry and its regulation. It first discusses the PBoC's central banking operations, as it is not only China's central bank and monetary authority but also an agent tasked with macroeconomic management to promote the country's economic development. The PBoC uses a basket of monetary policy tools to manage China's economy. The deposit RRR dictates the percentage of funds commercial banks must hold in reserve with the central bank. Relending and rediscounting mechanisms provide additional liquidity to commercial banks, often issued together through combined quotas. OMOs involve the buying and selling of securities in public financial markets to control the money supply. In addition, the PBoC has been utilizing some innovative monetary tools to adjust the money supply, such as the SLF, the MLF, PSL, and other structural monetary policy instruments.

Second, the chapter presents the key players in China's banking arena and addresses the key regulatory issues. There are eighteen large national banks, including six 'large state-owned commercial banks' (or the big six) and twelve 'joint-equity commercial banks'. Despite having over 3,900 deposit-taking institutions, banking assets are highly concentrated in China, with the big six accounting for RMB 176.8 trillion or 42.4% of total banking assets at the end of 2023. Additionally, there are thousands of smaller regional banks operating within cities, counties, villages, and towns, including 125 city commercial banks holding RMB 55.2 trillion in assets and over 3,000 rural financial institutions. During the 2010s, China initiated reforms allowing private investors to establish new banks, resulting in nineteen new private banks by 2024, such as WeBank, which has leveraged fintech to become a successful digital bank within a decade. To achieve effective banking regulation to promote competition and maintain financial stability, the NFRA has introduced latest reforms like the establishment of LPR as the market-based interest rate mechanism and the recent bank capital rules to echo the international standards like Basel III.

Third, the chapter examines China's vast and largely unregulated shadow banking sector. It highlights private lending—agreements between business

[118] Martin Yip, 'Death for fraud: China debates Wu Ying's sentence', *BBC News* (24 February 2012), http://www.bbc.co.uk/news/world-asia-china-17071311.

borrowers and investors without banks—as an example to discuss the causes, risks, and regulatory measures. The demand for capital from entrepreneurs and the supply from wealthy savers have driven the growth of China's trillion-yuan shadow banking system. Since 2011, China has faced lending crunches and corporate insolvencies, termed 'China's subprime crisis' by the media. This situation has made private financing one of the largest categories of civil litigation. In response, the government, judiciary, and financial regulators have committed to reforms. It discusses the latest regulation of private loans such as the PRC Civil Code on loan agreements, judicial interpretations, interest rate caps, and specific criminal offences.

Chapter 5
China's capital markets

5.1 Introduction

Chapter 5 assesses China's fast-growing capital markets and the country's securities law reform to construct a more efficient and transparent market-based financing system with enhanced investor protection and market integrity. China now has the world's second-largest capital market. Among the top ten global stock markets by market capitalization, China, with the Shanghai Stock Exchange (SSE), the Shenzhen Stock Exchange (SZSE), and the Hong Kong Stock Exchange (HKEX), ranks just behind the United States which holds the New York Stock Exchange (NYSE) and NASDAQ.[1] As of June 2024, China possessed 16 of the largest public companies out of the top 100 in the world, including Tencent (with a market cap of $457.63 billion), ICBC ($266.39 billion), Kweichow Moutai ($255.69 billion), PetroChina ($244.61 billion), and China Mobile ($215.46 billion).[2] China's capital markets are considered diverse and multi-layered, capable of satisfying the financing needs of various corporate entities, particularly those in the innovative and science and technology sectors. In addition to the main boards, the SSE also operates the Sci-Tech Innovation Board (Star Market), while the SZSE operates the Small and Medium-Sized Cap Board and the Growth Enterprises Market (ChiNext board). In 2021, China launched the Beijing Stock Exchange (BSE) to channel capital towards the country's growing technology companies, particularly small and medium-sized enterprises (SMEs) with limited access to traditional financing channels such as banks, venture capital (VC), and private equity (PE) funds.[3]

[1] Statista, 'Largest stock exchange operators worldwide as of September 2023, by market capitalization of listed companies', https://www.statista.com/statistics/270126/largest-stock-exchange-operators-by-market-capitalization-of-listed-companies/.

[2] CompaniesMarketCap, 'Largest companies by market cap', https://companiesmarketcap.com/, accessed 28 June 2024.

[3] James T. Areddy, 'China to Launch Beijing Stock Exchange to Steer Investment into Innovation', *The Wall Street Journal* (2 September 2021), https://www.wsj.com/articles/china-to-launch-beijing-stock-exchange-to-steer-investment-into-innovation-11630622825.

Towards Financial Superpower. Lerong Lu, Oxford University Press. © Lerong Lu (2025).
DOI: 10.1093/9780198948568.003.0005

Following this introduction, Section 5.2 introduces the market structure and main boards of China's capital markets, consisted of multiple market segments in Shanghai and Shenzhen accommodating the different financing demands of state-owned and private corporations of various sizes. Section 5.3 evaluates the launch of the Star Market (Sci-Tech Innovation Board) at the SSE in 2019, as the country's reform measure to boost technological innovations by offering more financing resources for tech ventures in the areas like artificial intelligence, Fintech, biometrics, 3D printing, and electric vehicles. Section 5.4 presents the latest addition to China's capital markets—the BSE—which was established in September 2021 to support the financing of SMEs. Section 5.5 evaluates China's securities law reform as the PRC Securities Law 2020 came into effect and discusses the key reform initiatives. The new legislation has overhauled China's financial markets regulatory framework, as it constrains regulators' administrative powers in deciding the outcome of IPOs as well as streamlining the securities offering procedure. Section 5.6 draws a conclusion.

5.2 China's multi-layer capital markets

Since 1990s, China has established a multi-level capital markets system comprising various exchange trading and over-the-counter (OTC) venues. The reason for having different trading venues is to satisfy the diverse financing demands of various corporate entities in China, as well as the differing capital scales and risk appetites of Chinese investors. In terms of exchange trading, mainland China has three stock exchanges: SSE, SZSE, and BSE.[4] Table 5.1 shows some basic information of the three stock exchanges in mainland China, including their issuers, market liquidity, and investor threshold. By the end of 2023, the number of listed companies on the Chinese domestic stock market reached 5,346, with 2,263 on the SSE, 2,844 on the SZSE, and 239 on the BSE.[5] Most public companies in China focus primarily on manufacturing, information transmission, software and information technology services, as well as the wholesale and retail sectors. Three provinces in China—Guangdong, Zhejiang, and Jiangsu—have the most public companies, with 872, 702, and 690 firms, respectively, collectively accounting for over 40% of all listed firms on the domestic stock markets.[6]

[4] This chapter only discusses the stock exchanges in mainland China; therefore, the analysis does not include stock exchanges in Hong Kong and Taiwan.

[5] *Xinhua*, 'Number of listed companies in China reaches 5,346 by end of 2023' (4 February 2024), https://www.chinadaily.com.cn/a/202402/04/WS65bef4cfa3104efcbdae98c9.html.

[6] Ibid.

Table 5.1 Overview of China's stock markets

	Shanghai Stock Exchange (SSE)		Shenzhen Stock Exchange (SZSE)			Beijing Stock Exchange (BSE)
	SSE Main Board	**SSE Sci-Tech Innovation Board (Star Market)**	**SZSE Main Board**	**SZSE Small and Medium-Sized Cap Board**	**SZSE Growth Enterprises Market (ChiNext board)**	
Typical Issuers	Large corporation, Blue chip	Technological and innovative enterprises	Large corporation, Blue chip	Small and medium-sized enterprises	Half-mature enterprises not meeting the listing requirements of the main boards	SMEs with 'specialization, refinement, differentiation, and innovation' (SRDI)
Market Liquidity	Highest	Moderate to low	Highest	High	Moderate	Moderate to low
Investor Threshold	Lowest	Moderate	Lowest	Lowest	Low	High

Source: Shanghai Stock Exchange, Shenzhen Stock Exchange, and Beijing Stock Exchange.

Becoming a listed company is considered a great prestige for Chinese entrepreneurs due to the strict listing standards in China, particularly those for the main boards of the SSE and SZSE. Any Chinese companies, in order to get a public listing, have to satisfy the following criteria according to the *PRC Securities Law*: (1) have a robust and well-run organizational structure; (2) have continuous operation ability; (3) the financial and accounting reports of last three years have been issued with an unqualified audit report; (4) the issuer, its controlling shareholders, or actual controllers have not committed crimes including corruption, bribery, embezzlement, misappropriation of property, and the disruption of the order of the socialist market economy, over the last three years; and (5) other conditions prescribed by the securities regulatory authority.[7] Each stock exchange also has its own listing standards, which include quantitative criteria regarding a company's revenue, profitability, and years of operation.

The SSE was established in November 1990, and the SZSE followed in December 1990, marking the start of modern Chinese stock markets in the early 1990s. Both stock exchanges are supervised by the China Securities Regulatory Commission (CSRC). In addition to equities, the exchanges facilitate bond and mutual fund trading. The listed bonds typically include treasury bonds, credit bonds, and convertible bonds. The SSE holds a main board as well as the latest sci-tech innovation board (Star Market). The SZSE has three different boards: main board, small and medium-sized cap board, and growth enterprises market. Each board or market targets the listing of different companies depending on their respective sizes, industries, financing needs, and development stages. The main boards of SSE and SZSE focus on the listing of large-cap and blue-chip companies. The SZSE small and medium-sized cap board mainly serves the champions of SMEs in the country. In order to list shares in the main boards and small and medium-sized cap board, companies have to make profits continuously over the past three accounting years with an accumulated profit amount of over RMB 30 million and to have the accumulated net cash flow amount of over RMB 50 million or the accumulated revenue of over RMB 300 million.[8] The SZSE growth enterprises market (ChiNext board) targets fast-growing enterprises with less stringent listing standards compared with main boards. Listing applicants have to make profits continuously over the past two years with an accumulated profit amount of over RMB 10 million or have to make profits for the past year with a revenue over RMB 50 million.[9]

[7] PRC Securities Law 2020, Article 12.

[8] Shanghai Stock Exchange, 'Listing on SSE', http://www.sse.com.cn/services/list/listedinsse/bluechips/a/20170825/b254004db4002ca4bd105c017adb374a.pdf.

[9] Ibid.

Regarding OTC markets, the National Equities Exchange and Quotations (NEEQ), also known as the New Third Board, provides a financing platform for innovative and entrepreneurial micro, small, and medium-sized businesses. As of the end of 2018, 10,691 companies are listed on the NEEQ, including 914 on the innovation tier and 9,777 on the base tier, with a total market capitalization of RMB 3.45 trillion.[10] In September 2021, the BSE was launched as a formal stock exchange, building upon the select tier of the NEEQ. This tier, the highest in the NEEQ system, has the strictest listing standards and trading rules, comparable to those of the SSE and SZSE. Aside from the NEEQ, there are also regional equity markets which offer the venue and facilitate non-public local companies to issue securities and raise funds locally as well as accommodate the transfer of such securities. It is estimated that over 100,000 companies are quoted in regional equity markets.

5.3 SSE star market (2019)

Established in 2019, the SSE sci-tech innovation board (star market) has been one of the latest regulatory experiments in China's capital markets to facilitate fundraising for high-tech enterprises. China is now the largest patent-filing country globally making 1,619,268 patent applications in 2022.[11] It is trying to become a global leader in areas like artificial intelligence, new energy, high-speed trains, and biopharmaceutics. The Star Market is expected to boost Shanghai's competitiveness as an international financial centre by attracting more tech businesses to list in China's economic hub. Shanghai is projected to become a leading financial centre in the twenty-first century, rivalling London, New York, Hong Kong, and Singapore.

Moreover, the star market spearheads China's reform of securities regulations as it promotes market efficiency and reduces government invention in the country's heavily regulated capital markets. The star market is implementing a registration-based IPO regime which streamlines the share offering process, supporting China's latest securities law reform. While loosening the listing standards to allow certain loss-making tech companies with dual-class shares and variable interest entities (VIE) structures to raise capital publicly in China, the new regulatory regime has introduced stricter rules regarding post-IPO information disclosure obligations and an investor suitability test to offer better protection for retail investors.

[10] National Equities Exchange and Quotations Company Limited, 'About NEEQ', http://www.neeq.com.cn/en/about_neeq/introduction.html.

[11] World Intellectual Property Organisation (WIPO), 'IP facts and figures', https://www.wipo.int/en/ipfactsandfigures/patents.

5.3.1 The history and status of star market

In late 2010s, China has established the science and technology innovation board at SSE, which is commonly referred to as the 'sci-tech innovation board' or 'star market', as the latest capital markets reform to assist the fundraising of tech enterprises and enhance the international competitiveness of SSE. At present, the total market capitalization of SSE and SZSE stands at RMB 45.6 trillion ($6.49 trillion), which is 56% of China's gross domestic product (GDP); in contrast, the total market cap of US stock markets is $36 trillion, equivalent to 180% of the US GDP.[12] This indicates that Chinese capital markets still have huge growth potential to match the scale of the Chinese economy as well as to meet the financing demands of Chinese businesses.

In November 2018, President Xi Jinping made a keynote speech at the opening ceremony of the first China International Import Expo in Shanghai where he announced the launch of the star market within SSE.[13] It is a brand-new trading platform with various experimental capital market reforms including the 'registration-based' IPO system. On 13th June 2019, the sci-tech innovation board was officially opened at the Shanghai Lujiazui Forum.[14] On 22nd July 2019, the first group of twenty-five companies, including China Railway Signal & Communication, Anji Technology, and Shanghai MicroPort Endovascular MedTech, were admitted to trading at the star market. On the debut date, the twenty-five companies saw an average share price rise of 139.55% and an average price-to-earnings (P/E) ratio of 120, and the total trading volume for the first five days exceeded RMB 140 billion.[15] On 8th August 2019, the second group of companies obtained a listing on the star market, including Amlogic, the semi-conductor maker, and Shanghai Friendess Electronic Technology Corp Ltd.[16] As of June 2024, there are 573 listed companies on the Science and Technology Innovation Board, with a total share capital of 217.52 billion shares and a total market value exceeding RMB 516.0 billion.[17] The average P/E ratio for all companies listed on start market is 34.7. More than 80% of these companies are in the fields of new generation information technology, biomedicine, and high-end equipment manufacturing.

[12] Song Xuetao, 'What is the historical significance of sci-tech innovation board?', *TF Securities* (2 March 2019), http://pdf.dfcfw.com/pdf/H3_AP201903041302384303_1.pdf.

[13] *China Daily*, 'Science and technology innovation board' (7 November 2018), http://www.chinadaily.com.cn/a/201811/07/WS5be23110a310eff303286fda.html.

[14] *Global Times*, 'China launches sci-tech innovation board, stressing further financial opening-up amid trade war' (13 June 2019), http://www.globaltimes.cn/content/1154078.shtml.

[15] *Xinhua*, 'The first week of sci-tech innovation board: How the first 25 listing companies performed?' (27 July 2019), http://www.xinhuanet.com/fortune/2019-07/27/c_1210216065.htm.

[16] *Xinhua*, 'The second group of companies obtained listing in sci-tech innovation board' (7 August 2019), http://www.xinhuanet.com/fortune/2019-08/07/c_1210232152.htm.

[17] Shanghai Stock Exchange Start Market Official Website, https://star.sse.com.cn/en/.

Given the various trading places serving different kinds of companies and investors, the star market is said to fill a major gap in China's capital markets by combining the advantages of both exchange trading platforms and off-exchange trading venues. The SSE and SZSE main boards, the Small and Medium-Sized Cap Board, and the ChiNext Board are formally regulated exchange trading platforms with high market liquidity, as most Chinese citizens can participate in trading activities without an investment threshold. However, those markets used to have strict and onerous listing rules. Before the recent reform, any IPO applicants of the SSE and SZSE had to obtain the administrative approval from CSRC and stock exchanges, apart from satisfying relevant standards in company law and securities regulations. It is referred to as the 'approval-based' IPO regime by the Chinese regulator.

On the contrary, it is relatively easy for businesses to get a listing in the OTC platforms like NEEQ and regional equity markets since they use the 'registration-based' IPO system and do not censor substantial business data of issuers like profitability and the value of assets. However, both markets suffer a severe problem of low liquidity as they have made extremely high thresholds for individual investor, which stops most Chinese citizens from trading at such forums. For example, investors need to possess at least RMB 5 million financial assets to be eligible to trade shares at the NEEQ.[18] Clearly, the star market has combined the benefits of both exchange trading and OTC trading by offering tech companies an easy access to a highly liquid market within the SSE. It has relatively lax listing standards similar to OTC trading while listed companies can enjoy sufficient liquidity and trading volumes comparable to the main boards. Obviously, the star market has differentiated itself from other existing markets and appeals to most domestic and international investors.

5.3.2 Rationales of introducing star market

There are two main reasons for the establishment of the sci-tech innovation board. First, the new trading platform is said to support the growth of high-tech industries by granting them more financing resources. The Chinese economy has been facing multiple challenges in the 2010s and early 2020s, such as the slowdown of GDP growth, the COVID-19 pandemic, and the China–US trade war. To boost the high-quality economic growth, China has made several policy initiatives, including the establishment of

[18] *National Equities Exchange and Quotations Investor Suitability Regulatory Rule* (2017), Article 5.

the star market, to support the growth of high-tech industries by granting entrepreneurs additional financing resources.

In the past, Chinese tech companies were mostly reliant on foreign venture capital (VC) or private equity (PE) funds to raise money. For example, Alibaba in 2000 received a $20 million investment from Japan's Soft bank, and Tencent in 2001 obtained $31 million capital from South Africa's Naspers.[19] That's why Alibaba and Tencent, two largest tech giants in China, now have foreign investors as their majority shareholders. Similarly, when raising funds in the capital markets, most Chinese tech businesses like NetEase, Sina, Sohu, Alibaba, JD, and NIO obtained a listing in overseas markets outside mainland China (like New York and Hong Kong) as Chinese law had not allowed unprofitable companies to go public until the recent law change. The CSRC also prohibits the foreign dominant ownership in Chinese public companies and restricts the use of dual-class shares and VIE which are commonly used by tech start-ups. Obviously, a lot of securities regulations in China seem outdated compared with the fast growth of tech companies and their innovative financing structures.

In recent years, promoting technological innovation has become a top priority for the Chinese government as the country has fostered a massive high-tech industry. China now has 206 unicorn companies, which are private tech businesses with a valuation of over $1 billion and less than a ten-year history, more than 203 unicorn companies in the United States.[20] China has launched the 'Made in China 2025' campaign aiming at upgrading its industry capacities to produce more high value-added products and services.[21] The initiative set out specific goals for ten prioritized industries including robotics, new generation information technology, aviation and aerospace equipment, maritime equipment and hi-tech ships, railway transport, new energy and energy-saving vehicles, energy equipment, agricultural equipment, new materials, and biopharma and hi-tech medical devices.

Moreover, a 2018 policy paper issued by the State Council (Chinese cabinet) and CSRC have been encouraging a group of so-called 'pilot enterprises' in the areas of internet, big data, cloud computing, artificial intelligence, software and integrated circuit, advanced equipment manufacturing,

[19] Vinnie Lauria, 'Instant replay: Naspers-Tencent echoes the SoftBank-Alibaba Story', *Forbes* (17 July 2019), https://www.forbes.com/sites/vinnielauria/2019/07/17/instant-replay-naspers-tencent-echoes-the-softbank-alibaba-story/.

[20] Hurun, 'Hurun global unicorn list 2019', http://www.hurun.net/CN/Article/Details?num=E719025 0C866.

[21] Alice Tse and Julianna Wu, 'Why "Made in China 2025" triggered the wrath of President Trump', *South China Morning Post* (11 September 2018), http://multimedia.scmp.com/news/china/article/made-in-China-2025/index.html.

biomedicine to issue Chinese depositary receipt (CDR) or new shares in mainland China, as long as they meet one of the following standards: for those enterprises which have already been listed abroad, the market capitalization should be no less than RMB 200 billion ($25.6 billion); and for those which are still private, they should have an annual revenue of no less than RMB 3 billion ($429 million) as well as a market capitalization of no less than RMB 20 billion ($2.86 billion), or they can demonstrate the rapid growth of revenue plus having self-developed and international leading technologies while maintaining an advantageous position among industry competitors.[22] It is clear that the development of capital markets in China is left behind its industrial and technological growth, so that's why China urgently needs to overhaul its capital markets law to create a more friendly financing market for tech businesses to raise capital. This serves as the first justification for introducing the star market.

Second, the launch of sci-tech innovation board is of strategic importance to promote Shanghai as a leading international financial centre. In the early twentieth century, Shanghai was the largest financial centre in the Far East, but its status has fallen due to the socialist revolution in the 1950s.[23] In the late 1970s, China started to re-embrace the market economy and underwent a series of economic and financial reforms guided by the 'reform and open-up' policy. This has led to the resurgence of Shanghai as an international financial centre. In 2018, the total transaction volume of the city's financial markets reached RMB 1,645.8 trillion, up 15.2% from the previous year.[24] There are 1,605 financial institutions in Shanghai, among which 30% are foreign institutions.[25] Shanghai is also the economic centre of Yangtze River Delta region, one of the most economically developed areas in the country. Based on its strong economic foundation and financial strength, Shanghai is said to become a top international financial centre like New York, London, Hong Kong, and Singapore in the 2020s.

According to the Global Financial Centre Index in 2024, Shanghai was ranked the sixth largest financial centre in the world.[26] Recently, Shanghai Municipal Government has released an action plan to accelerate the building

[22] State Council, 'The State Council office on forwarding the CSRC's notice on developing the pilot scheme of allowing innovative enterprises to issue shares or depository receipts in mainland China' (GUOFABAN 2018, No.21), Article 3.

[23] Lerong Lu, *Private Lending in China: Practice, Law, and Regulation of Shadow Banking and Alternative Finance* (Routledge, 2018), p. 21.

[24] Shanghai Government Official Website, http://www.shanghai.gov.cn/nw2/nw2314/nw2319/nw12344/u26aw58032.html.

[25] Ibid.

[26] Z/Yen Group, 'The Global Financial Centres Index 35' (21 March 2024), https://www.longfinance.net/publications/long-finance-reports/the-global-financial-centres-index-35/.

of Shanghai international financial centre. The goal for the 2020s is for Shanghai to establish itself as a global financial market dominated by Renminbi products, with robust financial resource allocation and market influence.[27] Shanghai aims to develop a fair, innovative, efficient, transparent, and open financial services system governed by the rule of law. The city seeks to become an international financial centre that matches China's economic strength and the global status of the Renminbi, positioning itself at the forefront of global financial centres. More specifically, Shanghai international financial centre is said to comprise '6 centres and 1 system' including: global asset management centre, cross-border investment and financing services centre (which is mainly to support the 'belt and road initiative'), financial technology (fintech) centre, international insurance centre (e.g. insurance market, re-insurance market, and Shanghai insurance exchange), global renminbi asset pricing, payment and settlement centre, financial risks management and stress-testing centre, and a world-class financial ecosystem.[28]

Apart from supporting the development of international financial institutions and financial markets, Shanghai's city congress passed the 'Local Finance Regulatory Provision' in April 2020.[29] The regulation aims to provide a better regulatory framework (including financial supervision, risk management, information sharing, and the protection of consumers' rights) for local financial organizations such as small-loan companies, financing guarantee companies, regional stock markets, pawnshops, financial leasing companies, commercial factoring companies and local asset management company. Evidently, the sci-tech board will support the bid of Shanghai to become a leading international financial centre as well as a technological innovation centre. It can boost the high-quality growth of Chinese economy and bring more and better investment opportunities for investors in China and beyond.

5.3.3 The pilot registration-based IPO regime

On 1 March 2019, the CSRC issued the 'Sci-Tech Innovation Board Initial Public Offering Share Registration Administrative Measures (Trial Implementation)' and the 'Sci-Tech Innovation Board Listed Companies Continuous Supervision Measures (Trial Implementation)', establishing basic rules

[27] People's Bank of China et al., 'The Action Plan on Building Shanghai International Financial Centre (2018–2020)', http://www.shanghai.gov.cn/nw2/nw2314/nw2315/nw4411/u21aw1360150.html.

[28] Ibid.

[29] *Shanghai Municipal Local Finance Regulatory Provision* (April 2020).

for listing and trading activities on the Star Market.[30] Subsequently, the CSRC and the SSE promulgated a series of regulatory rules for the star market, unleashing the latest capital markets law reform in China. The biggest change in the reform comes from the adoption of the 'registration-based' IPO system.

Previously, both the SSE and SZSE had adopted a so-called 'approval-based' IPO system under which listing applicants had been subject to strict financial censor and administrative approval by the CSRC's Public Offering Review Committee. The emphasis of China's securities regulation lies on the pre-listing financial checks rather than post-listing information disclosure. IPO applicants have to pass at least three rounds of administrative reviews to obtain a final approval from the securities regulator. On average, an IPO application takes around 589 days in China. The ultra-long waiting time makes some issuers giving up their listing plans in mainland China and turning to stock markets in Hong Kong and New York. Occasionally, the CSRC will freeze new IPOs completely as it can refuse to grant approvals in order to control the supply of new shares and stabilize share prices and the share index in a bear market.[31]

The 'approval-based' system is criticized as being inefficient and opaque, as the regulator has excessive power in deciding the outcomes of IPO applications. Therefore, China's capital markets have been gradually transitioning towards a more market-oriented 'registration-based' IPO system. In December 2015, the standing committee of the National People's Congress, the Chinese parliament, authorized the implementation of 'registration-based' IPOs. This provides a legal basis for the trial of 'registration-based' IPOs in the star market which significantly reduces governmental intervention in the capital markets. Thus, the CSRC will no longer conduct substantial examination over the issuing companies as long as their investment bankers, accountants, and lawyers provide valid legal and financial documentations in compliance with relevant regulations. The 'registration-based' system has reduced the costs of IPOs while shortening the time frame. However, it requires a higher level of information disclosure obligations for issuers after the IPO to protect the interests of investors.

The latest amendment of *PRC Securities Law* reaffirmed the adoption of 'registration-based' IPO for Chinese stock markets, and its specific scope and implementation steps will be decided by the State Council.[32] However, the

[30] Shanghai Stock Exchange, 'Regulations of launching the star market and experimenting registration-based IPO', http://www.sse.com.cn/lawandrules/sserules/tib/.

[31] Nan Ma and Gabriel Wildau, 'Beijing's visible hand lies heavy on China IPOs', *Financial Times* (26 March 2015), p. 18.

[32] PRC Securities Law 2020, Article 9.

transition towards 'registration-based' IPO is likely to be a gradual process, as it started with the trial at Sci-tech innovation board in Shanghai. Then it will be used by Shenzhen's ChiNext board, followed by the widespread experiments in other segments of Chinese markets.

There are three major distinctions between 'approval-based' and 'registration-based' IPO regimes. First, from a theoretical point of view, it is concerned with the question that who has the power to issue securities. Under the 'approval-based' system, legislators think securities issuance is closely related to public interests as thousands of retail and institutional investors will get involved in the subscription and trading of such securities. Therefore, issuing securities should be viewed as a chartered right, so applicants need a special administrative approval from public agencies such as the securities regulator. In contrast, the underlying ideology of 'registration-based' system is that issuing securities is a natural economic right belonging to modern enterprises. On this basis, companies should be allowed to issue shares without restrictions providing that they fulfil the information disclosure obligations.

Second, the two systems have different methods of checking the authenticity and accuracy of information relating to the issuers and their securities. Regarding the 'approval-based' system, the securities regulator is undertaking the sole responsibility of examining the substantial information of the issuers. It might be beneficial when the number of listed companies is smaller so the securities regulator could have the resource to check all the information for future investors. However, as the capital markets grow, with China now having over 5,000 listed companies and hundreds more obtaining a listing each year, it will be neither feasible nor desirable for the regulator to check each issuer's information on a case-by-case basis. Under the 'registration-based' system, the responsibility of scrutinizing information has been transferred to a diversity of bodies including the stock exchange, law firm, accountancy firm, and investment bank. This approach alleviates the burden on securities regulators and promotes a more market-based and transparent environment for share issuance.

Third, the two systems are reliant on different political and legal backgrounds in one country. The 'approval-based' system requires a big and strong government as the securities regulator monopolizes the power of issuing securities and it can determine the issuing price, the amount of capital to be raised, as well as the exact listing date. Under this kind of IPO arrangement, self-regulatory bodies and market participants play a more supplementary role in the process of securities offering. However, the free market has the say in the 'registration-based' IPO system since the securities regulator is not directly involved in the decision of granting or refusing an IPO. Accordingly, whether an IPO is successful depends on the complicated gaming between various market players including issuers, underwriters, legal professionals, accountants, and investors.

5.3.4 The regulation of star market

In response to the launch of star market and the introduction of 'registration-based' IPO system, the CSRC and SSE have learned from international experience to design a more effective and efficient legal framework for regulating securities issuance and trading. In particular, the 'registration-based' system is more dependent on the post-IPO information disclosure requirements to protect the legitimate interests of investors. Thus, the attentions of the securities regulators will be placed on ensuring the truthfulness and comprehensiveness of information provided by the issuers on a continuous basis. This section summarizes the main points of latest laws and regulations surrounding the star market as follows.

a. Differentiated listing standards: The star market no longer solely relies on traditional indicators set by CSRC, such as net asset and profit level, to evaluate a company's feasibility to obtain a listing. It gives more listing opportunities to innovative and technological enterprises whose businesses are at an early stage but have great potential to thrive and become industry leaders in the future. However, the new model could result in the difficulty for investment banks to determine a proper market valuation and offering price for prospective issuers. It produces extra risks for public investors as well, because the traditional valuation methods such as P/E ratio or price-to-book (P/B) ratio will be less effective in guiding the investments. Generally speaking, the star market has relaxed the listing standards for issuing companies. It has broken a long-term rule in China's A-share market that listing companies must make profits before floating their shares publicly. The star market allows some high-tech businesses to go public when still making losses, as long as they display strong business strength and potential in certain fields. The regulators and the stock exchange will comprehensively consider multiple factors concerning the listing applicants, such as market capitalization, profit, revenue, research and development (R&D) expenditure, cash flow, and technological achievement. The IPO applicants have to meet at least one of the following standards to be eligible for the star market:[33]

[33] *Shanghai Stock Exchange Sci-Tech Innovation Board Share Listing Rules* (2019), Article 2.1.2.

- The predicted market cap is no less than RMB 1 billion and the company has made positive profits over the past two years with an accumulated profit amount of no less than RMB 50 million, or the predicted market cap is no less than RMB 1 billion and the company has made positive profits for one year with a accumulated profit amount of no less than RMB 100 million;
- The predicted market cap is no less than RMB 1.5 billion, the revenue of the previous year is no less than RMB 200 million, and the R&D expenditure of the past three years should be no less than 15% of the accumulated revenues of the past three years;
- The predicted market cap is no less than RMB 2 billion, the revenue of the previous year is no less than RMB 300 million, and the accumulated net cash flow of the previous three years should be no less than RMB 100 million;
- The predicted market cap is no less than RMB 3 billion and the revenue of the previous year is no less than RMB 300 million; and
- The predicted market cap is no less than RMB 4 billion and the main business or product has obtained regulatory approvals from the relevant authorities which have a large potential market and have made staged achievements. Pharmaceutical companies need to have at least one core product that has obtained approval to carry out Phase-II clinical trials. Companies in other sectors should have significant technological advantages and satisfy relevant criteria.

b. Red-chip companies, VIEs, and dual-class shares: The sci-tech innovation board accepts the listing of red-chip companies which are incorporated in a foreign jurisdiction but have main business interests in mainland China.[34] Traditionally, foreign-registered companies are not allowed to obtain a listing on the main boards of SSE and SZSE. In practice, a large number of Chinese tech businesses have been incorporated in jurisdictions having favourable tax policies and legal frameworks such as Cayman Islands, British Virgin Islands, and Singapore. As a result, the red-chip companies, despite conducting most of their businesses in or with China, are not allowed to list their shares in China. It partly accounts for the popularity of overseas listing for Chinese tech companies. As for the star market, red-chip companies can issue either new shares or CDRs to be traded in the SSE. In April 2019, Segway-Ninebot Ltd, which produces two-wheeled personal

[34] *Shanghai Stock Exchange Sci-Tech Innovation Board Share Listing Rules* (2019), Chapter 13 'Red-chip companies and the coordination of cross-border issues'.

transporters and robotics, has filed the first application to apply for a CDR listing in the star market.[35] Moreover, it is common for red-chip companies to adopt VIEs which are complex off-shore financing and legal structures to help foreign investors evade Beijing's restriction of foreign ownership in companies from industries such as the internet, finance, and education.[36] VIEs are banned on the main board of the SSE but they are allowed in the star market. Besides, tech and innovative businesses including Facebook and Google often use dual-class shares with weighted voting rights to help business founders maintain the control of their businesses even if they only have a minority of shares. It is because external VC and PE investments often significantly dilute the ownership of tech entrepreneurs. Mr. Liu Qiangdong, the founder and CEO of the Nasdaq-listed JD.com, a leading online shopping platform in China, owns 15.4% of shares in JD.com but has 79% of voting rights thanks to the design of dual-class shares.[37] Although this kind of legal arrangement is extremely beneficial for the founder and management team of tech companies, it is widely criticized for breaching the principle of shareholder democracy and equality by giving some shareholders more votes per share than others.[38] Dual-class shares are prohibited in most Chinese capital markets but it is allowed in the latest star market subject to sufficient risk warning and explanation in the listing prospectus.

c. Daily price fluctuation limit: The SSE and SZSE have been implementing a daily price limit of 10% on common stocks listed on the main boards and 5% on special treatment stocks.[39] It is a market stabilization mechanism preventing the share price from fluctuating fiercely within one trading day, giving retail investors more time to react to the market change. Unlike countries having mature capital markets such as the United States or the United Kingdom where institutional investors play a main role in trading, in China retail investors contribute to over 90% of daily trading volume.[40] Therefore, China's stock markets have seen a high level of volatility and speculative bubbles often occur; for example, within twelve months, the SSE composite index rose from around 2,000 points in July 2014 to the peak of 5,166.35 points

[35] Ninebot Limited, 'CDR public offering prospectus' (April 2019), http://static.sse.com.cn/stock/information/c/201904/6cb9b97495db4b80aeeb99eac8e35c49.pdf.

[36] Ningyao Ye and Lerong Lu, 'How to Harness a Unicorn? Demystifying China's Reform of Share Listing Rules and Chinese Depositary Receipts (CDRs)' (2019) 30 *International Company and Commercial Law Review* 454, 457–458.

[37] *Eastmoney*, 'The latest shareholding structure of JD.com revealed' (10 May 2019), http://stock.eastmoney.com/a/201905091118284644.html.

[38] Henry Angest, 'In defence of dual-class shares with different rights', *Financial Times* (17 April 2019), p. 9.

[39] Ting Chen, Zhenyu Gao, Jibao He, Wenxi Jiang, and Wei Xiong, 'Daily Price Limits and Destructive Market Behaviour' (2019) 208 *Journal of Econometrics* 249.

[40] *The Economist*, 'China's stock market: A crazy casino' (26 May 2015).

on 12 June 2015.[41] The price limit rule seems necessary for China's markets as it can mitigate the irrational price movements and prevent excessive speculation. However, the price limit is criticized to cause an opposite effect sometimes by exacerbating the price rise and fall. Judged by behavioural finance, the price limit will have psychological impacts on both trading parties, which subsequently changes their trading behaviours. For instance, if the share price hits the upper limit (+10%), it is likely that the seller will raise his or her expectation of the selling price and determine to sell the shares on later dates at a higher price. Similarly, if buyers are unable to purchase the shares owing to the upper circuit breaker, their determination to buy such shares will be reinforced so they will be more likely to purchase the shares at a higher price in the following trading day. The star market has introduced a loosened daily price cap, as there will be no price movement limits during the first five trading days when a company first goes public; after that, the daily limit of price fluctuation will be set at 20%.[42] This gives investors twice space to respond to the market price movement, which is conducive to the effective price-discovery mechanism and improves market liquidity.

d. Stricter market exit rules: For a long time, China's A-share market is described as having 'no exits' because very few public companies are delisted as a result of underperformance and other illegal issues. Therefore, in the eyes of most Chinese entrepreneurs, getting an IPO is the symbol of ultimate success which brings them numerous practical benefits.[43] It means that literally public companies enjoy endless financing resources from banks and capital markets and will obtain an extra layer of protection against bankruptcy as the businesses will never 'die' after becoming a public company. Clearly, it is a disaster for the investors as the shares of some worst-performing business are still afloat. As a response, the star market has announced stricter delisting rules for underperforming companies. There are several situations which might lead to the delisting of a public company, such as the fraudulent issuance of shares, the violation of information disclosure requirements, and if a company violates laws in relation to national security, public safety, ecological safety, production safety, and public health security.[44] The company can also be delisted by the exchange if it fails to meet the regulatory standards

[41] Lerong Lu and Longjie Lu, 'Unveiling China's Stock Market Bubble: Margin Financing, the Leveraged Bull and Governmental Responses' (2017) 32 *Journal of International Banking Law and Regulation* 146 at 147.

[42] *Shanghai Stock Exchange Sci-Tech Innovation Board Share Trading Special Regulation* (2019), Article 18.

[43] Lerong Lu, *Private Lending in China: Practice, Law, and Regulation of Shadow Banking and Alternative Finance* (Routledge, 2018), p. 57.

[44] *Shanghai Stock Exchange Sci-Tech Innovation Board Share Listing Rules* (2019), Chapter 12 'Delisting'.

regarding share transactions and key financial indicators. For example, the SSE will delist companies encountering the following situations:[45]

- The accumulated trading volume for 120 consecutive trading days is less than two million shares;
- The closing price for twenty consecutive trading days is less than the par value of the share;
- The market cap for twenty consecutive trading days is less than RMB 300 million ($42.67 million);
- The number of shareholders for twenty consecutive trading days is less than 400; and
- Other situations specified by the SSE.

e. Strengthened information disclosure rules: The 'registration-based' IPO system and other market-oriented listing and trading rules call for stronger information disclosure obligations to be imposed on the issuers. Information disclosure lies at the heart of modern securities regulation as investors should be provided with sufficient and accurate information relating to the securities that they are trading. Investors can only make informed investment decisions when an adequate amount information is given to them. Under the 'approval-based' IPO regime, the securities regulator is undertaking the primary responsibility of substantially assessing the quality of issuers before the shares are offered to the public and therefore investors can rely on the regulator to screen out qualified investment objectives. However, the 'registration-based' IPO system restricts the role of the securities regulator in the share offering process and as a result, the post-IPO information disclosure becomes especially important and necessary for investors who can only rely on themselves to judge the quality of the securities that they are going to subscribe or purchase. As for the star market, listed tech and innovative companies are required to fully disclose any risk factors that might have significant adverse impacts on the company's core competitiveness, operation activities, and future growth.[46] Moreover, if the issuers have not made profits, they should fully disclose the reasons for why they are not making profits, and its impact on the company cash flow, business development, talent recruitment, the stability of the entrepreneurial team, R&D investment, strategic investment, and growth sustainability.[47] The new *PRC Securities Law* also

[45] *Shanghai Stock Exchange Sci-Tech Innovation Board Share Listing Rules* (2019), Article 12.3.1.

[46] *Sci-Tech Innovation Board Listed Companies Continuous Supervision Measures (Trial Implementation)* (2019), Article 12.

[47] *Sci-Tech Innovation Board Listed Companies Continuous Supervision Measures (Trial Implementation)* (2019), Article 12.

strengthened the requirement of information disclosure for the issuer as it has to notify the CSRC and stock exchange about the following important incidents and explain the cause and potential impact:

(1) Major change in the company's operating principles and the scope of business;
(2) The company's major investment activities, e.g. the company's major asset purchases and sales within one year the amount of which exceeds 30% of the company's total assets, or the company decides to mortgage, pledge, sell, or discard its principal business assets if the transaction involves the disposal of over 30% of the value of such assets;
(3) The company enters into major business contracts, provides significant guarantee, engages in connected transactions, which might have significant influence on the company's assets, liabilities, legal rights, and operating results;
(4) The company incurs major debts or faces default situations like failing to pay major debts when they fall due;
(5) The company faces major losses;
(6) The company faces significant changes in external conditions in relation to its production and operation;
(7) The change of the company's directors or the change of over one-third of its supervisors or managers, or when the chairman of the board of directors or managers are unable to perform their duties;
(8) Major changes in shareholders having over 5% of shares in the company or the change of company's actual controller about its shareholding or controlling companies, or the major changes in the actual controller and its controlling companies engaging in the same or similar businesses as the issuer;
(9) The company's plan to pay dividends and increase capital, the major changes in the company's ownership structure, the company's decisions regarding capital reduction, merger, division, dissolution, and bankruptcy application, or the company enters into the bankruptcy proceeding according to law or the company is ordered to close down;
(10) Major litigation and arbitration relating to the company, or the decisions of the general meeting of shareholders and the board of directors have been revoked or declared null and void in accordance with the law;

(11) The company is suspected of a crime and being investigated in accordance with the law, or the company's controlling shareholders, actual controllers, directors, supervisors, and senior management personnel are suspected of a crime and under compulsory measures according to law; and

(12) Other matters prescribed by the securities regulatory authority under the State Council.[48]

f. Investor suitability test: The CSRC and SSE try to ensure that the investments in the star market are only suitable for those retail investors with appropriate funding, investment experience, and risk tolerance ability. As companies listed in the star market are mostly tech businesses whose futures are highly uncertain, the relevant investments tend to be riskier. It needs investors to have better knowledge, extra experience, and more money to participate in the market. The latest regulation requires that individual investors must have at least two-year trading experience, and hold financial assets worth no less than RMB 500,000 for twenty trading days, to open an account to trade shares at the star market.[49] Clearly, this stops investors with a lower risk appetite and less funding from directly participating in the trading, which might be the best protection for them. The *PRC Securities Law* also distinguishes ordinary investors from professional investors based on their overall asset, financial asset, investment knowledge and experience, and professional ability, as ordinary investors will receive extra protection when they have disputes with securities companies who bear the burden of proof.[50] If investors do not pass the above thresholds, they will still be able to invest in the star market indirectly through purchasing units in mutual funds that have access to the star market. Share issuance in the star market will be conducted via both online and offline channels. Regarding online issuance, the issuer will use the online trading network of the SSE to list and sell the new shares, while the investors will subscribe to these shares by the same network. Online issuance mainly targets individual investors. In contrast, offline issuance does not go through the trading system of the SSE and primarily it is open privately to professional and institutional investors such as securities firms, mutual funds, trust companies, insurance companies, qualified foreign institutional investors (QFII), and non-public investment funds. The newly issued shares

[48] PRC Securities Law 2020, Article 80.

[49] *Shanghai Stock Exchange Sci-Tech Innovation Board Share Trading Special Regulation* (2019), Article 4.

[50] PRC Securities Law 2020, Article 89.

at the star market will be sold to institutional investors who enjoy certain priority over individual investors. At least 50% of offline issuance will be firstly allotted to mutual funds, social security funds, pension funds, enterprise annuity funds, and insurance firms.[51] If the total number of shares after the public offering does not exceed 400 million, the offline issuance should be no less than 70% of the total issuance; if the total number of shares is over 400 million or the issuer is not yet making profits, the offline issuance should be no less than 80%.[52]

g. Extra judicial supports: A sound securities regulatory system cannot exist without a supportive and effective law enforcement mechanism. On 21 June 2019, the Supreme People's Court of China issued the '*Some Opinions on Providing Judicial Supports for the Establishment of Sci-Tech Innovation Board and the Experiment of Registration-Based System*' (the '*Opinions*') as the principles guiding judicial practices in relation to securities and futures disputes as well as the protection of investors' interests in the star market. It is the first time in the history of Supreme People's Court to make some special and comprehensive judicial opinions for capital markets law enforcement. In terms of the jurisdiction, any civil and commercial disputes relating to securities issuance, IPO underwriting contracts, IPO sponsorship contracts, and securities frauds in the star market will be heard by Shanghai Financial Court.[53] Established in August 2018, Shanghai Financial Court specializes in finance-related lawsuits and it is the first of its kind in China which aims to provide a better business environment and dispute resolution forum for investors from home and abroad.[54] The *Opinions* also stipulate the civil liabilities for breaching relevant information disclosure obligations. The controlling shareholders or actual controller of the issuing companies will owe directly civil liabilities to investors if they conduct fraud issuance or make false statements.[55] In addition, the court will fully respect special corporate governance arrangements of tech and innovative companies which are compatible with technological innovations, such as weighted voting rights and stock option incentives for senior managers as

[51] *Shanghai Stock Exchange Sci-Tech Innovation Board Share Issuance and Underwriting Implementing Measures* (2019), Article 12.

[52] *Shanghai Stock Exchange Sci-Tech Innovation Board Share Issuance and Underwriting Implementing Measures* (2019), Article 12.

[53] Supreme People's Court, 'Some Opinions on Providing Judicial Supports for the Establishment of Sci-Tech Innovation Board and the Experiment of Registration-Based System' (FAFA 2019 No.17), Article 3.

[54] Supreme People's Court, 'First-of-its-kind financial court gets down to work in Shanghai' (22 August 2018), http://english.court.gov.cn/2018-08/22/content_36806558.htm.

[55] Supreme People's Court, 'Some Opinions on Providing Judicial Supports for the Establishment of Sci-Tech Innovation Board and the Experiment of Registration-Based System' (FAFA 2019 No.17), Article 5.

long as such arrangements do not violate laws and regulations.[56] Furthermore, the court will try to enhance the judicial protection for the intellectual properties (IP) belong to listed companies in the star market when dealing with IP cases relating to patents and technological contracts and punishing IP infringements.[57]

5.4 Beijing Stock Exchange (2021)

In September 2021, China established the BSE to channel capital into the country's burgeoning technology companies. This initiative particularly targets SMEs with limited access to traditional financing channels such as banks, VC, and PE funds. As the arrival of the fintech era, more innovative and technological companies have been actively seeking an official listing or alternative financing options.[58] The BSE is particularly valuable for Chinese entrepreneurs given the current geopolitical tensions between China and the United States, which have led to reduced access to New York stock markets for Chinese businesses.

While the traditional option for a company floating its shares for the first time is to have its securities admitted to listing on a domestic stock exchange, there is an increasing number of primary and secondary listing options in a foreign jurisdiction.[59] Many Chinese technology companies, including Alibaba, Baidu, JD, and NetEase, have chosen to list their shares on the NYSE and Nasdaq. However, the trend seems to come to a halt in 2021. For example, China Mobile and some other Chinese state-owned enterprises have been asked by NYSE to delist their shares due to the US investment ban on foreign corporations that might pose a national security threat.[60] Besides, China's ride-hailing group Didi Chuxing recently expressed a plan to withdraw its listing from the NYSE as the Chinese authorities have increased regulatory

[56] Supreme People's Court, 'Some Opinions on Providing Judicial Supports for the Establishment of Sci-Tech Innovation Board and the Experiment of Registration-Based System' (FAFA 2019 No.17), Article 6.

[57] Supreme People's Court, 'Some Opinions on Providing Judicial Supports for the Establishment of Sci-Tech Innovation Board and the Experiment of Registration-Based System' (FAFA 2019 No.17), Article 7.

[58] Lerong Lu and Alice Lingsheng Zhang, 'Regulating Fintech Corporations Amidst Covid-19 Pandemic: An Analysis of Ant Group (Alipay)'s Suspension of IPO and Business Restructuring' (2021) 42 *Company Lawyer* 341.

[59] Eilís Ferran and Look Chan Ho, *Principles of Corporate Finance Law* (2nd Edition, Oxford University Press, 2014), p. 357.

[60] Chong Koh Ping and Alexander Osipovich, 'NYSE to Delist Chinese Telecom Carriers After Rejecting Appeals', *The Wall Street Journal* (7 May 2021), https://www.wsj.com/articles/nyse-to-delist-chinese-telecoms-carriers-after-rejecting-appeals-11620394719.

scrutiny over the country's overseas-listed technology groups due to the data safety concern.[61]

The BSE was established based on the select tier board of China's NEEQ, an OTC market for trading shares of public limited companies not listed on the SSE or the SZSE. The BSE fully implements China's latest PRC Securities Law 2020, which brought about the most significant overhaul of securities regulation and capital markets law in the past decade, including the introduction of a registration-based IPO regime.[62] The following section discusses the latest capital markets reform measure—the launch of BSE as well as its new listing and trading rules. When discussing the BSE's listing standards, it refers to the similar rules for the ChiNext Board of SZSE, the Sci-tech Innovation Board (Star Market) of SSE, and the select tier of NEEQ, to provide readers with a holistic view of China's capital markets and their regulations.

5.4.1 The background of introducing Beijing Stock Exchange

SMEs play an essential and indispensable role in the Chinese economy as they account for 99% of the total number of enterprises and contribute to over 50% of tax revenue, 60% of GDP, 70% of technological innovations, and more than 80% of employment.[63] However, Chinese SMEs have long faced financing difficulties due to the inefficiencies in resource allocation within the country's state-dominated banking system. To address the SME financing dilemma, the Securities Trading Automatic Quotation (STAQ) and National Electronic Trading System (NET) were founded but both were terminated in 1999 because of the lack of supervision.

In 2001, in order to solve the historical problem of the suspended trading of STAQ and NET and to host the corporations delisted from the bourses of Shanghai and Shenzhen, China established the Agency Share Transfer System (Third Market).[64] In 2006, the Chinese regulators, to help more innovative SMEs raise funds from the capital markets, launched the New Third Market with a pilot project accepting the quotation of unlisted enterprises

[61] Ryan McMorrow, Sun Yu, and Tom Mitchell, 'China's Didi to delist from New York and switch to Hong Kong', *The Financial Times* (3 December 2021), https://www.ft.com/content/c30cf911-51da-4b40-a969-161351de6f04.

[62] Lerong Lu, 'Reforming Corporate Share-Listing Rules in China: Understanding the Rationale and Advantages of the Registration-Based IPO Regime' (2021) 42 *Company Lawyer* 236.

[63] Chinese Government, 'We will give policy support to small and medium-sized enterprises' (1 April 2021), http://www.gov.cn/zhengce/2020-04/01/content_5497938.htm.

[64] National Equities Exchange and Quotations (NEEQ), 'About NEEQ', http://www.neeq.com.cn/en/about_neeq/overview.html.

of Zhongguancun Science and Technology Park in Beijing (which is viewed as China's Silicon Valley). From 2006 to 2012, the pilot project was gradually expanded to Tianjin Binhai, Shanghai Zhangjiang, and Wuhan Donghu high-tech parks. Eventually, in September 2012, it led to the official launch of National Equities Exchange and Quotation Co., Ltd (NEEQ or New Third Board).

In 2013, the achievements of the pilot listing project in high-tech parks were highly recognized, so the State Council, which is China's cabinet, decided to roll out the experimental project to the rest of the country.[65] This has indicated the maturity of NEEQ as an OTC market for Chinese SMEs to raise capital, which is also a springboard for SMEs to float their shares on either SSE or SZSE at a later stage once they grow bigger. Nevertheless, due to the lack of market liquidity of NEEQ and the absence of an effective transferring mechanism from NEEQ to SSE and SZSE, the financing difficulties of Chinese SMEs have not been fully addressed. It has remained a prioritized policy task for the Chinese government for several years.

On 2 September 2021, President Xi Jinping, when speaking at the Global Trade in Services Summit of 2021 China International Fair for Trade in Services (CIFTIS), introduced a number of new measures to reform the Chinese capital markets, leading to the immediate launch of the BSE.[66] The new BSE not only deepens the reform of Beijing's NEEQ market, but also provides an extra financing channel for the so-called '*Zhuan, Jing, Te, Xin*' SMEs which stand for those companies with special characteristics of 'specialization, refinement, differentiation, and innovation' (SRDI) that are the robust mainstay of the Chinese economy. The BSE has been built upon the select tier of NEEQ, which is the highest tier of the entire NEEQ system having the strictest listing standards and trading rules close to those on SSE and SZSE.[67] Companies listed on the select tier for over a year that meet the IPO requirements of Shanghai's Star Market or Shenzhen's ChiNext board can switch their listing venues upon approval from the stock exchanges. This process does not require additional reviews or approvals from the CSRC.

Clearly, the select tier of NEEQ provides a convenient and fast channel for growing SMEs to obtain a listing in the more liquid exchange markets and to receive a higher valuation. The introduction of BSE and its further capital

[65] China News, 'The launch of new third board to nationwide, listed enterprises up to more than 2000' (7 November 2013), https://www.chinanews.com.cn/stock/2013/11-07/5473975.shtml.

[66] James T. Areddy, 'China to Launch Beijing Stock Exchange to Steer Investment into Innovation', *The Wall Street Journal* (2 September 2021), https://www.wsj.com/articles/china-to-launch-beijing-stock-exchange-to-steer-investment-into-innovation-11630622825.

[67] Zhou Lanxu, 'NEEQ to ease funding woes of small firms', *China Daily* (28 July 2020), https://www.chinadailyhk.com/article/138272.

market reform based on the select tier has been coined as the 'major strategic deployment' by CSRC.[68] In the first five trading days of the BSE, a batch of eighty-one companies embarked on their IPOs with a cumulative turnover of over RMB 21 billion, attracting 340,000 qualified investors.[69] The successful launch of the BSE is said to perfectly solve one long-lasting problem of NEEQ, i.e. the ultra-low trading volume, which has depicted a bright future for China's capital markets.

5.4.2 The listing standards of Beijing Stock Exchange

The success of BSE could not be achieved without China's latest reform of securities laws. The BSE is devoted to creating an attractive marketplace for SMEs that has inclusive listing thresholds. Furthermore, following the enaction of *PRC Securities Law 2020*, the BSE fully implements the registration-based IPO regime, in line with the practices of the Star Market and the ChiNext Board. The information disclosure requirements have been enhanced by considering the recent developments of China's innovation-orientated companies. To build a fair and transparent capital market, the BSE also upgraded the investor protection and accountability mechanisms.

The listing standards of BSE have been tailored for *'Zhuan, Jing, Te, Xin'* or SRDI SMEs. In 2011, the concept of *'Zhuan, Jing, Te, Xin'* SMEs was initiated by the Ministry of Industry and Information Technology (MIIT).[70] They are likely to become large corporations and BigTechs in the future, such as Alibaba, Tencent, and Huawei. 'With the profound and continuous development, the SMEs inventing high tech gadgets which are the ancillary or radical constituent part of advanced products will finally grow into giant enterprises', commented by China's state media.[71] Take the BSE-listed Wuhan Welltrans Optoelectronic Co Ltd (Welltrans) as an example. Although the market capitalization of Welltrans ($86.9 million as of September 2021) is not particularly large, it has been spending a high proportion (9.45%) of its revenue on R&D.[72] The Welltrans' businesses focus on the development of fibre

[68] Shen Lu, 'China to set up Beijing Stock Exchange', *Protocol* (2 September 2021), https://www.protocol.com/bulletins/china-to-set-up-beijing-stock-exchange.

[69] *Global Times*, '1st trading week of Beijing Stock Exchange meets expectations with 340,000 new investors coming online' (21 November 2021), https://www.globaltimes.cn/page/202111/1239536.shtml.

[70] Ministry of Industry and Information Technology (MIIT), 'China Industry Development and Industry Policy Report (2011)'.

[71] People's Daily Overseas, 'Let specialized special new small and medium enterprises thrive' (19 October 2021), http://www.gov.cn/xinwen/2021-10/19/content_5643541.htm.

[72] Beijing Stock Exchange, 'Welltrans Optoelectronic Co Ltd: Annual report 2020' (26 April 2021), http://www.bse.cn/disclosure/2021/2021-04-26/1619442101_852034.pdf.

communications, video processing, and electronic technologies, providing a wide range of high-speed video surveillance products widely used in highways, urban intelligent transportation, railways, and urban social public security.[73] This shows the innovative part and great potential of SRDI SMEs.

In order to facilitate the listing of such businesses, the BSE has introduced certain permissive and inclusive threshold standards under the *Listing Rules of Beijing Stock Exchange*, which is mostly modelled on the rules of the NEEQ select tier. For instance, companies will be able to obtain a listing if meeting one of the following four sets of standards: (1) Market Cap + Net Profit + Ratio of an Exponentially Weighted Averages (ROEWA); (2) Market Cap + Operating Revenue + Revenue Growth Rate + Cashflow; (3) Market Cap + Operating Revenue + the Proportion of R&D Investment; or (4) Market Cap + R&D Investment.[74] The former two sets of criteria stress on the financial indicators, while the latter two sets of standards pay more attention to the innovation ability of the companies. Furthermore, if a company has made higher profits and possesses more cash flow, the relevant requirement for market cap will be lower. Also, the higher R&D investments could make up for fewer profits, cash flow, as well as the revenue. So far, around half of the companies debuting on BSE have benefited from the first set of standard, which has demonstrated the effectiveness and flexibility of the new listing rules.[75] Moreover, the minimum market cap standard for a profitable company wanting to go for a list at BSE is just CNY200 million.[76] If the predicted market cap of a company exceeding CNY1.5 billion it will not need to make any profits, the standard of which is much lower than that of Star Market and ChiNext.[77] It shows the BSE's position to serve SME finance. Moreover, government backing and policy support such as financial subsidies will be available for SMEs to go listing. For example, the Guangzhou government in South China indicated that they are willing to cover half of the IPO expense of its SRDI SMEs.[78]

In addition, innovative SMEs adopting the dual class share structure (DCSS) are also welcomed by the BSE.[79] In so doing, the founder of SMEs

[73] Beijing Stock Exchange, 'Welltrans Optoelectronic Co Ltd: Semi-annual report 2021' (27 August 2021), http://www.bse.cn/disclosure/2021/2021-08-27/1630054790_168417.pdf.

[74] Listing Rules of Beijing Stock Exchange 2021 (Trial), Section 2.1.3.

[75] Zeyi Yang, 'The New Beijing Stock Exchange's companies are older and less tech-forward than Promised', *Protocol* (14 November 2021), https://www.protocol.com/china/beijing-stock-exchange-old-nontech.

[76] Listing Rules of Beijing Stock Exchange 2021 (Trial), Section 2.1.3.

[77] Listing Rules of Beijing Stock Exchange 2021 (Trial), Section 2.1.3.

[78] *Nanfang Daily*, 'Guangzhou seized the establishment of the North Exchange opportunity to listed enterprises one-time capital subsidies' (24 November 2021).

[79] Listing Rules of Beijing Stock Exchange 2021 (Trial), Section 4.4.1.

who enjoy the weighted voting rights do not need to worry about the corporate control issue. This has been a main concern for many Chinese entrepreneurs who finally decided to list their companies on stock exchanges in Hong Kong or New York. Moreover, the *Listing Rules* has no restriction on the red-chip companies and VIE, which has sent out a positive message that the BSE is open to the financial and corporate innovations happening across the world. Accordingly, the more favourable listing rules could make BSE an attractive listing venue for SMEs in China and globally, which also enhances Beijing's status as a rising international financial centre in Asia along with other more established financial centres in China like Hong Kong, Shanghai, and Shenzhen. Table 5.2 provides a summary of listing standards of the BSE with some comparison with the rules from the SSE Star Market and the SZSE ChiNext.

5.4.3 The IPO regime and information disclosure requirements

Though the BSE was established on the basis of the NEEQ's select tier, it gave up the inefficient approval-based IPO system under which listing companies would need to be extra censored and approved by the securities regulator. As a result, the BSE has fully adopted the registration-based IPO regime, as a more market-orientated and cost-effective listing procedure that is reliant on adequate information disclosure instead of substantial regulatory check.[80] This also resembles the latest rules of the Star Market and ChiNext, as the BSE aims to build a bespoke IPO system for SMEs. In terms of the prospectus regime, the validity period of financial statements has been extended by two months from 6+1 months for the select tier, which is now consistent with the period rule held by the Star Market and ChiNext.[81] Furthermore, the new Listing Rule of BSE has provided a more speedy and streamlined process for the listing entities, as the time for reviewing the application documents has been shorted from three to two months.[82] Thus, it only takes approximately six to eight months for a company meeting the formalities and pre-set standards of the BSE to float their shares. This is welcomed by many SMEs who

[80] Lerong Lu, 'Reforming Corporate Share-Listing Rules in China: Understanding the Rationale and Advantages of the Registration-Based IPO Regime' (2021) 42 *Company Lawyer* 236.

[81] Rules for Review Offering Shares to Non-Specific Qualified Investors of Beijing Stock Exchange 2021 (Trial), Article 43.

[82] Rules for Review Offering Shares to Non-Specific Qualified Investors of Beijing Stock Exchange 2021 (Trial), Article 38.

Table 5.2 The listing standards of Beijing Stock Exchange, Star Market, and ChiNext

	BSE	**Star Market (SSE)**	**ChiNext (SZSE)**
The genre of industries supported	Innovative SMEs in advanced manufacturing and modern service industries	Information technology, high-end equipment, new materials, new energy sources, biomedicine etc.	Growing innovative and entrepreneurial enterprises
Minimum market capitalization	For Profitable Organization (PO), Market Cap ≥ CNY200 million For Non-Profitable Organization (NPO), Market Cap ≥ CNY1.5 billion	For PO, Market Cap ≥ CNY1 billion For NPO, Market Cap ≥ CNY4 billion	For PO, Market Cap ≥ CNY1 billion For NPO, Market Cap ≥ CNY5 billion
Attitudes towards red-chip companies, VIE, and DCSS	Accepting DCSS companies with limitations; no explicit restriction for VIE or red-chip companies	Welcome	Welcome but with a high standard

Source: Shanghai Stock Exchange, Shenzhen Stock Exchange, and Beijing Stock Exchange.

are in urgent need of funding and prefer a fast financing conduit comparable to bank loans and PE funds.

Meanwhile, there is a strong demand for stricter information disclosure requirements to address the information asymmetry between corporate issuers and their investors when a company goes public. This is of particular importance as, under the new registration-based IPO regime, the securities regulator is no longer responsible for inspecting substantial contents of public documents offered by the issuers. Aside from the prospectus disclosure rules under the *Prospectus Regime of BSE*, there are also periodic and episodic disclosure requirements contained in the *Listing Rules* that have imposed ongoing obligations on the issuers.[83] This is in line with the information disclosure regime under *PRC Securities Law 2020*, which is similar to that implemented for the select tier and other segments of SSE and SZSE.[84] For instance, issuers are asked to disclose critical incidents and explain relevant causes and further impacts, as they have to ensure the authenticity, integrity, and precision of the information.[85] There is no doubt the strengthened information disclosure regime will boost market confidence and help investors make informed investment decisions. It will be conducive to the construction of a more transparent and efficient marketplace.

Nevertheless, to accommodate the interests of SMEs, some listing rules have been adjusted. For example, the interpretation of material changes in the performance projection system varies across different market segments. According to the regulations for ChiNext and Star Market, any material changes refer to the circumstance where a company's net profit changes over 50% year on year.[86] However, the *Listing Rules of BSE* suggests that interpretation of the material changes has been limited, as the fluctuation of 50% also needs to exceed the amount of CNY5 million.[87] Similarly, issuers are required to reveal transactions if the profits generated from such transactions are more than CNY1.5 million, which is higher than of the criteria for ChiNext or Star Market.[88] Moreover, issuers have to disclose the substantial matters and incidents like the shares of anyone holding over 5% of corporate equities have been frozen, put under judicial auction, placed under conservatorship, or there is setting up of a trust or any legal restrictions of voting rights.[89]

[83] Standards on The Content and Format of Information Disclosure of Publicly issued Securities by Companies No. 46 Prospectuses regime of Beijing Stock Exchange 2021.

[84] PRC Securities Law 2020, Article 80.

[85] Listing Rules of Beijing Stock Exchange 2021 (Trial), Section 5.3.2.

[86] Listing Rules of Star Market of Shanghai Stock Exchange 2020, Section 6.2.1; Listing Rules of ChiNext of Shenzhen Stock Exchange 2020, Section 6.2.2.

[87] Listing Rules of Beijing Stock Exchange 2021 (Trial), Section 6.2.2.

[88] Listing Rules of Beijing Stock Exchange 2021 (Trial), Section 7.1.2.

[89] Listing Rules of Beijing Stock Exchange 2021 (Trial), Section 8.2.1.

In general, the new BSE regulation focuses more on the appropriateness and flexibility to serve the special financing demand from SRDI SMEs. Whether the adjustment of rules is effective remains to be tested by practice in future.

5.4.4 The investor suitability and accountability mechanisms

The spectre of fraud will never disappear if a regulatory regime only relies on mandatory information disclosure. In order to foster an active, transparent, and efficient capital market of high integrity, the BSE gives it its best shot by introducing double safeguards: for one thing, it tries to comply with the *Rules of Investor Suitability*; for another, it aims to establish a sound accountability mechanism.[90] With respect to investor suitability, the requirements for eligible personal investors are identical to that for Star Market, which states 'personal investors who are eligible to open accounts to trade shares at the BSE should have two years of trading experience and hold financial assets worth more than CNY0.5 million for 20 trading days'.[91] The financial asset threshold for personal investors at BSE has been reduced by CNY0.5 million compared to that prescribed for the NEEQ's select tier, which shows a signal that the BSE hopes to attract more retail investors. In addition, the BSE has introduced a more relaxing daily price fluctuation limit, which is as much as 30%, compared with the 20% limit for Star Market and ChiNext and 10% for the mainboards of SSE and SZSE.[92] Apparently, this will encourage more investors to trade at the BSE, supplying more capital and liquidity to the nascent market. However, it also comes with greater risks and investors need to behave in a vigilant manner when investing in SMEs which tend to have less mature business models and a less predictable business outlook in a long term.

Moreover, a sound accountability mechanism contributes to market fairness and integrity. For corporate issuers who violate *the Listing Rules* in a less severe way, the BSE set out a series of self-regulatory measures such as criticizing in a circulated notice, publicly denouncing, and making corrections within a time limit etc.[93] However, as for the substantial breach of securities laws and regulations, the BSE will launch an investigation and

[90] Rules of Investors Suitability of Beijing Stock Exchange 2021 (Trial).

[91] Rules of Investors Suitability of Beijing Stock Exchange 2021 (Trial), Article 5.

[92] Trading Rules of Beijing Stock Exchange 2021 (Trial), Section 3.3.11.

[93] Rules for Review Offering Shares to Non-Specific Qualified Investors of Beijing Stock Exchange 2021 (Trial), Chapter 6; Listing Rules of Beijing Stock Exchange 2021 (Trial), Chapter 11.

report the case to the CSRC, as *PRC Securities Law* has made stricter penalties such as a fine of 100% of the raised fund for financial fraud, which be a massive blow to SME issuers. Most recently, China's State Council issued a decree to pass the '*regulation on securities, futures violations*', which came into effect on 1 January 2022.[94] Under the new regulation, corporations that break securities laws but are likely to rectify illegal behaviours to eliminate adverse effects or are likely to compensate investors for their losses, will have their investigation terminated if it is approved by the securities regulator. Obviously, all the above rules have been made to safeguard the investor interests by considering the special characteristics of SRDI SMEs, which are able to create a forward-looking and sound capital market legal regime.

5.5 Capital markets law reform: PRC Securities Law 2020

The following sections analyse the legislative background and some major changes in the *People's Republic of China (PRC) Securities Law 2020*. On 28 December 2019, the revised *PRC Securities Law* was passed by the Standing Committee of National People's Congress, which is the Chinese Parliament. The new legislation has formally endorsed the implementation of the 'registration-based IPO regime' across many segments of the Chinese capital markets. It will remove the excessive power of the securities regulator in deciding the outcome of IPOs, as in the future, any listing applicants who satisfy the formalities and pre-set standards will obtain a listing without the extra censorship and administrative approval from the securities regulator. The new legislation has created a disclosure-based regulatory system, introducing harsh penalties for illegal activities such as fraudulent issuance, misrepresentation, and false information disclosure, in a response to high-profile scandals of securities fraud in some Chinese companies such as *Kangmei Pharmaceutical* and the US-listed *Luckin Coffee*. Moreover, the *PRC Securities Law 2020* offers better protection for retail investors in terms of the special treatment of ordinary investors (distinct from professional investors), the delegation of shareholder rights, as well as the US-style class action regime.

[94] *Xinhua*, 'China unveils regulation on securities, futures violations' (30 November 2021), http://en.people.cn/n3/2021/1130/c90000-9926128.html.

5.5.1 The legislative background for PRC Securities Law 2020

When China first established its stock market—the SSE—in 1990, there were only eight listed companies including Feilo Acoustics and Shanghai Shenhua Holdings. Thirty years later China now has the second-largest capital market in the world with thousands of publicly listed companies, 156 million investors, and more than 130 securities companies or stockbrokers.[95] As discussed, China has fostered a multi-level capital markets system that calls for a better regulatory framework that is in line with the best international practices.

Reforming the capital markets law and securities regulation has always been a key task for Chinese authorities. In 1998, China introduced its first piece of securities markets legislation—the *PRC Securities Law* which laid down comprehensive regulatory rules for securities issuance and trading. It took effect from 1 July 1999. Over the past two decades, despite the rapid growth of China's capital markets, the legislation has only gone through one major revision in 2005, along with minor amendments in 2004, 2013, and 2014. Due to the rapid growth of China's capital markets in the early twenty-first century, the regulatory system built upon the original *PRC Securities Law* was considered not comprehensive and effective enough to deal with the increasingly popular and complicated securities issuance and trading activities.

Accordingly, China's lawmakers planned to fully revise the *PRC Securities Law* in April 2015 when it issued the first consultation draft. After four years of preparation and public debates, on 28 December 2019, the second revision of the *PRC Securities Law* was passed by the Standing Committee of the National People's Congress.[96] The Law came into effect on 1 March 2020 and has been considered the biggest overhaul of China's securities regulatory regime since the Law was firstly enacted in 1998. The revision has changed over 100 articles in the *PRC Securities Law* and promulgated two new chapters on information disclosure and investors protection. The revised legislation has 226 articles covering securities issuance, investor protection, information disclosure, irregularity punishment, and intermediary management, among others.

[95] *Xinhua*, 'From zero start, China now has the second largest capital market in the world' (8 October 2019), http://www.xinhuanet.com/fortune/2019-10/08/c_1210303693.htm.

[96] *Global Times*, 'New Securities Law takes effect, targets overseas activity' (1 March 2020), http://www.globaltimes.cn/content/1181185.shtml.

5.5.2 The full implementation of the registration-based IPO regime

For a long time, the CSRC and two major stock exchanges in mainland China—the SSE and the SZSE—had been using the 'approval-based IPO system' to select qualified companies to obtain a listing in either Shanghai or Shenzhen. It reflects the interventionist approach of Chinese financial regulators, as listing candidates have to pass a stringent financial censor to obtain administrative approval for their IPOs by the CSRC's Public Offering Review Committee. The 'approval-based IPO system' has been criticized as inefficient and sometimes corruptive. Under such a regime, IPO opportunities are not always given to good companies in need of capital, which often forces Chinese companies to seek a listing outside mainland China on the NYSE, NASDAQ, or Hong Kong Stock Exchange.

In contrast, the new securities law calls for the full implementation of the 'registration-based IPO regime' that will remove the excessive power of the securities regulator in deciding the outcome of IPOs, as IPO applicants meeting the formalities and pre-set standards will obtain a listing without the extra censorship and approval from the regulator. Clearly, the new market-oriented IPO system will improve the efficiency of capital allocation as it reduces the social and economic costs of share issuance and shortens the turnover time of selling shares publicly. It allows capital-starved Chinese companies to obtain funding more quickly, while offering Chinese and international investors better and more investment choices. Table 5.3 summarizes the key differences between 'approval-based IPO' and 'registration-based IPO'.

As discussed, the 'registration-based IPO regime' was first tested on the latest star market (sci-tech innovation board) of the SSE. The *PRC Securities Law 2020* has restated the adoption of the registration-based IPO for the Shanghai and Shenzhen stock exchanges, and its specific scope and implementation steps will be further defined by the State Council.[97] Following the trial of the 'registration-based IPO regime' on the star market, the experiment is likely to be expanded into other segments of Chinese capital markets, and will finally be introduced to the main boards of SSE and SZSE.

In June 2020, the Chinese regulator announced the adoption of the registration-based IPO system by the ChiNext board of SZSE, which is the country's Nasdaq-style board that mainly hosts growth enterprises and

[97] PRC Securities Law 2020, Article 9.

Table 5.3 Comparison between approval-based IPO and registration-based IPO

	Institutional backgrounds	**Listing standards**	**Pre-listing substantial examination of listing standards**	**Post-listing financial supervision from securities regulator**	**Marketization level**	**IPO efficiency**
Approval-based IPO	Stock markets are in the early stage of development as retail investors dominate trading.	High. The applicant has to: 1) provide public and accurate information; and 2) pass strict checks of financial criteria in terms of revenue and profitability.	Securities regulator; and securities brokers or investment banks have to assess the listing companies against strict listing standards.	Weak. Securities regulation focuses on pre-listing substantial financial checks.	Low.	Low.
Registration-based IPO	Stock markets are more developed with more institutional investors.	Low. The applicant has to provide public and accurate information.	Securities brokers or investment banks. *Securities regulator will only check the formalities of the applicants' materials.	Strong. Securities regulation focuses on the enforcement of post-listing information disclosure requirements.	High.	High.

Source: The chart is compiled by the author.

innovative start-ups.[98] In October 2020, China's Vice Premier Liu He chaired a special meeting of the Financial Stability and Development Committee of the State Council where he emphasized the need to adopt further reform and open-up China's financial system, including the full implementation of the registration-based IPO system.[99]

5.5.3 The stricter penalties for financial frauds and other illegal activities

The *PRC Securities Law 2020* has greatly increased the penalties for the violation of securities law. For example, for the fraudulent issuance of securities, the fine was previously capped at 5% of the total funds raised, but it has now been increased to 100% of the raised funds.[100] When listed companies violate the information disclosure requirements, the upper limit of fines has increased from RMB 600,000 to RMB 10 million.[101] Apart from fines, the *PRC Securities Law 2020* has clarified the presumption of fault and the joint liability of the issuer's controlling shareholder and actual controller whenever there is a case of fraudulent issuance or illegal information disclosure. The new penalties are said to level the playing field for Chinese stock markets and other major stock exchanges in the world, as it is now more in line with the practice of other jurisdictions like the United States.

The law has been changed in response to the recent financial frauds committed by Chinese companies, such as the high-profile cases of *Luckin Coffee* and *Kangmei Pharmaceutical*, prompting the new Securities Law to impose a tough crackdown. Dubbed as the Starbucks of China, *Luckin Coffee* has built a successful coffee empire owning over 10,000 cafes across China. In 2019, within less than two years of opening its first coffee shop, *Luckin* floated its shares on the NASDAQ in the United States. However, in 2020 it was reported that *Luckin Coffee* had deliberately fabricated over $300 million of retail sales through the use of related-party transactions.[102] The company tried to conceal the fraud by inflating its expenses by more than $190 million, through the creation of a fake operations database and changed its bank records and accounting books. *Luckin Coffee* was fined $180 million by the

[98] *Xinhua*, 'Registration-based IPO reform of ChiNext a boon for innovative enterprises' (17 June 2020), http://www.xinhuanet.com/english/2020-06/17/c_139146066.htm.

[99] *Global Times*, 'IPOs to enter era of full registration, delisting process to be normalized' (1 November 2020), http://www.globaltimes.cn/content/1205330.shtml.

[100] PRC Securities Law 2020, Article 181.

[101] PRC Securities Law 2020, Article 197.

[102] Alistair Gray, 'Luckin Coffee to pay $180m in accounting fraud settlement', *Financial Times* (17 December 2020), https://www.ft.com/content/4db3b074-829f-4f1c-a256-11c7e28a31d1.

US Securities and Exchange Commission for conducting accounting frauds. *Kangmei Pharmaceutical* was found by regulators to have engaged in one of China's largest financial frauds totalling $12.6 billion.[103] From 2016 to 2018, *Kangmei* inflated its revenue by 29 billion yuan and its operating profit by 4.1 billion yuan. It also inflated cash positions by a total of 88.7 billion yuan in its 2016 and 2017 annual reports and its 2018 interim report.

5.5.4 The strengthening of the investor protection regime

The *PRC Securities Law 2020* has incorporated a new chapter (Chapter 6) to set out the investor protection mechanism which has made several progressive arrangements. First, the new legislation distinguishes between ordinary investors and professional investors, based on their asset amount, the amount of financial assets, investment knowledge and experience, professional ability, and other factors, to make targeted arrangements for investor rights protection.[104] If investors are classified as ordinary investors by the *Securities Law*, they will enjoy a higher level of protection. For instance, when there is a dispute between ordinary investors and the securities companies in which they invest, the securities companies will undertake the proof of burden to demonstrate that their actions have complied with relevant laws and regulations, and they have not undertaken any misleading and fraudulent practices. If not, the securities companies will be liable for the losses of the investors.

Moreover, the *PRC Securities Law 2020* has established a collection system (delegation) for shareholder rights in listed companies in order to protect minority shareholders and improve corporate governance. The board of directors of the listed company, the independent directors, the shareholders holding over 1% of the total voting shares, and the investor protection institutions, can act as the collector on their own or entrust the securities companies and securities service agencies, to make a public request to all shareholders of the listed company in order to represent them to attend the shareholder general meeting and to make proposals on behalf of shareholders, to represent them in order to exercise voting rights and other rights.[105]

There are also new provisions concerning bondholder meetings and the bond trustee system as well as the new cash dividend allocation system of

[103] Xie Yu, 'Why is Kangmei Pharmaceutical, found to have committed one of China's biggest financial frauds, rallying?', *South China Morning Post* (23 August 2019), https://www.scmp.com/business/companies/article/3024084/why-kangmei-pharmaceutical-found-have-committed-one-chinas.

[104] PRC Securities Law 2020, Article 89.

[105] PRC Securities Law 2020, Article 90.

listed companies.[106] Among the new measures, it is worth noting that, in order to facilitate the registration-based IPO system, the new legislation has explored a new securities civil litigation system. The *PRC Securities Law 2020* has formally introduced the class action for the first time in Chinese capital markets whereby an investor protection institution can act as the litigation representative.[107] An investor protection institution mandated by fifty or more investors can register the qualified investors with the People's Court, unless any investor explicitly refuses to be registered, which, according to the Supreme People's Court's statement in the press conference, serves as an 'opt-out' legal regime for the securities class action. The integration of the 'opt-in' representative litigation with the 'opt-out' class action is undoubtedly a major innovation in Chinese legislation. However, it remains to be tested in China's judicial practice due to the lack of relevant litigation experience.

5.6 Conclusion

The chapter has discussed both the practices and latest regulation of China's fast-growing capital markets. It has provided an overview of the so-called multi-layer capital markets that consist of the main boards of SSE, SZSE, as well as the Sci-Tech Innovation Board (Star Market), ChiNext board, and BSE. The deep and diverse market segments ensure that Chinese corporations of various sizes and business sectors can find a suitable financing venue that matches their scale and needs. In detail, the chapter has assessed three most recent reform measures in the Chinese capital markets, including Star Market, the BSE, and the latest amendment to PRC Securities Law.

The SSE Star Market, established in 2019, integrates technology and finance to offer robust financing for tech and innovative enterprises in China. It addresses the capital needs of China's vast tech industry by removing restrictive regulations and supports Shanghai's ambition to become a leading international financial centre in the twenty-first century. The market's key feature is its trial 'registration-based' IPO system, which shifts IPO decision-making from the securities regulator to the stock exchange and market participants, potentially enhancing efficiency and liquidity. This system requires rigorous post-IPO information disclosure and strong enforcement to protect public investors. Other reforms include diverse listing standards, strict market exit rules, enhanced information disclosure obligations, stringent investor suitability tests, and judicial support against securities fraud

[106] PRC Securities Law 2020, Articles 91, 92.
[107] PRC Securities Law 2020, Article 95.

and IP infringements. While promising for Chinese tech companies and investors, the effectiveness of these reforms will be evaluated over time with more empirical data.

The launch of the BSE in 2021 and the introduction of targeted rules for tech corporations and SRDI SMEs demonstrate the Chinese authorities' clear determination to address the financing difficulties of smaller businesses. The inclusive threshold, time-effective registration-based IPO system, and appropriate and flexible information disclosure are likely to create an active, transparent, and efficient capital market, unleashing the potential of SRDI SMEs. By learning from the existing standards and leading market practices of the NEEQ Select Tier, ChiNext, and the Star Market, the BSE adheres to premier rules adjusted to suit the economic reality and financing demands of SRDI SMEs. With favourable policy support, the BSE is likely to complement the more established SSE and SZSE by facilitating SME finance in the Chinese capital market. Currently, China hosts three major bourses located in the North (BSE), Middle (SSE), and South (SZSE) of the country, forming an institutionally sound, multi-tier, and nationally connected capital market financing system.

The PRC Securities Law 2020 reflects China's latest efforts to create a sound and effective legal environment for capital markets. This legislation fully implements the registration-based IPO regime, promoting the long-term growth of healthy, dynamic, and efficient capital markets in China. It mandates more stringent post-listing information disclosure for public companies, ensuring that investors can make informed investment choices. Additionally, the law introduces better protection for retail investors through special treatment of ordinary shareholders, delegation of shareholder rights, and a US-style class action regime. It also increases penalties for share issuers and other entities that commit securities fraud and misrepresentation. Clearly, this market-oriented law reform will unlock the growth potential of Chinese stock markets and create more business opportunities for investors, investment bankers, and international financial lawyers involved in Chinese capital markets.

Chapter 6
China's central bank digital currency

6.1 Introduction

Chapter 6 discusses the innovation of financial services and Fintech in China by using the country's central bank digital currency (CBDC) as an example. The global Fintech revolution has produced various new financial services and products such as P2P lending, crypto trading, insurtech, digital banking, mobile wealth management, and more recently CBDCs.[1] Fintech not only provides more convenient and affordable financial services for consumers, but also offers existing financial institutions and entrepreneurs an opportunity to use artificial intelligence (AI), big data, and blockchain to increase business efficiency and profitability. China has become a leader in Fintech in the 2010s when it comes to the application of information technologies in the financial markets and institutions. For example, China possesses the world's largest mobile payment sector which is dominated by two Fintech giants—Alipay and WeChat Pay. Launched by the e-commerce company Alibaba as a payment tool to support its online sales, Alipay now has over 1.25 billion users across the world.[2] Most Chinese citizens now use QR code-based mobile payments to replace traditional cash and card payments, making the country a cashless society. More recently, the People's Bank of China (PBoC) has launched the pilot CBDC reform, known as 'digital yuan' or 'Digital Currency Electronic Payment (DC/EP)', to promote the state-backed digital money and the internationalization of Chinese currency.[3] Clearly, financial digitalization and Fintech has been a key driver behind the rapid rise of China's financial industry and its increasing international influence.

Chapter 6 focuses on the latest pilot reforms and regulatory issues relating to China's CBDC pilot project, and analyses if CBDC could contribute to the internationalization of Chinese currency and help the country become

[1] Lerong Lu, *Global Fintech Revolution: Practice, Policy, and Regulation* (Oxford University Press, 2024), p. 11.

[2] Alipay's Official Website, www.alipay.com.

[3] The People's Bank of China (PBoC), 'The White Paper on the Research and Development of China's Digital Yuan' (July 2021), http://www.pbc.gov.cn/goutongjiaoliu/113456/113469/4293590/2021071614200022055.pdf.

Towards Financial Superpower. Lerong Lu, Oxford University Press. © Lerong Lu (2025).
DOI: 10.1093/9780198948568.003.0006

a financial superpower. After this introduction, Section 6.2 introduces the background of rising digital money in the twenty-first century as both private entities and states compete to join the game of creating new digital currencies. Section 6.3 discusses why China has been proactively introducing CBDCs and promoting their usage both at home and abroad. Section 6.4 assesses the operating mechanisms and main design features of China's CBDC pilot project. Section 6.5 continues to analyse the regulatory challenges posed by the CBDC experiment, especially how the PBoC and financial regulators could strike a balance between personal data protection and anti-money laundering (AML) enforcement. Section 6.6 evaluates the cross-border use of Chinese CBDCs in both retail and wholesale settings, considering how it facilitates the goal of RMB internationalization. Section 6.7 makes a conclusion for the chapter.

6.2 The rise of digital money in the twenty-first century

The twenty-first century has witnessed the rapid rise of digital money, which could be attributed to multiple reasons. First, the Global Financial Crisis of 2007–2008 made people distrust the current financial and monetary systems, so businesses and consumers have been actively seeking alternative solutions to replace or undergrade traditional fiat money.[4] Second, the latest technological breakthroughs in relation to AI, big data, cloud computing, and blockchain have contributed to the transformation of financial industry. The technological readiness leads to the emergence of innovative services and products in most areas of the financial industry like banking, securities dealing, online lending, payment, wealth management, insurance, and virtual currency.[5] Third, the COVID-19 pandemic has accelerated the societal transition towards virtual economy since a large proportion of population has been working, playing, and shopping from home.[6] This results in a greater demand for Fintech and digital money services that could be easily accessed online, through mobile apps, or in the metaverse. Digital money is easier to carry as users would only need to bring their mobile phones when going out.

[4] Fiat money (i.e. banknotes and coins) is issued by one country's central bank or financial authority, such as the US dollar, Euro, the British pound, and Chinese yuan. See Robert J. Barro, 'Money and the Price Level Under the Gold Standard' (1979) 89 *The Economic Journal* 13–33.

[5] Lerong Lu, 'Financial Technology and Challenger Banks in the UK: Gap Fillers or Real Challengers?' (2017) 32 *Journal of International Banking Law and Regulation* 273 at 274.

[6] Lerong Lu and Lingsheng Zhang, 'Regulating Fintech Corporations Amidst Covid-19 Pandemic: An Analysis of Ant Group (Alipay)'s Suspension of IPO and Business Restructuring' (2021) 42 *Company Lawyer* 341–343.

Digital money and electronic payment are also considered as most hygienic payment methods, which reduce the use of physical banknotes and coins that could carry lots of bacteria and germs.

Accordingly, various forms of digital money have sprung up in the 2000s and 2010s. Both private and public sectors have proposed to develop their own digital money for tomorrow's economy with different technological standards and application scenarios. On the one hand, privately issued digital currencies such as crypto coins and stablecoins have gained great popularity as both a new asset class and a payment tool.[7] Most cryptocurrencies operate using blockchain technology, a distributed public ledger that is updated and maintained by coin holders. New units of Bitcoin are created through a process known as mining, where investors use computer power to solve complex mathematical problems.[8]

More than 10,000 different crypto coins are currently listed on cryptocurrency exchanges, including Bitcoin, Ethereum, BNB, XRP, Cardano, Solana, and Dogecoin. Bitcoin is the most well-known crypto asset globally, as it has the largest market capitalization among all cryptocurrencies. In 2008, Bitcoin, as the first generation of cryptocurrency, was invented by Satoshi Nakamoto who published an online paper advocating a new form of electronic cash that users can send to each other without going through banks and other financial intermediaries.[9] The crypto sector had grown rapidly during the 2010s. In July 2024, one Bitcoin was worth around $63,000, with the total market value amounting to $1.24 trillion.[10] China once accounted for 90% of global crypto trading activities before it banned the local crypto exchanges in 2017.[11] The stablecoins, such as Tether (USDT), CACHE Gold, and Meta's Diem, are a more advanced version of digital money. Corporations and other private entities have created stablecoins to address certain shortcomings of cryptocurrencies, particularly their extreme price volatility and value instability.[12] Stablecoins are designed to maintain a relatively stable value by being backed by real assets like traditional currencies and commodities and are intended to trade at par with benchmark assets such as

[7] Lerong Lu, 'Bitcoin: Speculative Bubble, Financial Risk and Regulatory Response' (2018) 33 *Butterworths Journal of International Banking and Financial Law* 178–182.

[8] Ibid.

[9] Satoshi Nakamoto, 'A peer-to-peer electronic cash system' (2008), https://bitcoin.org/bitcoin.pdf.

[10] CoinMarketCap, 'Bitcoin price today', https://coinmarketcap.com/currencies/bitcoin/, accessed 1 July 2024.

[11] *Reuters*, 'China bans financial, payment institutions from cryptocurrency business' (18 May 2021), https://www.reuters.com/technology/chinese-financial-payment-bodies-barred-cryptocurrency-business-2021-05-18/.

[12] Gary B Gorton and Jeffery Y Zhang, 'Taming Wildcat Stablecoins' (2023) 90 *The University of Chicago Law Review* 909–971.

the US dollar or gold. Therefore, they can be more effectively used as a unit of account or store of value compared with the volatile cryptocurrencies.

Cryptocurrencies and stablecoins function as a medium of exchange across a network of computers, operating independently of any centralized authority like a central bank or government agency. The rise of private digital money has greatly challenged the status quo of global financial system, especially central banks' supreme power in money creation and circulation. As a result, central banks and monetary authorities must find a response. So far, they have been proactively experimenting with official digital currencies, which are commonly known as CBDC or sovereign digital money, as a more efficient and safer payment option.[13] The wider use of CBDC could preserve central banks' status and to promote financial inclusion and stability. According to the Bank for International Settlements (BIS), 86% of surveyed central banks have been actively engaging in CBDC-related research projects, proofs of concept, and pilot schemes.[14] CBDC is likely to be the most important working task for global central banks in the 2020s.

Major economies, including the G20, have initiated a series of CBDC projects, such as the European Central Bank's (ECB) digital euro and the US Federal Reserve's digital dollar.[15] The first movers of currency competition are likely to be in an advantageous position. The countries with the earliest experiment of CBDC could have a greater say in the future's international financial order which has been constructed around dominant financial powers like US dollar, Euro, British pound, and Japanese yen. So far, China has been one of the leading countries in the research, design, and experiment of CBDCs. In 2014, the PBoC started to test the feasibility of digital fiat currency when it established the PBoC Digital Currency Research Institute. In 2020, the PBoC first launched a pilot CBDC project in south China's Shenzhen City. In 2022, Chinese CBDCs had been widely tested in the Beijing Winter Olympics with two million worth digital yuan used by the participants each day.[16] Chinese CBDCs are known as 'e-CNY', 'digital yuan', 'digital renminbi (RMB)', or 'Digital Currency Electronic Payment (DC/EP)'. Moreover,

[13] Ross P Buckley et al., 'Sovereign Digital Currencies: Reshaping the Design of Money and Payments Systems' (2021) 15 *Journal of Payments Strategy & Systems* 7 at 8–10.

[14] Codruta Boar, Henry Holden, and Amber Wadsworth, 'Impending Arrival—A Sequel to the Survey on Central Bank Digital Currency', BIS Papers No. 107 (January 2020), https://www.bis.org/publ/bppdf/bispap107.pdf.

[15] The European Central Bank (ECB), 'A digital euro', https://www.ecb.europa.eu/paym/digital_euro/html/index.en.html; and The US Federal Reserve, 'Federal Reserve Board releases discussion paper that examines pros and cons of a potential U.S. Central Bank Digital Currency (CBDC)' (January 2022), https://www.federalreserve.gov/newsevents/pressreleases/other20220120a.htm.

[16] Marc Jones, 'Over $315,000 in digital yuan used every day at Olympics, PBOC official says', *Reuters* (16 February 2022), https://www.reuters.com/technology/around-300-mln-digital-yuan-used-every-day-olympics-pboc-official-says-2022-02-15/.

China plans to use its CBDCs to support the national strategy of RMB internationalization by promoting their use in retail, wholesale, and cross-border scenarios at both domestic and international levels.[17]

6.3 The rationales for China's proactive adoption of CBDCs

There are several reasons which could explain China's active experiments of CBDCs: (1) CBDCs' comparative advantages as a new generation of money; (2) CBDCs' suitability under the state-led economic model; (3) the strategic use of CBDCs to achieve the objective of RMB internationalization; and (4) China's market maturity and technology and infrastructure readiness for embracing the CBDC era. This section will analyse the four justifications in detail.

First, CBDCs, compared with crypto coins and stablecoins, are considered as the most viable choice for the global economy and financial markets in the future. CBDCs have various economic and social benefits like their advanced regulatory functions, stable value, official endorsement, and the wider acceptability.[18] Most countries have witnessed the co-existence and competition between privately issued and government-issued money. Blockchain-based crypto coins are praised for having obvious advantages like decentralization, cost-effective transaction, and anonymity.[19] Nonetheless, they are also criticized for having extreme price volatility, causing huge energy consumption, and being used for illicit purposes like money laundering.[20] Therefore, crypto coins are more likely to be used for financial investment and speculation, instead of being a widely accepted form as medium of exchange. However, the absence of governmental backing for crypto coins and stablecoins in most countries indicates their limited usage in most financial and commercial transactions. Most people still trust cryptos much less than their national currencies. In contrast, CBDCs present clear benefits that are typically found in any central bank-issued money, such as settlement finality,

[17] Lerong Lu and Lingsheng Zhang, 'China experiments with cross-border payments of Central Bank Digital Currencies', *Columbia Law School's Blog on Corporations and Capital Markets* (17 December 2021), https://clsbluesky.law.columbia.edu/2021/12/17/china-experiments-with-cross-border-payments-of-central-bank-digital-currencies/.

[18] Lerong Lu and Lingsheng Zhang, 'Could the "Dragon" Now Fly Beyond Borders? Contextualizing Regulatory Aspects and Risks for China's CBDC Cross-Border Use' (2022) 14:S *Tsinghua China Law Review* 19–44.

[19] Lerong Lu, 'Bitcoin: Speculative Bubble, Financial Risk and Regulatory Response' (2018) 33 *Butterworths Journal of International Banking and Financial Law* 178 at 178–182.

[20] Ibid.

liquidity, integrity, and public trust. CBDCs will be governed by a centralized system similar to that for conventional banknotes, so all transaction records and data could be accessed by financial authorities. In addition, CBDCs facilitate the effective making of monetary policies as an interest leverage tool, and they could be charged with extra regulatory functions regarding AML and combating the financing of terrorism (CFT). As a result, the PBoC and Chinese government perceive the use of CBDCs as an advancement in monetary and payment systems, due to the CBDCs' advantages over traditional banknotes and crypto coins.

Second, the rise of various digital currencies is a battle for money-making power between market and state. The emergence and popularity of Bitcoins and other cryptocurrencies have suggested the resurgence of liberal capitalism or neoliberalism.[21] Entrepreneurs, private corporations, and financial institutions have been trying to regain the power of creating money and governing its circulation through innovative payment and settlement networks. Traditionally, central banks have monopolized the money-making businesses, as their mandates have been protected by monetary law in most countries.[22] Nowadays, private entities could easily launch their own coins due to the relatively low costs and modest technological requirements, resulting in over 10,000 digital coins being traded. This decentralized movement has posed a real threat to the status, functions, and even the very existence of central banks and monetary authorities, which has made us rethink the traditional relationship between market and state in the financial domain. To fight against the rise of private coins, central banks and financial authorities across the world have been devising their official digital currencies, namely CBDCs or sovereign digital money. CBDCs are created to maintain central banks' supreme status, economic influence, as well as the effectiveness of monetary policies. This phenomenon has been clearly observed in China, where it used to account the world's most Bitcoin transactions during 2010s. The governments were worried about the excessive use of private digital money that could harm the financial stability and government's authority in the financial sector. In 2021, we have seen the total ban of cryptocurrencies-related activities such as mining, trading, and currency exchange in China, issued by the PBoC jointly with other nine government agencies.[23] This has suggested the

[21] David Harvey, *A Brief History of Neoliberalism* (Oxford University Press, 2005), p. 64.

[22] The Federal Reserve Bank of Richmond, 'The note issue function of central banks', *Monthly Review* (July 1962), https://fraser.stlouisfed.org/files/docs/publications/frbrichreview/pages/65387_1960-1964.pdf.

[23] The People's Bank of China, 'Notice on further preventing and resolving the risks of virtual currency trading and speculation' (15 September 2021), http://www.pbc.gov.cn/en/3688253/3689012/4353814/index.html.

intensified currency competition between liberal capitalism and state capitalism, as the latter tends to predominate in China's case. Therefore, it is not difficult to understand China's decision to prioritize the use of CBDCs over any other private digital currencies.

Third, China's promotion of CBDCs beyond its border echoes its long-term national strategy of RMB internationalization. It has been a key strategy for Chinese policymakers to boost the use of Chinese yuan or RMB to compete with other major currencies, such as US dollar, Euro, British pound, and Japanese yen in international payments.[24] Although China has been the world's second-largest economy for many years and possesses one of largest financial industries, its currency has been underrepresented in international commercial and financial transactions. In 2021, US dollar accounted for 40.51% of SWIFT international payments in terms of transaction value, Euro for 36.65%, British pound for 5.89%, while Chinese yuan only takes up 2.7% of total payments.[25] Thus, there is a huge demand for the increasing use of RMB, as China imports and exports a significant number of goods and services to the rest of the world every year. In addition, China has proposed the Belt and Road Initiative (BRI) in 2013 to improve connectivity and deepen economic cooperation on a transcontinental scale.[26] This calls for the more extensive use of RMB in the neighbouring countries and main trading partners. Clearly, it is high time that the PBoC and Chinese authorities seized the opportunity of currency revolution by advancing the use of digital Chinese yuan within and beyond its borders.

Last but not least, China possesses the mature market conditions, technologies, and infrastructures that are necessary for any large-scale experiment of CBDCs. China is a leading country in the fintech sector, including online P2P lending, crypto assets, mobile payment, and robo-advisor.[27] China accounts for over half of the global digital payment market as well as three-quarters of global online lending transactions.[28] Over one billion Chinese consumers have been familiar with e-money and mobile payment services offered by Alipay and WeChat Pay, as the country has first-class telecom infrastructure and a very high smartphone penetration rate. China has built up the ultra-high-speed internet and 5G mobile network for its mobile

[24] The People's Bank of China, '2021 report on RMB internationalization', http://www.pbc.gov.cn/goutongjiaoliu/113456/113469/4344602/2021091814193942128.pdf.

[25] *Statista*, 'Most active currency for international payments in 2021, based on transaction value', https://www.statista.com/statistics/1189498/share-of-global-payments-by-currency/.

[26] The World Bank, 'Belt and road initiative' (29 March 2018), https://www.worldbank.org/en/topic/regional-integration/brief/belt-and-road-initiative.

[27] Robin Hui Huang, *Fintech Regulation in China: Principles, Policies and Practices* (Cambridge University Press, 2021) at 2–7.

[28] *The Economist*, 'The Age of the Appacus: Fintech in China' (25 February 2017), p. 65.

users. Making payment by smartphones has become a default option for Chinese consumers, many of whom do not carry any cash when going out shopping, dining, and for entertainment. Therefore, the CBDC pilot project is less likely to face technological challenges in China. Nor will it encounter the resistance from consumers and businesses as they are already using Chinese yuan in digital format in most transactions. It is safe to say that China is technologically and commercially ready for the advent of the CBDC age. If China combines its advanced technologies with its enormous financial industry, it is likely to create the most forward-looking currencies for the twenty-first century.

6.4 The operating mechanisms and design features of China's CBDCs

Currency (or money) lies at the heart of any country's financial system. Money is crucial for modern transactions as it solves the trust issue between different parties. Without it, transactions would require a double coincidence of wants, the basis of a bartering economy. Over time, money has evolved from physical commercial commodities like shells and grains to precious metals such as gold and silver, and eventually to paper notes issued by central banks. More recently, central banks and monetary authorities have been leveraging on fintech and CBDCs to modernize the established fiat money system. CBDCs denote cash-like direct claims on the central bank, so the holder of digital yuan is likely to have a direct account with the PBoC. In contrast to private digital money, CBDCs are perceived as a new form of official money being issued by central banks as legal tender.[29] Determined by each jurisdiction, legal tender is recognized by law as satisfactory payment to extinguish debts, which means that if someone offers to fully pay off a debt to their creditors in legal tender, they cannot be sued for failing to repay.[30] CBDCs have gathered significant interest as a potential digital alternative to conventional fiat currencies. Issued and backed by central banks, CBDCs aim to maintain the integrity and stability of the financial system. This distinguishes them from privately issued cryptocurrencies like Bitcoin and Tether.

[29] Tommaso Mancini Griffoli et al., 'Casting Light on Central Bank Digital Currency' (2018) IMF Staff Discussion Notes No. 18/08, https://www.imf.org/en/Publications/Staff-Discussion-Notes/Issues/2018/11/13/Casting-Light-on-Central-Bank-Digital-Currencies-46233.

[30] Bank of England, 'What is legal tender?', https://www.bankofengland.co.uk/explainers/what-is-legal-tender.

In China, e-CNY is considered as legal tender which is real money in the legal and economic sense.[31] Previously, the Chinese CBDCs had been known as DC/EP until it was renamed to e-CNY by the PBoC. Mr. Zhou Xiaochuan, the former governor of the PBoC, explained the differences between DC/EP and e-CNY by stating that the concept of the DC/EP was a form of two-tier research and constituted a pilot project with various potential payment products, while the e-CNY was the chosen product at the end of the process, i.e. the digital money in the wallet.[32] The former vice president of the Bank of China, Mr. Yongli Wang, also expressed that the name change was to avoid a common misunderstanding that digital yuan will create a new monetary system other than existing renminbi.[33] It is clear that digital yuan, initially used as a substitute for cash to compete with other digital currencies, has great potential to become a mainstream form of currency as well as an effective regulatory toolkit if CBDCs were tested on a large scale.

From the technical point of view, the operating mechanisms of e-CNY could be understood in the following aspects.[34] First, e-CNY substitutes cash in circulation (known as M0 in the economic term). Digital yuan is designed to operate as M0 to substitute cash as the basic layer of currencies. M0 refers to the money in people's daily use in commercial transactions, which is different from the reserve money stored in banks. It is monopolistically issued by the central bank in a sovereign state and is categorized as money in the narrowest sense since there are other widely accepted means of payments like cheques and credit cards. Judged by liquidity, currencies are divided into different layers: M0 is the direct claim on the central bank with the highest liquidity; M1 contains both currency in circulation and tradable deposits, which represents the direct purchasing power of society as a whole; M2 generally consists of M1 and other non-tradable deposits such as the time deposit; and finally, M3 consists of M2 and other current assets such as government bonds, bank acceptances, and commercial paper.[35] Therefore, as e-CNY is defined as M0, it should, on the one hand, be seen as direct purchasing power in the commodity market and be categorized as cash (rather than deposit or

[31] Lerong Lu and Hang Chen, 'Digital Yuan: The Practice and Regulation of China's Central Bank Digital Currency' (2021) 36 *Butterworths Journal of International Banking and Financial Law* 601–603.

[32] Zhou Xiaochuan, 'The evolution principles of currencies and payments in the digital age', *Sina Finance* (2020), http://finance.sina.com.cn/zl/china/2020-12-02/zl-iiznctke4306697.shtml.

[33] Wang Yongli, 'What changes will digital RMB bring?' *Sina Finance* (2020), https://finance.sina.com.cn/blockchain/coin/2020-11-09/doc-iiznctke0425584.shtml.

[34] Lerong Lu and Hang Chen, 'Digital Yuan: The Practice and Regulation of China's Central Bank Digital Currency' (2021) 36 *Butterworths Journal of International Banking and Financial Law* 601–603.

[35] Swiss National Bank, 'The monetary base and the M1, M2 and M3 monetary aggregates' (February 2007), https://www.snb.ch/en/mmr/reference/histz_geldmengen_book/source/histz_geldmengen_book.en.pdf.

other current assets) when the PBoC calculates the inflation rate and when making monetary policies. On the other hand, the essence of issuing digital yuan is the digitalization process of cash with its intrinsic value being as stable as legal tender.

Second, e-CNY primarily targets the retail sector in China. The use of CBDCs could be divided into three categories: retail, wholesale, and cross-border transactions. At retail level, the simplest and most common model for completing transactions is the direct cash payment without any settlement activities through banks or other financial institutions. It is an initial and immediate method of transaction, during which services or goods are transferred from buyers to sellers without the involvement of any third-party intermediaries. In this scenario, the advantages of cash payments are obvious, such as flexibility, speediness, and wide acceptance. It makes cash the ideal method of payment in retail transactions, which is also what e-CNY intends to achieve. In addition, the electronic version of RMB is likely to reduce customers' storage costs and the risk of carrying cash, to cut the transfer costs between different commercial banks and mitigates the time lag, to lower a country's public expense for maintaining banknotes and coins, and to alleviates criminal activities relating to paper money transactions such as counterfeiting and money laundering.

Third, the operation of e-CNY is largely reliant on China's two-tier banking system that consists of the PBoC and financial institutions such as commercial banks. Major payment platforms and telecom operators are also involved in the distributional activities. The issuance of e-CNY by the central bank represents direct liabilities between financial users and the PBoC, leading to the disintermediation of financial institutions. However, the PBoC does not intend to replace the intermediary role of financial institutions. Mr. Qian Yao, the former director of the PBoC's DC/EP project, suggested that the introduction of CBDC was not aimed at disrupting the existing currency issuance mechanism; on the contrary, it is necessary for the PBoC to mobilize and cooperate with commercial banks to promote the use of CBDC, to allocate financial risks, and to accelerate innovation.[36] Under the two-tier system of DC/EP, the fundamental elements of digital yuan's operating network can be summarized as 'one currency, two funds, and three centres'. One currency refers to the e-CNY, issued by the central bank and backed by the state's credit. Two databases (funds) refer to the issuance database where the PBoC stores the issuance fund and the database where commercial banks manage

[36] Qian Yao, 'Experimental Study on Prototype System of Central Bank Digital Currency' (2018) 29 *Journal of Software* 2716.

their data of e-CNY. The central bank has established a digital currency fund to directly issue electronic money to commercial banks and other agencies, which is recorded in commercial banks' digital currency settlement systems. Meanwhile, commercial banks would pay that same amount of digital currency issuance back to the central bank. The issuance fund of e-CNY is more like a currency conversion fund rather than the traditional deposit reserve. Three centres stand for the Registration Centre, the Authentication Centre, and the Analysis Centre. It used to be the Banknotes Identification Centre of the PBoC which undertook the function of identifying counterfeit banknotes. Now, it has been reformed to become the Registration Centre as there is no need to identify banknotes anymore for digital currency. The Authentication Centre is asked to record the issuance, ownership, transfer, and withdrawal of digital yuan, while banks and other financial institutions specifically manage the daily operation of the payment and settlement systems. The Authentication Centre also authenticates the identity of payees and payers. The Analysis Centre conducts data analysis regarding abnormal payment and settlement behaviours of financial customers. The three centres are all managed by the PBoC.

Moreover, there are a number of distinctive design features that we could observe in the pilot e-CNY project:[37] (1) unlimited legal credit: as discussed, the digital yuan is the fiat currency issued by the central bank. As legal tender, it is subject to the same legal indemnity regime as physical currency consisting of banknotes and coins. Accordingly, when digital yuan is used to pay any public and private debts within the territory of China, no units or individuals could refuse to accept it if the conditions for acceptance were satisfied; (2) loosely coupled account: digital yuan is based on the general account system. It supports the loosely coupled accounts of banks, which indicates that an e-CNY wallet can open without a bank account, and individuals are able to decide whether to connect it to a bank account. Thus, the e-CNY and its related services are accessible for those who are not able to have bank accounts, which contributes to financial inclusion; (3) controllable anonymity: as for privacy and data protection, the authentication of e-CNY users' identity relies on the so-called controllable anonymity mechanism, the design of which makes the full use of the digital currency's special features: front-end voluntary and back-end real-name. It is anonymous when transactions are made among users; however, all transaction data will be kept by the central bank under users' real names; and (4) non-interest bearing and no

[37] Lerong Lu and Hang Chen, 'Digital Yuan: The Practice and Regulation of China's Central Bank Digital Currency' (2021) 36 *Butterworths Journal of International Banking and Financial Law* 601–603.

exchange fees: the development of digital yuan is still in its initial stage as substitute for cash. There has been no interest-bearing design so far. The e-CNY seeks to maximize social benefits to make it more accessible for everyone. To build the public financial infrastructure, the PBoC has made the policies consistent with cash for digital currency and aims to build a free digital currency value transfer system. There will be no costs of issuing, distributing, and exchanging services for end users.

6.5 The regulatory challenge: balancing anti-money laundering with personal data protection

As China plans to promote the cross-border use of CBDCs to pursue RMB internationalization, the PBoC would need to carefully consider the design of its AML function, and how this could be reconciled with personal data protection.[38] In 2021, China introduced its first comprehensive legislation on personal information and data privacy—The Personal Information Protection Law (PIPL)—which is akin to the European Union's General Data Protection Regulation (GDPR) and is likely to have an enormous impact internationally by changing the ways in which parties do businesses both within and outside of China.[39] The new data protection law regulates the use of personal information and grants citizens the right to request information about themselves. Clearly, the effective enforcement of AML regulations requires authorities and financial institutions to collect, share, and even disclose sensitive information relating to citizens' daily transactions, which could be hard to achieve under a strict set of data protection laws. This is of particular importance to the design and operation of CBDCs, as their cross-border application would involve regulatory efforts and law enforcement activities across multiple jurisdictions.

The cross-border circulation of money could result from either the ordinary course of international business transactions or other illegal activities such as money laundering. In principle, complying with the AML and CFT regulations shall be a prerequisite for any countries that intend to encourage the cross-border use of their CBDCs in international financial markets. In China's case, the key AML compliance issues relating to CDBCs can

[38] Lerong Lu and Lingsheng Zhang, 'Could the "Dragon" Now Fly Beyond Borders? Contextualizing Regulatory Aspects and Risks for China's CBDC Cross-Border Use' (2022) 14:S *Tsinghua China Law Review* 19–44.

[39] Julia Zhu, 'The Personal Information Protection Law: China's Version of the GDPR?' *The Bulletin Blog—Columbia Journal of Transnational Law* (14 February 2022), https://www.jtl.columbia.edu/bulletin-blog/the-personal-information-protection-law-chinas-version-of-the-gdpr.

be summarized in the following two aspects. First, the cross-border use of CBDCs shall be in line with the existing AML law in China and international conventions. Although meeting AML and CFT requirements is less likely to be a core regulatory objective or the primary motivation for any countries to issue CBDCs, central banks are expected to design CBDCs in a way that their operation will conform to such requirements.[40] This asks central banks and financial regulators, when experimenting CBDCs domestically or internationally, to incorporate the compulsory requirements under current AML frameworks into CBDCs' payment and settlement process. Second, promoting the cross-border use of CBDCs is progressively conducive to the enforcement of Chinese AML law at both domestic and international levels. Based on an empirical study regarding AML enforcement in key jurisdictions, 'identity' is found to be the most common factor for triggering influential AML enforcement cases leading to a fine of over $100,000.[41] Failures to conduct customer due diligence (CDD) or identify account ownership have been the common reason accounting for the hefty fines imposed on financial institutions and other corporations. This suggests that AML investigations are primarily focused on the verification of clients' identities and accounts, before the law enforcers starting to assess the source and flow of funds, business relationships and suspicious transactions, and to prepare relevant reports and evidence for the AML regulatory authorities.

The anonymity design is likely to be a common feature for CBDCs in most issuing countries. When central banks launch sovereign digital money for the cross-border use, balancing the AML compliance requirements with the protection of personal data privacy across multiple jurisdictions could be a universal concern that merits regulatory attention and multi-party coordination. As individual jurisdictions possess unique economic, political, and legal environments, they might adopt different approaches in improving the compatibility of their existing legislative frameworks to accommodate the CBDC experiments. For example, in the European Union (EU), the 'proportionality test' is a requirement for Member States to ensure that the regulatory power given to any governments under a particular law does not unduly restrict other fundamental rights under Article 52(1) of the Charter of Fundamental Rights in the European Union.[42] Besides, the AML

[40] BIS, 'Central Bank Digital Currencies: Foundational principles and core features' (2020), https://www.bis.org/publ/othp33.pdf.

[41] Lerong Lu and Lingsheng Zhang, 'Could the "Dragon" Now Fly Beyond Borders? Contextualizing Regulatory Aspects and Risks for China's CBDC Cross-Border Use' (2022) 14:S *Tsinghua China Law Review* 19–44.

[42] Harbo Tor-Inge, 'The Function of the Proportionality Principle in the EU law' (2010) 16 *European Law Journal* 158–185.

transaction monitoring process could be referred to and evaluated by the Court of Justice of the European Union (CJEU) for further justification on whether a case requiring banks to implement detection and report suspicious activities of their customers is compliant with the Article 23 of the GDPR interpreted in light of Article 52(1) of the Charter.[43] In contrast, regulators in Hong Kong hold a view that personal data is exempt from data protection rules where such data will be used for the prevention and detection of crimes.[44] As for China (mainland), data security and privacy has been a hot topic of academic and policy discussion in recent years due to the enactment of PIPL. Though there exist no special clauses that deal with the AML compliance issue with personal data collection, the PIPL does require that administrative officials and regulators should collect personal information within the range and level not exceeding necessary limitation.[45]

Accordingly, there exist two types of legal regimes with the objective to strike a delicate balance between AML and data protection laws:[46] (1) the EU model, where the domestic regulatory enforcement would be referred to and measured by the European court system for the revaluation of balancing interests on both sides; and (2) the China model (including Hong Kong SAR), which seems to prioritize the task of detecting potential money-laundering activities, and meanwhile it takes account of the necessary protection of personal data during the process of investigation. It is worth mentioning that one major distinction between the Chinese and EU models reveals that the current financial judicial system in China does not lead or shape regulatory attitudes. Instead, the court decisions relating to financial disputes usually follow the regulatory policies and decisions implemented by financial regulators, which suggests that Chinese financial regulators have more power in maintaining financial stability and financial order, compared with their European counterparts. Accordingly, as one of the financial authorities, the Chinese central bank is likely to prioritize the compliance of AML regulations over other regulatory goals when issuing CBDCs, for the sake of safeguarding financial stability and security.

[43] Astrid Bertrand, Winston Maxwell, and Xavier Vamparys, 'Do AI-Based Anti-Money Laundering (AML) Systems Violate European Fundamental Rights?' (2021) 11 *International Data Privacy Law* 276–293.

[44] The Personal Data (Privacy) Ordinance (2012), 63B (DPP 3); Data Protection Principles in the Personal Data (Privacy) Ordinance (2010), Chapter 7, 7.45.

[45] PRC Personal Information Protection Law (PIPL), Article 34.

[46] Lerong Lu and Lingsheng Zhang, 'Could the "Dragon" Now Fly Beyond Borders? Contextualizing Regulatory Aspects and Risks for China's CBDC Cross-Border Use' (2022) 14:S *Tsinghua China Law Review* 19–44.

Therefore, constructing a token-based CBDC system with full anonymity tends to be a risky attempt and is less likely to be welcomed by Chinese regulators in the future.[47] As for the EU Member States, since the protection of data privacy as a fundamental human right will need to be firstly satisfied, the results of enforcing AML laws might be subject to extra judicial reviews in the future. To balance individuals' basic rights with public interest and minimize compliance costs when enforcement results are challenged or reaffirmed by the European Court of Justice (ECJ), EU Member States are likely to initially incorporate anonymity mechanisms in their CBDC designs and gradually enhance features to address AML risks. The latest research project of ECB on CBDCs' anonymity has further supported this view.[48] However, the various and divergent designs of CBDCs' anonymity rules made by central banks in different countries are likely to restrict the feasibility and compatibility of CBDCs' cross-border use, which presents a major challenge for the regulation and compliance of CBDCs' cross-border payment activities.

6.6 The cross-border use of China's CBDCs: the retail and wholesale scenarios

Bearing in mind the rising popularity of CDBDs in the context of global currency competition (between private and public digital money, and between each sovereign digital money), one way for China's central bank to stimulate the further growth and mass application of e-CNY is to expand its cross-border usability.[49] Obviously, this echoes China's national goal of achieving currency internationalization, which is likely to reshape the international financial order that is currently dominated by US dollar and Euro.[50] According to the Financial Stability Board (FSB), there is a consensus among major economies, such as the G20, to enhance cross-border payments.[51] It is clear

[47] Changchun Mu, 'Reflection on Controlled Anonymity CBDC', *Sina Finance* (25 March 2021), http://finance.sina.com.cn/zl/china/2021-03-25/zl-ikknscsk1349458.shtml.

[48] Anonymity voucher is a new concept introduced by the ECB to create flexibility for users who want to transfer CBDC without revealing information to the AML authority if they have enough vouchers to spend (a ratio of one voucher per CBDC unit transferred). See ECB, 'Exploring anonymity in Central Bank Digital Currencies' (December 2019), https://www.ecb.europa.eu/paym/intro/publications/pdf/ecb.mipinfocus191217.en.pdf.

[49] Lerong Lu and Lingsheng Zhang, 'Could the "Dragon" Now Fly Beyond Borders? Contextualizing Regulatory Aspects and Risks for China's CBDC Cross-Border Use' (2022) 14:S *Tsinghua China Law Review* 19–44.

[50] The People's Bank of China, '2021 report on RMB internationalization', http://www.pbc.gov.cn/goutongjiaoliu/113456/113469/4344602/2021091814193942128.pdf.

[51] FSB, 'Enhancing cross-border payments: Stage 3 roadmap' (13 October 2020), https://www.fsb.org/wp-content/uploads/P131020-1.pdf.

that providing faster, cheaper, and more transparent and inclusive cross-border payment services would be beneficial for citizens, businesses, and national economies. As the BIS noted, the COVID-19 pandemic has made global policymakers rethink the significance of optimizing global payment and settlement systems, leading some countries to further explore the possibility of developing cross-border CBDCs.[52] Mr. He Dong, from the International Monetary Fund (IMF), suggested that, 'CBDCs would not qualitatively change the economic force that lead to the international use of currencies, but they could enhance the incentives behind currency substitution and currency internationalisation.'[53] Obviously, facilitating the cross-border use of CBDCs is beneficial for the global economy, as it contributes to higher efficiency in international payment and settlement systems and is likely to enhance multilateral economic cooperation in neighbouring countries and beyond; however, the potential financial risks and regulatory challenges should not be underestimated.

Accelerating the cross-border use of CBDCs is critical to realizing China's long-term national strategy of RMB internationalization to compete with other major currencies like US dollars, Euros, British pounds, and Japanese yens in international payments. In response, China has sped up its own CBDC experiment by joining the 'Multiple CBDC (m-CBDC) Bridge' project, whose other members are the Hong Kong Monetary Authority and the central banks of Thailand and the United Arab Emirates.[54] As discussed, the PBoC has legally defined retail-CBDCs (DC/EP) as digital fiat money, meaning it is currently incapable of being freely exchanged beyond the country's borders, which may severely restrict DC/EP's acceptance and application at both domestic and international level. This issue is of particular importance for China's policymakers, as the country has been actively promoting the use of retail-CBDCs on a large scale within its borders. Accordingly, exploring the cross-border use of CBDCs has become an urgent task for the PBoC. China, as the world's second-largest economy, should be cautious when it experiments with cross-border CBDCs and carefully consider regulatory challenges like financial stability and regulatory compatibility.

Special attentions shall be paid to the design of CDBCs in both retail and wholesale settings and related financial risks, to enable the large-scale and effective cross-border use of Chinese CBDCs. We would need to assess the

[52] BIS, 'Central bank digital currencies for cross-border payments: Report to the G20' (July 2021), https://www.bis.org/publ/othp38.pdf.

[53] Dong He, 'Digitalization of Cross-border Payments' (2021) 14 *China Economic Journal* 26–38.

[54] BIS, 'Multiple CBDC (mCBDC) bridge', https://www.bis.org/about/bisih/topics/cbdc/mcbdc_bridge.htm.

use of retail CBDCs in foreign markets and relevant regulatory issues in relation to financial stability, liquidity spillovers, balance-sheet reorganization, and floating interest rates. Retail CBDCs provide convenience for retail consumers using the CBDC payment method that involves a direct claim on central banks, as it is a vital component of a completed CBDC family tree.[55] Clearly, the cross-border flow of retail CBDC (M0) would affect the circles of flowing money creation, in particular its quantity and frequency, among countries, leading to a higher level of regulatory burden of predicting risks and carrying liquidity for both commercial banks and central banks.[56] At the early stage of any CBDC pilot schemes, retail CBDCs flowing cross-border is more likely to happen at small or medium amounts. Even though the development of CBDCs is expected to progress rapidly along with the recovery and further growth of international e-commerce activities and global tourism after the COVID-19 pandemic, whether retail CBDCs could be aptly inserted into the whole economy, especially the large-scale businesses and industries, is still unknown. Therefore, as the medium of seamless and inexpensive cross-border payments, the transactions in use of retail CBDCs are likely to be requested mainly by end-users like retail consumers and small and medium-sized enterprises (SMEs) for daily business and consumption like small trading, vehicle use, and grocery payment.

In the countries that are supporting the cross-border usability of China's retail CBDCs, money liquidity and money creation would be affected bilaterally by both monetary policies in their home countries and China.[57] It is largely due to the most significant features of retail CBDCs as consumers' direct claims on the balance sheet of central banks when having access to their non-interest DC/EP wallets. This is likely to incur extra transactional costs to the commercial banks under the two-tier operation system, when they must comply with the due diligence rules among multiple risks like money laundering and fake accounts.

If and when retail CBDCs become popular in foreign markets as the equivalent of publicly available cash, this is highly likely to increase the circulation speed of RMB currencies in general, leading to the rapid fluctuation of interest rates for RMB-denominated deposits and financial products, which might affect financial stability. Under the two-tier distribution model

[55] Raphael Auer and Rainer Böhme, 'The technology of retail Central Bank Digital Currency', *BIS Quarterly Review* (March 2020), https://www.bis.org/publ/qtrpdf/r_qt2003j.htm.

[56] Lerong Lu and Lingsheng Zhang, 'Could the "Dragon" Now Fly Beyond Borders? Contextualizing Regulatory Aspects and Risks for China's CBDC Cross-Border Use' (2022) 14:S *Tsinghua China Law Review* 19–44.

[57] The People's Bank of China, 'Progress of Research & Development of E-CNY in China (Whitepaper)' (July 2021), http://www.pbc.gov.cn/en/3688110/3688172/4157443/4293696/2021071614584691871.pdf.

of Chinese retail CBDCs (DC/EP), domestic commercial banks and offshore RMB business clearing banks are exposed to the liquidity risk caused by frequent fund movements between customers' ordinary RMB deposit accounts (interest-bearing) and their DC/EP accounts (non-interest bearing). As a response, both onshore and offshore commercial banks are likely to reorganize their balance sheets by partly switching long-term RMB assets into short ones. Moreover, the cross-border payment convenience of Chinese CBDCs, coupled with the price stability of RMB, might expose certain developing countries with immature financial systems to the threat of currency substitution. Finally, in the event of an overheated domestic economy caused by a large inflow of foreign money via DCEP, the PBoC is likely to raise interest rates to curb the consequent inflation. In practice, however, the regular fluctuation of currency exchange rates and interest rates is determined by multiple factors that are either positively or negatively correlated with each other, which further complicates the problem. Such challenges require domestic commercial banks to closely watch the global inflow and outflow of Chinese CBDCs when they are setting interest rates for their savings products and rate-sensitive businesses.

We will now evaluate the wholesale CBDC scenario and make some suggestions for revising relevant international settlement rules. Distinctive from retail CBDCs that mainly focus on household transactions and SME trading, wholesale CBDCs is a digital payment method designed for the settlement of inter-bank money transfers and related wholesale transactions.[58] Wholesale CBDCs are less known and used by the public as its transactions flow among financial intermediaries only. When policymakers and researchers are considering RMB globalization through the use of CBDCs, whether wholesale CBDCs, as a way of inter-bank payments and settlements, could be used at a large scale in international capital markets is a key criterion in assessing the maturity of CBDC's cross-border usability.[59] The resilience of Chinese economy to the Global Financial Crisis of 2007–2008 and the COVID-19 pandemic, coupled with the higher-yielding Chinese assets, have attracted large amounts of overseas capital flowing to China's bond markets with a total amount of RMB 3.3 trillion.[60] In China's bond markets, China Interbank

[58] The Bank for International Settlements, 'BIS Annual Economic Report: III. CBDCs: An opportunity for the monetary system' (2021), https://www.bis.org/publ/arpdf/ar2021e3.pdf.

[59] Lerong Lu and Lingsheng Zhang, 'Could the "Dragon" Now Fly Beyond Borders? Contextualizing Regulatory Aspects and Risks for China's CBDC Cross-Border Use' (2022) 14:S *Tsinghua China Law Review* 19–44.

[60] *The Bloomberg*, 'China's Epic Battle With Capital Flows Is More Intense Than Ever' (6 April 2021), https://www.bloomberg.com/news/articles/2021-04-06/china-s-epic-battle-with-capital-flows-is-more-intense-than-ever.

Bond Market (CIBM) accounts for the most value of transactions. Therefore, analysing wholesale CBDCs' potential advantages and limitations as a de facto medium of settlement in the inter-bank bond markets would constitute a necessary part of further exploration of the legal framework of Inter-bank Market Clearing House Co., Ltd. (hereinafter referred to as Shanghai Clearing House), a financial intermediary that assumes statutory duties and owns the rights to provide services for qualified foreign investors through centralized registration, custody, clearing, and settlement.

In contrast to retail CBDCs, wholesale CBDCs generally flow through financial intermediaries, which is likely to impact the institutional settlement framework. The inter-bank bond market accounts for 80% of the bond trading volume in China, and its settlement and clearing scheme for qualified foreign investors is made up of multiple accounts and a tier structure.[61] The PBoC, the Market Clearing House Co., Ltd. (Shanghai Clearing House), and commercial banks have collectively been granted statutory rights and duties to provide services of centralized registration, custody, clearing, and settlement. Technically speaking, if and when wholesale CBDCs are used in international financial markets in the future, this would allow foreign investors to complete the settlement process by bypassing third parties, as they are supposed to have direct claims on the PBoC. The peer-to-peer mechanism of CBDC settlement and clearing is likely to reduce transaction costs for foreign investors, but it may also weaken the status of financial intermediaries, especially traditional commercial banks. Considering the need to protect financial stability, the PBoC is expected to maintain the role of Shanghai Clearing House as the central counterparty and might even embed wholesale-CBDCs into the existing Clearing House system.

6.7 Conclusion

This chapter has discussed the practices and regulatory issues regarding China's proactive adoption of CBDCs. The e-CNY is perceived as legal tender in China, and it is likely to play a central role in China's fast-growing financial system with a possibility to reshape the international financial order, if Chinese CBDCs were widely tested in all retail, wholesale, and cross-border settings. Promoting the international use of e-CNY echoes China's long-term strategy of RMB internalization, which could significantly strengthen the

[61] Lerong Lu and Lingsheng Zhang, 'Could the "Dragon" Now Fly Beyond Borders? Contextualizing Regulatory Aspects and Risks for China's CBDC Cross-Border Use' (2022) 14:S *Tsinghua China Law Review* 19–44.

country's economic power and international influence. There is no doubt that a financial superpower needs to possess a strong currency that could be widely used in international financial transactions, like the US dollars. It is high time that China made good use of its advanced Fintech with mass consumer markets to devise the future generation of official currency.

China is actively embracing CBDCs for the following reasons. First, compared with privately issued crypto coins and stablecoins, CBDCs seem to be the most feasible currency option for the global economy and financial markets in the future, thanks to CBDCs' competitive edges such as the advanced regulatory functions, stable value, public trust, and the potential use as a monetary policy tool. Second, as analysed, CBDCs are likely to be more welcomed by countries with a state-led economic model (e.g. China), as opposed to sovereign states with free-market capitalism might be more in favour of traditional currencies or private digital money. Third, the use of CBDCs beyond national borders resonates with the initiative RMB internationalization, allowing more frequent use of Chinese yuan in international payments and financial transactions. Fourth, China now possesses a mature consumer market, as citizens and businesses have been used to mobile payments and e-money for a long time. It has the world-class information technology, hardware, and infrastructure, suggesting the commercial and technological readiness for any large-scale CBDC pilot projects.

The chapter has assessed the operating mechanisms and design options of China's CBDCs. The e-CNY is designed to operate as M0 to substitute cash in the economy, as the basic layer of currencies, and it will create a direct claim on the central bank's balance sheets with the highest liquidity. At present, e-CNY primarily targets the domestic retail sector at the initial stage, with the potential to be extended to cover wholesale and cross-border scenarios in the upcoming years. Moreover, the operation of e-CNY relies on China's two-tier banking system that consists of the PBoC as the central bank and other commercial banks, as each institution has respective functions and mandates in the process of payment and settlement. In the current CBDC experiment programmes, we could observe some distinctive design features for e-CNY: unlimited legal credit, loosely coupled account, controllable anonymity, and non-interest bearing and no exchange fees. This offers valuable lessons for other countries which wish to research or test CBDC schemes.

The chapter has evaluated three main regulatory issues relating to China's potential cross-border use of CBDCs, to facilitate RMB internationalization and to increase its influence in the international financial arena. First, considering the anonymous design of CBDCs, how to strike a finance balance between the AML compliance task and the protection of personal data and privacy will be a major task for the PBoC and Chinese financial regulators when dealing with the cross-border use of CBDCs. The solution lies in multi-party coordination as relevant transactions denominated in e-CNY are likely to involve regulatory scrutiny and law enforcement across several jurisdictions. Also, controlled anonymity could be a future mainstream design for China's CBDCs. Second, when retail CBDCs become popular in foreign markets as the equivalent of cash, this will increase the circulation speed of RMB currencies in general, leading to the rapid fluctuation of interest rates for RMB-denominated deposits and financial products, which might affect financial stability. It requires regulatory to watch out for the liquidity spillover problem, and commercial banks to reorganize their balance sheets and to carefully set the interest rates for relevant products. Third, the potential wholesale use of Chinese CBDCs will impact the institutional settlement framework, such as the inter-bank bond market. The peer-to-peer mechanism of CBDC settlement and clearing is likely to reduce transaction costs for foreign investors, but it may also weaken the status of financial intermediaries, like commercial banks. The PBoC is likely to maintain the role of Shanghai Clearing House as the central counterparty and even embed wholesale CBDCs into the existing clearing system.

Chapter 7
China's financial courts

7.1 Introduction

Chapter 7 considers China's financial courts that are specialized law courts dealing with legal cases relating to financial transactions in relation to securities, banking, and insurance. After four decades of rapid economic growth (1980–2020), China now has one of the largest financial industries in the world. The fast growth in financial transactions naturally leads to an increasing number of finance-related legal disputes. From 2018 to 2023, the Shanghai Financial Court handled 17,137 cases related to securities (such as shares, bonds, and futures), 8,091 cases related to banking, 1,468 related to insurance, and 2,270 cases concerning other financial matters.[1] In order to process financial law cases more effectively, China has been actively reforming its judicial system to increase its capacity and efficiency in hearing financial disputes. As of December 2023, China has set up three financial courts across the country: Shanghai Financial Court (established on 20 August 2018), Beijing Financial Court (18 March 2021), and Chengdu-Chongqing (Chengyu) Financial Court (28 September 2022).[2]

Chapter 7 aims to introduce China's financial courts and discuss how they can make a positive difference in creatively solving financial law disputes. It will proceed as follows. Section 7.2 presents the background and motivations of the National People's Congress in setting up financial courts in China. Section 7.3 introduces the historical development of three financial courts in Beijing, Shanghai, and Chengdu-Chongqing. Section 7.4 discusses the financial courts' institutional structure. Section 7.5 focuses on the jurisdictions of the financial courts. Section 7.6 conducts analysis regarding the leading cases heard by financial courts and the impacts of those cases. Finally, Section 7.7 draws a conclusion.

[1] *Securities Times*, 'Over 17,000 cases in five years, the disputes in securities industry greatly exceed banking and insurance' (24 August 2023), https://www.stcn.com/article/detail/957115.html.

[2] Shanghai Financial Court, 'Introduction to the Shanghai Financial Court', http://www.shjrfy.gov.cn/jrfy/English/about.jsp; Beijing Financial Court, 'Court overview', https://bjfc.bjcourt.gov.cn/cac/1615256934535.html; and Chengdu-Chongqing Financial Court, 'Court introduction', http://cyjrfy.cqfygzfw.gov.cn/article/detail/2023/11/id/7615653.shtml.

Towards Financial Superpower. Lerong Lu, Oxford University Press. © Lerong Lu (2025).
DOI: 10.1093/9780198948568.003.0007

7.2 The background for introducing financial courts

Having a sound legal system is a prerequisite for the effective operation of financial markets and institutions. Domestic and international investors will have greater confidence in a country's financial industry if it can offer fast, fair, and easily accessible dispute resolution mechanisms. With the development of vibrant financial markets in the first two decades of the twenty-first century, China's financial law cases have become more complex, involving issues such as securities misrepresentation, financial leasing disputes, and bills recourse disputes. To approach financial legal issues with more professional knowledge, the financial law courts system, as judicial innovation, has been introduced in mainland China. So far, three specialized financial courts have been set up in Shanghai, Beijing, and Chengdu-Chongqing since 2018.

Financial courts are a newly established category of specialized law courts that specifically handle financial civil or commercial cases (e.g. securities, futures, and trusts-related issues), financial administrative cases, and financial-related appeal or retrial petition cases. The establishment of specialized financial courts, along with the introduction of dedicated internet courts and Intellectual Property courts, is considered a transformative innovation within the Chinese judicial system. The judicial innovation aims to provide specialized legal recourse for financial issues and streamline financial services by consolidating financial trials in China. According to the National Administration of Financial Regulation (NAFR), China's financial industry has three primary regulatory objectives: emphasizing its service to the real economy, managing financial risks, and deepening financial reforms.[3] The establishment of financial courts in China undoubtedly brings positive impacts in achieving these missions. Meanwhile, centralizing financial trials enhances the international influence of China's financial justice by providing high-quality and professional judicial and financial assistance. This serves as a model for other countries in addressing commercial disputes.

At present, the Chinese judicial system is categorized into three distinctive tiers: the Supreme People's Court, local people's courts operating at different levels, and specialized people's courts.[4] Trial activities in specialized people's courts are subject to diligent supervision by the Supreme People's Court, which serves as the highest judicial authority.[5] The authority to establish, organize, and define the jurisdiction of financial courts, as well as the

[3] Shanghai Securities News, 'NAFR Chief Li Yunze: The three main tasks in financial sector' (May 2023), https://news.cnstock.com/news,bwkx-202305-5062916.htm.

[4] The Organic Law of the People's Courts of the People's Republic of China (2018 Revision), Article 12.

[5] The Organic Law of the People's Courts of the People's Republic of China (2018 Revision), Article 10.

appointment and removal of judges within these courts, rests with the Standing Committee of the National People's Congress (SCNPC), which is the legislative body of China. Clearly, the establishment of new financial courts has demonstrated China's commitment and effects to strengthen its legal framework and sound governance in the realm of financial sector. Before the formal establishment of financial courts, financial tribunals were first introduced in China. The Basic People's Court Financial Tribunal was set up in November 2008, which was the first financial tribunal based in Shanghai Pudong New Area People's Court. Financial tribunals were financial specialized trial branches to handle cases relating to financial market turbulence resulted from the financial crisis of 2007–2008.

The establishment of financial courts in China results from the growing demands associated with the evolving economy and financial landscape. Two primary reasons underscore the need for these specialized law courts. First, the rapid expansion of the financial sector, encompassing both traditional and emerging activities relating to the internet and artificial intelligence, necessitates a more sophisticated regulatory system. In particular, the rise of financial technologies (Fintech) presents more legal challenges, in the areas of consumer protection, data privacy, smart contacts, and the property rights of cryptocurrencies.[6] As the financial industry diversifies, corresponding risks emerge, highlighting the need for specialized legal treatment. Financial courts address this demand by providing a more focused and professional approach to handling complex financial cases. Second, the presence of specialized financial courts contributes to the development of a robust financial legal framework. This specialized system enhances the financial trial structure, fostering healthier economic and financial growth. Legal regulations not only guide financial practices by setting the expectation of transaction parties, but also provide mechanisms for safeguarding and judicial remedies. By offering timely and professional assistance, financial courts instil confidence in market participants, including both retail and institutional investors, encouraging their active involvement in financial activities. Financial courts enable China's legal system to support the development of the financial and commercial industry actively and reliably.

Two widely adopted patterns can be observed for the judicial branches to supervise financial activities. One is to regulate financial activities within the existing court system, for example, by the general civil courts, while the other

[6] Lerong Lu, 'Financial Technology and Challenger Banks in the UK: Gap Fillers or Real Challengers?' (2017) 32 *Journal of International Banking Law and Regulation* 273–282.

is to manage them separately, launching specialized financial courts. Some countries used to have specialized courts or tribunals to deal with financial issues and later include such courts into traditional civil courts, for example, the United Kingdom. The United Kingdom used to have the Financial Services and Markets Tribunal, which could review the decisions issued by the financial regulator such as the entry of official list issues.[7] The Transfer of Tribunal Functions Order 2010 resulted in the abolition of the Financial Services and Markets Tribunal, with its functions being transferred to the Upper Tribunal.[8] Some countries designate financial courts especially for financial activities, such as the Financial Services Division of the Grand Court established under the Grand Court Rules in Cayman Islands.[9] The other example is Astana International Financial Centre Court established under Law on Regional Financial Center of Almaty City in Kazakhstan.[10] Generally, those financial courts were established based on the existing legislations and operate independently from the administrative bodies. While for Chinese financial courts, their establishments were not based on the clauses of any special laws but were based on a direct decision made by the SCNPC. The legislator saw the importance and necessity of financial-specialized court and place expectation on them for the development of Chinese financial sector.

7.3 The development of financial courts in China

7.3.1 Shanghai Financial Court

Where there is a high occurrence of financial crimes, incidents, or legal disputes, there is a need for a specialized financial court. The first specialized financial court in China is located in Shanghai, the country's economic and financial heartland. Shanghai often ranks as the most competitive financial centre in China.[11] Shanghai boasts an active financial market with an annual transaction volume surpassing RMB 25 trillion in 2021, indicating a year-on-year growth of 10.4%.[12] Additionally, the value contributed by the

[7] The Financial Services and Markets Act 2000, Section 132.

[8] The Upper Tribunal, also known as the Administrative Appeals Chamber, serves as an appellate tribunal responsible for hearing, reviewing, and deciding on cases that arise from lower tribunals.

[9] Cayman Islands Judicial Administration, 'Financial services division', https://www.judicial.ky/courts/grand-court/financial-services-division.

[10] AIFC, 'An introduction', https://court.aifc.kz/en/an-introduction.

[11] China Development Institute, 'The China Financial Center Index (CFCI)' (27 December 2022), http://www.cdi.com.cn/Article/Detail?id=18078&cid=160.

[12] The People's Bank of China, 'Shanghai Financial Operation Report (2022)', http://shanghai.pbc.gov.cn/fzhshanghai/113589/4599988/2022070814444473871.pdf.

financial industry in the same year reached RMB 797.325 trillion, reflecting a 7.5% increase compared to the previous year.[13]

The enormous financial service sector in Shanghai makes it a suitable test ground for establishing a financial law court to solve the increasing legal disputes in China's leading financial centre. Moreover, the new financial law court contributes to the sound legal environment of Shanghai, further improving the city's competitiveness as a global financial hub. With the first-class financial and legal infrastructure, Shanghai is likely to compete with London, New York, Singapore, and Hong Kong to become a top destination for global investors.

The journey from the preparation to the actual launch of the Shanghai Financial Court spanned nearly a decade starting from the early 2010s. In 2010, three members of the Shanghai Municipal Chinese People's Political Consultative Conference (CPPCC) Standing Committee—Ning Zhang, Hongbing Lu, and Rongxing Xie—submitted a proposal to establish a specialized financial court. The proposal aims to centralize the adjudication of financial cases, presented at the Third Meeting of the Eleventh Session of the Shanghai Political Consultative Conference in 2010.[14] After a careful review of the proposal, Xiaoming Zhu and Xiaomei Gao, then vice chairmen of the Shanghai CPPCC, referred the proposal to the Shanghai Higher People's Court. The president of the Shanghai Higher People's Court at that time, Yong Ying, expressed a favourable view of the proposal and forwarded it for consultations within the court, with the decision marked to 'hold for future reference'.[15] Since then, there has been a continuous push for a financial court led by members of the Shanghai Municipal CPPCC Standing Committee and scholars.

In 2015, during the opening ceremony of the third session of the twelfth Shanghai Municipal Political Consultative Conference, the renewed proposal on the establishment of a financial court in Shanghai was submitted once more.[16]At this time, this proposal was drafted by Hongbing Lu with a joint submission from Ning Zhang and other eleven members of the Shanghai CPPCC. It proposed that the financial court could be first launched within the Shanghai First Intermediate People's Court, based on the precedent that the Shanghai Intellectual Property Court was firstly set up

[13] Ibid.

[14] *Sohu*, '50 good proposals from members of CPPCC' (21 December 2022), https://www.sohu.com/a/619521214_120119476.

[15] Ibid.

[16] *Xinhua*, 'Focusing on NPC and CPPCC', http://www.xinhuanet.com/politics/2015lh/zhibo/20150302a/index.htm.

in Shanghai Third Intermediate People's Court.[17] Once the time comes, there could be the establishment of an independent Shanghai Financial Court. Yadong Cui, the then president of Shanghai Higher People's Court, saw the necessity to establish a financial court and this proposal was included as one of the key proposals for the consideration of the Shanghai Municipal Political Consultative Conference, leading to the active result of 'included in plans to be finalised'.[18]

In 2017, Yiping Li, the then vice chairman of the Shanghai CPPCC, led a research team to Macau and Hong Kong with a focus on addressing financial cases and concluded that the establishment of a special financial court in Shanghai was 'very necessary'.[19] During the meeting of NPC and CPPCC in 2018, Hongbing Lu, as a member of the National CPPCC, Wei Huang, the associate professor at Shanghai International Studies University and others made another attempt to propose the establishment of Shanghai financial court. Finally, this 'very necessary' proposal welcomed its approval in the year of 2018.

On 28 March 2018, the co-signed proposal of establishing the Shanghai Financial Court by the Supreme People's Court, the People's Bank of China, and Shanghai Municipal Government was formally approved at the first meeting of the Central Committee for Comprehensively Deepening the Reform. This Committee, led by the Chinese President Xi Jinping, is the top coordination body in charge of China's social and economic reforms which was set up under the Central Committee of the Communist Party of China (CPC).[20] On 27 April 2018, the Chief Justice and President of the Supreme People's Court Zhou Qiang delivered the working report of the Supreme People's Court to the SCNPC. In this report, he addressed that 'the financial court would bolster the international influence of China's financial justice, forestall financial risk, steer the financial sector to serve the real economy, and reinforce Shanghai's transformation into an international financial centre by 2020'.[21] On the same day, the SCNPC adopted the Decision on the

[17] *People*, 'Loss of deposit? Shanghai CPPCC foretell the Shanghai Financial Court' (by Xinrong He and Linlin Wang, 24 January 2015), http://finance.people.com.cn/n/2015/0124/c1004-26443897.html.

[18] *Sohu*, '50 good proposals from members of CPPCC' (21 December 2022), https://www.sohu.com/a/619521214_120119476.

[19] Ibid.

[20] Lance L P Gore, 'China's Central Commission on Comprehensively Deepening Reforms: Seven Years on' (EAI Background Brief No. 1581, 18 March 2021), https://research.nus.edu.sg/eai/wp-content/uploads/sites/2/2021/03/EAIBB-No.-1581-Chinas-Central-Commission-7-yrs-on-exsum.pdf.

[21] Shanghai Financial Court, 'Introduction to the Shanghai Financial Court', http://www.shjrfy.gov.cn/jrfy/English/about.jsp.

Establishment of the Shanghai Financial Court, which was later formally launched on 20 August 2018.[22]

7.3.2 Beijing Financial Court

Beijing Financial Court is the second financial court in China. Beijing is not only the capital city of China but also an international financial centre. Beijing Financial Street stands as the epicentre of China's financial sector, holding major financial institutions with a collective value of RMB 99.5 trillion in financial assets, constituting 40% of the total financial holdings in the country.[23] Beijing is not only home to major Chinese regulatory bodies like the People's Bank of China, China Securities Regulatory Commission (CSRC), and NAFR, but also hosts the headquarters of the Asian Infrastructure Investment Bank (AIIB) and most state-owned financial conglomerates. Additionally, Beijing accommodates the regional offices of prominent international financial institutions such as Goldman Sachs, Citibank, JPMorgan Chase, Morgan Stanley, VISA, Mastercard, and Societe Generale.

Beijing, designated as the regulatory hub for Chinese financial policy, serves as the national financial management centre as specified by the Central Committee of the CCP and the State Council.[24] It holds the top position in the number of financial institutions and is a favoured destination for hosting headquarters of numerous international financial institutions. The financial industry in Beijing thrives significantly. The Central Committee of the CCP and the State Council explicitly stated in the response to the Beijing Urban Master Plan (2016–2035) that Beijing will be developed into a national centre for technological and financial innovation.[25] It will also become an international hub for financial functions and a modern service industry cluster, centred around the Beijing Central Business District. In this context, the creation of the Beijing Financial Court is seen as an essential step in fulfilling the significant strategic objectives outlined by the central government. It is crucial for ensuring the execution of the national financial strategy, enhancing the financial trial system, mitigating and resolving

[22] Decision of the Standing Committee of the National People's Congress on the establishment of Shanghai Financial Court (adopted at the 2nd session of the Standing Committee of the 13th National People's Congress on 27 April 2018).

[23] *ChinaNews*, 'Beijing Financial Street financial institutions asset scale is approaching RMB100 trillion' (29 April 2018), http://www.chinanews.com/fortune/2018/04-29/8503009.shtml.

[24] The Supreme People's Court, Illustration on the Decision to the Establishment of Beijing Financial Court (2021).

[25] *Xinhua*, 'Beijing releases full text of new city plan' (29 September 2017), http://www.xinhuanet.com/english/2017-09/29/c_136649259.htm.

systemic financial risks, and fostering high-quality economic development in Beijing.

Furthermore, it holds great significance in elevating the international influence of Chinese judicial decisions relating to financial matters. Following the review of the plan for establishing the Beijing Financial Court by the Central Committee for Comprehensively Deepening the Reform, the proposal was approved in the seventeenth meeting of the Central Committee on 30 December 2020.[26] The purpose of establishing a financial court in Beijing is to create a high-standard institution with a centralized jurisdiction over financial cases, considering local functions and characteristics.[27] This aims to advance systematic and institutional reforms in financial case adjudication and enhance the professional standards of such adjudication. The Beijing Financial Court is at the same judicial level as the Intermediate People's Court of a municipality.[28] It hears financial civil or commercial cases, financial administrative cases, and enforcement cases that should be originally accepted and heard by the Intermediate People's Court in the jurisdiction of Beijing. After its official inauguration, the first trial batch consisted of twenty-five judges.[29] All of these judges are members of the CPC, with ten female judges. Eleven of them hold doctoral degrees, and the rest have master's degrees.

7.3.3 Chengdu-Chongqing (Chengyu) Financial Court

The Chengdu-Chongqing (Chengyu) Financial Court is the third and also the latest financial court in China, serving as the first financial court in the southwestern part of the country. In early 2022, the SCNPC announced the decision to establish the Chengyu Financial Court, covering Chengdu and Chongqing as the two largest metropolitan cities in southwest China.[30] The purpose of such a decision, according to SCNPC, is to strengthen financial judicial protection, create a sound legal environment for financial industry, and maintain financial security. Unlike the Shanghai Financial Court and Beijing Financial Court, the Chengyu Financial Court is the first one that

[26] Chinese Government, 'Xi Jinping chairs the 17th meeting of the Central Committee for Comprehensively Deepening Reform and Delivers an Important Speech' (30 December 2020), http://www.gov.cn/xinwen/2020-12/30/content_5575462.htm.

[27] Beijing Financial Court, 'Court overview', https://bjfc.bjcourt.gov.cn/cac/1615256934535.html.

[28] A municipality is a singular administrative division that operates directly under the Central Government.

[29] Beijing Financial Court, 'Court overview', https://bjfc.bjcourt.gov.cn/cac/1615256934535.html.

[30] Standing Committee of the National People's Congress, 'Decision on establishing the Chengyu Financial Court' (28 February 2022).

can exercise its jurisdiction over two provinces, Chongqing Municipality and Sichuan Province, within the scope of the Chengdu-Chongqing Economic Circle.

According to the Plan for the Development of the Chengdu-Chongqing Economic Circle, formulated by the Central Committee of the CCP and the State Council, it is a shared objective for Chengdu and Chongqing to establish the Chengdu-Chongqing economic circle as the western financial centre.[31] In the economic circle, financial market reforms and innovations will be fully encouraged and supported by the State, and the goal to improve the financial trial system is of great significance in fulfilling the objectives of regional financial reforms. The Supreme People's Court aligns with the Central Committee of the CCP and the State Council. In the document titled 'Opinions of the Supreme People's Court on Providing Judicial Services to Safeguard the Development of the Chengdu-Chongqing Economic Circle', the Supreme People's Court emphasizes maximizing 'the role of judicial organs' to create 'a legal environment favourable for the development of the Economic Circle'.[32] To be more specific, the trial of financial cases should be enhanced with the aim of preventing fatal financial risks. The Supreme People's Court will actively support regional financial reforms and innovations, promote the establishment of financial courts with high standards, improve the financial trial system, and continuously strengthen the professionalization and internationalization of financial trials. On 1 January 2023, Chengyu Financial Court started accepting and reviewing cases.[33]

7.4 The institutional structure of financial courts

The institutional structure illustrates how a financial court organizes itself, with a primary focus on its internal divisions and their respective powers, mandates, and responsibilities. Common internal divisions in a financial court include the case-filing division, the general adjudication division, the enforcement bureau, the personnel department, and the general office. Figure 7.1 provides an overview of the trial procedure for financial courts when they accept relevant cases.

[31] Chinese Government, 'The plan for the development of the Chengdu-Chongqing Economic Circle' (21 October 2021), http://www.gov.cn/zhengce/2021-10/21/content_5643875.htm.

[32] Supreme People's Court, 'Opinions of the Supreme People's Court on providing judicial services to safeguard the development of the Chengdu-Chongqing Economic Circle' (13 January 2021), https://lawinfochina.com/display.aspx?id=35000&lib=law.

[33] Chengdu-Chongqing Financial Court, 'Media paid close attention to the first press conference of Chengyu Financial Court' (4 January 2023), http://cyjrfy.cqfygzfw.gov.cn/article/detail/2023/01/id/7086414.shtml.

Figure 7.1 The general trial procedure in China's financial courts
Source: This figure is compiled by the author.

The case-filing division primarily handles the registration and filing of cases accepted by the financial court. There are typically multiple general adjudication divisions responsible for reviewing financial cases and providing relevant trial guidance within their jurisdiction. The enforcement bureau oversees the execution of legal documents mandated by the law to be enforced by the financial court. The personnel department is responsible for the organization and personnel management of the financial court, guiding ideological and political work, recognizing rewards, overseeing education and training, and managing the judicial police of the financial court. The general office is tasked with process management and quality assessment of cases, supervising and inspecting the implementation of statutory trial limits, and drafting judicial interpretations, as well as researching, soliciting opinions on draft laws, regulations, and rules, and compiling guiding cases.

In its institutional structure, the Shanghai Financial Court comprises six internal divisions: the Case-filing Division, First General Adjudication Division, Second General Adjudication Division, Enforcement Bureau, Personnel Department (including the Judicial Police Unit), and General Office (which includes the Research Office and Trial Management Office).[34] The Beijing Financial Court features seven internal divisions, including the Case-Filing Division (Adjudication Management Office), the First Division, the Second Division, the Third Division, Enforcement Department, Political Department (Judicial Police Branch), and General Office. In contrast, Chengyu Financial Court has nine internal divisions, comprising the General Office (Trial Management Office), Political Department (Judicial Police Detachment), Case-filing Division (Litigation Service Centre), First General Adjudication Division, Second General Adjudication Division, Third General Adjudication Division, Fourth General Adjudication Division, Trial Supervision Division, and Enforcement Bureau.[35]

[34] Shanghai Financial Court, 'Introduction to the Shanghai Financial Court', http://www.shjrfy.gov.cn/jrfy/English/about.jsp

[35] Chengdu-Chongqing Financial Court, 'Chengdu-Chongqing Financial Court held its first press conference' (January 2023), http://cyjrfy.cqfygzfw.gov.cn/article/detail/2023/01/id/7086361.shtml.

The institutional structures of Shanghai Financial Court, Beijing Financial Court, and Chengyu Financial Court exhibit notable similarities. Each court comprises the Case-Filing Division, Enforcement Department, Political Department, General Office, and a minimum of three General Adjudication Divisions. Beijing Financial Court encompasses seven divisions, while Shanghai Financial Court adds an Appeal Review and Trial Supervision Division, and Chengyu Financial Court includes an additional General Adjudication Division and Trial Supervision Division. Regarding the location of internal divisions, those in Shanghai and Beijing Financial Courts are all within the respective cities. In contrast, Chengyu Financial Court, with jurisdiction over both Chengdu and Chongqing, situates two of its nine divisions, the Third and Fourth General Adjudication Divisions, in Chengdu, while the others are in Chongqing.[36]

7.5 The jurisdiction of financial courts

The court system plays a crucial role in addressing disputes with efficiency and fairness in modern society.[37] In the realm of public international law, the term 'jurisdiction' is frequently understood as a state's ability to exert its sovereignty, including applying domestic rules and laws to address matters beyond its borders. In the context of financial courts, the term 'jurisdiction' focuses on the specific range of cases that these courts can accept and adjudicate. Therefore, it is essential to have a precise understanding of the types of cases that financial courts can handle. The Supreme People's Court instructed on this matter. Generally, financial courts, as the specialized people's courts, possess the authority to exercise jurisdiction that is equivalent to that of local intermediate people's courts.[38] The jurisdiction of the intermediate people's court encompasses the following: (1) cases of first instance under its jurisdiction as prescribed by the law; (2) cases of first instance submitted by the primary people's court; (3) cases of first instance appointed by the higher people's court or the Supreme Court; (4) appellate cases judged and ruled by the primary people's court; and (5) retrial cases filed in accordance with the trial supervision procedures.[39] In sum, a local intermediate people's court has the authority to handle a wide range of cases, including

[36] Ibid.
[37] Alisdair Gillespie and Siobhan Weare, *English Legal System* (9th Edition, Oxford University Press, 2023), p. 14.
[38] Organic Law of the People's Courts of the People's Republic of China (2018 Revision), Article 15.
[39] Organic Law of the People's Courts of the People's Republic of China (2018 Revision), Article 23.

hear civil (including commercial and financial) cases, criminal cases, and administrative cases within its administrative jurisdiction.

Contrary to the general rule, financial courts, operating under dedicated obligations, narrow their focus to primarily handle financial civil or commercial cases, financial administrative cases, as well as judgments, disputes, and appeals or retrial petitions within their designated administrative area. This specialization enables financial courts to effectively address the intricacies and complexities that emerge in the financial industry, offering specialized expertise and efficiency in handling a variety of disputes in financial activities. Accordingly, the Supreme People's Court has explicitly defined the jurisdiction scope of the Shanghai Financial Court and the Beijing Financial Court.[40] In the Decision of the Standing Committee of the National People's Congress on Establishing the Chengyu Financial Court, the SCNPC outlines the exclusive jurisdiction granted to the Chengyu Financial Court. The formal recognition of jurisdiction for the Chengyu Financial Court was also introduced by the Supreme People's Court at the beginning of 2023.[41] As discussed, financial courts specialize in three categories of cases: financial civil or commercial cases (including securities, futures, and trusts), financial administrative cases, and judgments, distributions, appeal, or retrial petition cases. The substantive content of regulatory clauses remains consistent across all three financial courts, despite their jurisdiction being exercised in different local municipalities, namely Shanghai, Beijing, and the Chengyu district. In the subsequent discussion, cases will be categorized according to their inherent nature.

7.5.1 Category I: financial civil or commercial cases

The scope of financial civil or commercial cases is very broad. Generally speaking, any cases related to the capital market, financing, and financial institutions can be brought to financial courts. First, financial courts have the authority to accept and adjudicate financial civil or commercial disputes within the designated local municipality, subject to the acceptance of the intermediate people's courts in the first instance. If such cases fall within the scope of the following, they will be heard by financial courts: (1) financial civil and commercial disputes over, among others, securities, futures

[40] Supreme People's Court, 'Rule on the Jurisdiction of the Beijing Financial Court by the Supreme People's Court' (16 March 2021); Supreme People's Court, 'Rule on the Jurisdiction of the Shanghai Financial Court by the Supreme People's Court' (Amendment, 1 March 2021).

[41] Supreme People's Court, 'Rule on the Jurisdiction of the Chengyu Financial Court by the Supreme People's Court' (1 January 2023).

trading, business trust, insurance, bills, letters of credit, independent letters of guarantee, factoring, financial loan contracts, bank cards, financial leasing contracts, entrusted wealth management contracts, savings deposit contracts, pawn, and bank settlement contracts; (2) financial civil and commercial disputes arising from asset management business, asset-backed securities business, private fund business, foreign exchange business, financial product sales and suitability management, credit reference business, payment business, and other financial business approved by competent authorities; (3) company-related disputes involving financial institutions; (4) bankruptcy disputes where financial institutions are debtors; (5) cases involving judicial review of arbitration of financial civil and commercial disputes; and (6) cases involving applications for recognition and enforcement of the judgments and rulings on financial civil and commercial disputes rendered by courts of Hong Kong Special Administrative Region, Macao Special Administrative Region and Taiwan region, and cases involving applications for recognition and enforcement of judgments and rulings on financial civil and commercial disputes rendered by foreign courts.[42] The above six categories of cases fall with normal and frequent financial or commercial cases. The separation of these cases from the jurisdiction of the immediate people's courts could help financial courts to specialize and focus on financial disputes.

It should be noted that Chinese financial courts also have jurisdiction over financial disputes that happened outside the territory of China. Financial courts will hear cases that (1) domestic investors with the regional financial court on the ground that the securities offerings or trading or futures trading activities that occur outside the territory of the People's Republic of China infringe upon their lawful rights and interests; and (2) domestic individuals or institutions with regional financial court on the ground that the financial products sold or financial services provided by financial institutions outside the territory of the People's Republic of China infringe upon their lawful rights and interests.[43] This clause recognizes the principle of territorial jurisdictional competence. It refers that if the appellants claim their damages in the territory of China, financial courts will have the competence to regulate the relevant conducts in question. It is viewed as an acknowledgement of territoriality of sovereignty.

Moreover, Shanghai Financial Court hear stock market related civil and commercial cases of disputes that in relation to the issuance of securities,

[42] Supra notes 40 and 41.
[43] Ibid.

disputes over securities underwriting contracts, disputes over securities listing sponsor contracts, disputes over securities listing contracts, and disputes over liability for securities fraud related to companies listed on the STAR market.[44] Beijing Financial Court exercises jurisdiction on first-instance civil and commercial cases related to securities issuance disputes, securities underwriting contract disputes, securities trading contract disputes, securities fraud liability disputes, as well as disputes arising from securities recommendation sponsorship and continuous supervision contracts, and disputes arising from securities listing contracts, involving companies that publicly issue stocks to non-specific qualified investors and are listed on the selected tier of the National Equities Exchange and Quotations (NEEQ) system for Small and Medium-sized Enterprises (SMEs).[45] Clearly, the geographical location of financial institutions plays an important role in determining the jurisdiction of the local financial courts. The Shanghai Stock Exchange being situated in Shanghai and NEEQ in Beijing aligns with the logical exercise of jurisdiction by the respective local financial courts. In the case of Chengyu Financial Court, lacking a local stock exchange, its jurisdiction extends to cases related to any legally established financial infrastructure institutions within the Chengdu-Chongqing Economic Circle, whether they are defendants or third parties.

Last but not least, financial courts accept and adjudicate stock market involved civil and commercial cases. Shanghai Financial Court exercises its power if the Shanghai Stock Exchange is the defendant or a third party and where the disputes involve the regulatory functions of the stock exchange.[46] Beijing Financial Court is responsible when NEEQ is the defendant or the third party and which are related to the regulatory functions of securities trading venues. Also, financial courts have jurisdiction over cases in relation to financial infrastructure institutions that legally formed and domiciled in regional municipality. If they are defendants or third parties and which are related to the performance of their respective functions shall be under original jurisdiction of the local financial court.

7.5.2 Category II: financial administrative cases

If one party in the dispute financial case plays an administrative role, financial courts can accept and adjudicate such cases. Shanghai Financial

[44] Ibid.
[45] Ibid.
[46] Ibid.

Court can hear financial-related administrative cases within the jurisdiction of Shanghai Municipality filed against administrative actions taken by financial regulators and organizations empowered by laws, regulations, and rules in performing their financial regulatory duties that shall be accepted by intermediate people's courts.[47] Beijing Financial Court can exercise its jurisdiction if the administrative actions taken by the People' Bank of China, the NAFR, the CSRC, the State Administration of Foreign Exchange and other financial management departments of the state and other component departments of the State Council and organizations empowered by laws, regulations, and rules for performance of financial regulatory duties.[48] Likewise, Chengyu Financial Court has jurisdiction over first-instance financial civil and commercial cases and financial administrative cases related to financial infrastructure institutions established in accordance with the law, with their place of residence located within Chongqing Municipality and Sichuan Province, which belong to the Chengdu-Chongqing Economic Circle.[49] Besides, the Chengyu Financial Court also hear first-instance administrative cases related to financial regulation, where the plaintiffs are dissatisfied with the administrative actions taken by financial regulatory institutions and organizations authorized by laws, regulations, and rules within the scope of the Chengdu-Chongqing Economic Circle, including Chongqing Municipality and Sichuan Province, which should be accepted by the intermediate people's court.

7.5.3 Category III: judgments, distributes and appeal or retrial petition

In the process of conducting appeal or retrial petition, financial courts will accept and adjudicate cases filed against judgments or rulings rendered by the basic people's courts on cases of first instance.[50] In the case of retrial, the retrial of financial civil and commercial cases and financial-related administrative cases within the jurisdiction of regional Municipality that shall be accepted by intermediate people's courts. When enforcing the effective judgments, financial courts will hear first instance and financial-related administrative cases and commercial disputes within the

[47] Ibid.
[48] Ibid.
[49] Ibid.
[50] Ibid.

jurisdiction of local Municipality that shall be enforced by intermediate people's courts.[51] Additionally, they also exercise jurisdiction over enforcement objection cases and cases involving enforcement objection actions arising during the enforcement by the Shanghai or Beijing Financial Court and the enforcement reconsideration cases and cases of appeals against enforcement objection actions arising during the enforcement of financial-related cases by the basic people's courts of Shanghai or Beijing Municipality.[52] In the process of appeal matters, cases that filed by the parties against the first-instance judgments or rulings rendered by the regional financial courts shall be heard by local Higher People's Courts. Former cases that have been accepted by intermediate people's courts of local Municipality before the establishment of the Shanghai or Beijing Financial Court but not yet concluded shall continue to be heard by such intermediate people's courts.

7.5.4 Summary of the jurisdiction of financial courts

Table 7.1 provides a summary of the jurisdiction of the three financial courts in China. The Supreme People's Court categorizes traditionally accepted financial-related cases within the civil tribunal divisions of intermediate courts. Clear jurisdiction for financial courts is essential for several reasons. First, the complexity and diversity of financial activities, including emerging practices like cryptocurrencies, necessitate specialized knowledge that traditional courts may lack. Financial courts, therefore, have the authority to handle these cases. Second, the explicit guidance on jurisdiction from the People's Supreme Court distinguishes financial courts from local intermediate people's courts, optimizing judicial resources and efficiency. Finally, the establishment of financial courts responds to the dynamic economic and social landscape, and sharing jurisdictional arrangements among them facilitates efficiency and consistency. Although the Supreme People's Court has not issued specific guidance on Chengyu Financial Court's jurisdiction, it can draw from the experiences of Shanghai Financial Court and Beijing Financial Court, ensuring a smooth and timely initiation of its operations. This interplay of experience-sharing ensures

[51] Ibid.
[52] Ibid.

Table 7.1 Overview of jurisdiction of Shanghai, Beijing, and Chengyu Financial Courts

<table>
<tr><th></th><th></th><th>Shanghai Financial Court</th><th>Beijing Financial Court</th><th>Chengyu Financial Court</th></tr>
<tr><td rowspan="5">Financial civil or commercial cases</td><td>Within the jurisdiction of local municipality that shall be accepted by intermediate people's courts</td><td colspan="3">Financial civil and commercial disputes over:
(1) financial products;
(2) capital markets;
(3) financial institutions;
(4) bankruptcy disputes;
(5) judicial review of arbitration; and
(6) applications for recognition and enforcement of the judgments and rulings in Hong Kong, Macao, and Taiwan.</td></tr>
<tr><td>Financial disputes, including lawsuits filed by</td><td colspan="3">(1) trade activities that occur outside China that infringe domestic investors; and
(2) financial products sold or financial services provided by financial institutions outside China that infringe domestic individuals or institutions.</td></tr>
<tr><td>Stock market related civil and commercial cases of disputes</td><td>Related to STAR market</td><td>Related to NEEQ</td><td>n/a</td></tr>
<tr><td>Stock market involved civil and commercial cases</td><td>Related to the Shanghai Stock Exchange</td><td>Related to NEEQ</td><td>n/a</td></tr>
<tr><td>Financial infrastructure institutions involved civil and commercial cases</td><td>Yes</td><td>Yes</td><td>Yes</td></tr>
<tr><td>Financial administrative cases</td><td>Financial regulators and organizations</td><td>Yes</td><td>The People's Bank of China, the National Administration of Financial Regulation, the China Securities Regulatory Commission, the State Administration of Foreign Exchange</td><td>Yes</td></tr>
</table>

		Shanghai Financial Court	Beijing Financial Court	Chengyu Financial Court
Judgments, distributes and appeal or retrial petition	Appeal or retrial petition	As set out in Supreme People's Courts' guideline		
	Retrial	Yes	Yes	Yes
	Enforce the effective judgments	Yes	Yes	Yes
	Appeals	Yes	Yes	Yes
	Former cases	Yes	Yes	Yes

Source: The table is compiled by the author.

that subsequent financial courts can always refer to existing structures for guidance.

7.6 Case studies and the latest judicial practices of financial courts

Since their establishment, the financial courts have assumed a crucial role in resolving disputes associated with China's financial markets and financial institutions. From August 2018 to December 2021, the Shanghai Financial Court handled a total of 23,456 cases and successfully resolved 22,033 of them, resulting in a case closure rate of 93%.[53] The Beijing Financial Court heard a total of 6,275 cases during a one-year period, covering the period from March 2021 to March 2022.[54] Among these cases, approximately 71% were categorized as financial civil or commercial cases. From March to December 2022, Beijing Financial Court received 13,259 cases and successfully concluded 11,274 of them, indicating a closure rate of 85%.[55] Each judge at the Beijing Financial Court successfully handled an average of 403 cases, showcasing both the substantial workload and impressive efficiency of the court. Chengyu Financial Court heard its first case on 3 January 2023.[56] The

[53] Shanghai Financial Court, 'Work report on trial activities of from 2018 to 2021', http://61.129.132.51/jrfy/gweb/xx_view.jsp?pa=aaWQ9NjU0OAPdcssPdcssz.

[54] Beijing Politics & Law, 'One-year overview of Beijing Financial Court with 6,275 cases' (24 March 2022), https://www.bj148.org/ztk/2022nzt/bjjrfyyzn_202009/ttxw/202203/t20220329_1630981.html.

[55] QianLong, 'The performance of Beijing Financial Court' (31 December 2021), https://beijing.qianlong.com/2022/1231/7945973.shtml.

[56] Chengdu-Chongqing Financial Court, 'The full launch of Chengyu Financial Court, outlook oriental by Xinhua News Agency' (28 January 2023), http://cyjrfy.cqfygzfw.gov.cn/article/detail/2023/01/id/7113102.shtml.

following are leading cases selected by Shanghai Financial Court and Beijing Financial Court to guide the further financial practices, which will be discussed to understand the latest judicial practices in resolving financial law disputes.

7.6.1 Xu et al. v. Shanghai Potevio Co., Ltd. [2020] Shanghai Financial Court

In financial law cases, misrepresentation and insider dealing frequently happened that often associated with huge economic loss. Misrepresentation can be interpreted as a false representation of material facts, which is misleading or untrue. This statement is used knowingly by one party to induce another party who relies on such a representation and then enters the contract. The case of *Xu et al. v. Shanghai Potevio Co., Ltd.* was selected by Shanghai Financial Court as an example to address issues related to misrepresentation in Chinese context.[57] This is a case concerning misrepresentation in the securities market between investors (the plaintiffs) and Potevio (the defendant), a listed company in Shanghai Stock Exchange. Plaintiffs bought shares of the defendant but suffered financial losses. Plaintiffs attributed the losses to the misrepresentation of information disclosed by the defendant. The defendant disagreed and responded that the investment of plaintiffs was not triggered by the information disclosed by the defendant because the plaintiff bought purchased Potevio shares from the commission date to the exposure date who continued buying in shares after the exposure of the misrepresentation. Therefore, according to the defendant whether the misrepresentation had occurred did not affect the two investors' decision-making.

The Court identified a number of critical issues in this case's first hearing: (1) the identification of the exposure date, base date, and base price; (2) the causal link between purchase the share and the misrepresentation; (3) the causal link between losses and misrepresentation; and (4), the difference between damage and investment losses.[58] First, the court found that the exposure date was meant to send sufficient warning signals to the securities market to remind investors of re-evaluating stocks, and this date carried out the function of cutting off transaction causation. Further, whether the exposure had a substantial impact on securities transactions

[57] Xu et al. v. Shanghai Potevio Co., Ltd. concerning Dispute over Liability for Misrepresentation in the Securities Market, Shanghai Financial Court, 11 June 2020, case report: http://61.129.132.51/jrfy/English/news_view.jsp?pa=aaWQ9NTAwNQPdcssPdcssz.

[58] Ibid.

should be considered. Second, according to 'presumed reliance' principle, it should be presumed that investors trading shares during the period when the market was affected by the misrepresentation were induced to trade shares in reliance on such misrepresentation, and that their transactions were causally connected to such misrepresentation.[59] Third, according to the Supreme People's Court's Misrepresentation Provisions, if it is proved that the losses are in whole or in part caused by the systemic risks of the securities market, it should be determined that there is no causation between the misrepresentation and such losses.[60] Finally, the Court appointed a professional institution as an assessor to determine the damages for plaintiffs' losses of investment difference. The Shanghai Financial Court found the defendant liable for plaintiffs' allegation. However, the defendant refused to accept the above judgment and appealed to Shanghai People's High Court. Shanghai People's High Court dismissed the appeal and affirmed the judgment of the first instance by adding there was causation between the misrepresentation and the losses suffered by investors by referring to Articles 18 and 19 of the Misrepresentation Provisions as well as confirmed there was no mistake in loss assessment. Evidently, misrepresentation is a complicated issue in practice. Shanghai Financial Court by carefully drafting its judgment gives an example of how to interpret the Trial of Civil Cases for Damages for the Tort of Misrepresentation, which is a clear guidance in solving disputes in financial activities.

7.6.2 Jiang et al. vs. China Securities Regulatory Commission Xiamen Office and China Securities Regulatory Commission [2022] Beijing Financial Court

Jiang vs. CSRC is the case concerning the recognition of insider information which is a common offence in securities markets.[61] Insider information or insider trading involves making trading decisions based on non-public

[59] See, for example, Supreme People's Court, 'Several provisions of the Supreme People's Court on the trial of civil cases for damages for the tort of misrepresentation in the securities market' (2022), http://www.lawinfochina.com/display.aspx?id=37627&lib=law.

[60] Ibid., Article 19.

[61] Jiang et al. vs. China Securities Regulatory Commission Xiamen Office and China Securities Regulatory Commission on the Confiscation of Illegal Gains, Fines, and Administrative Reconsideration, Beijing Financial Court (19 October 2022).

information.[62] If such information were made to the public, it could have significant impacts on the price of the financial instrument in question. In the Chinese context, as per the Beijing Financial Court, insider trading is considered a violation of the principles of openness, fairness, and impartiality in the securities market. It is seen as a serious disruption to market trading order, interference with market functions, and an infringement upon the legitimate rights and interests of investors.[63] The rationale for dealing with insider information, according to the Beijing Financial Court, is that securities regulatory institutions may, in accordance with laws, determine whether non-public information that has a significant impact on a listed company falls within the scope of insider information.

In this case, CSRC Xiamen Office made the sued penalty decision that 'X holding group is the controlling shareholder of a listed chemical company, and holds in total more than 30% of the shares of a listed environmental company through direct and indirect shareholding'.[64] The holding group faced a debt crisis as its failure in issuing RMB 1.2 billion of the super-short-term commercial papers which caused the suspension of its stock trading. Later, the statement of the control of the company may change as long as the holding group was unable to properly handle its debt repayment made by the chemical company and the environmental company, respectively. Jiang, who attended the company's management meetings, learnt about the sensitive information and cashed out over RMB 8.15 million and avoided a loss of over RMB 3.36 million.[65] Zhu interacted with relevant insiders and cashed out over RMB 11.37 million and avoided a loss of over RMB 4.72 million.[66] The CSRC Xiamen Office made the sued penalty decision on the basis of Jiang and Zhu committing insider trading which was refused by Jiang and Zhu. Jiang and Zhu then filed a lawsuit with the Primary People's Court of Xicheng District of Beijing Municipality which entered a judgment to dismiss the claims of Jiang and Zhu after trial. Jiang and Zhu still refused to accept the judgment and appealed to the Beijing Financial Court. The Beijing Financial Court held the decision from Xiamen Office 'that the "major debt crisis" matter with the possibility of triggering a change of control of the environmental

[62] Harry McVea, 'What's Wrong With Insider Dealing?' (1995) 15 *Legal Studies* 390–414.

[63] Jiang et al. vs. China Securities Regulatory Commission Xiamen Office and China Securities Regulatory Commission on the Confiscation of Illegal Gains, Fines, and Administrative Reconsideration, Beijing Financial Court (19 October 2022); Beijing Financial Court, '"Major debt crisis" matter that may trigger a change in the controlling right of a company shall be regarded as insider' (19 October 2022), https://bjfc.bjcourt.gov.cn/cac/1666162394152.html.

[64] Ibid.

[65] Ibid.

[66] Ibid.

company and the chemical company shall be regarded as insider information before its disclosure in accordance with the law'.[67] Insider information is complicated in its sources and diversified in its transmission channels. Therefore, it is of necessity and importance for the court to clarify determination rules and applicable standards. In this sense, this case is of great significance. On the one hand, it affirms the principle that the securities regulatory institution enjoys the capability to determine what is insider information. On the other hand, it draws a conclusion on how to recognize insider information, stating that any major debt crisis matter that may trigger a change of control of a company shall be regulated as insider information prior to its disclosure in accordance with the law.

7.6.3 Selected cases heard by Chengyu Financial Court

Due to the relatively short history of operation, Chengyu Financial Court has not published its judgments on the cases that it heard. However, we could find some selected cases from the news reports covered by Xinhua News Agency. The first case of the first instance was heard in Chengyu Financial Court's Chengdu office. This case was concerning false statement in capital market.[68] The plaintiff is an investor who buys and sells shares in the Chinese stock market, while the defendant is a company limited by shares listed on the Shanghai Stock Exchange. As this company has registered its domicile in Suining City, Sichuan Province, Chengyu Financial Court has jurisdiction over this case. The plaintiff brought a lawsuit to the court on the grounds that the defendant's false statements caused investment losses, demanding that the defendant compensate its investment, commission, stamp duty, and other losses with a total amount of more than RMB 240,000.[69] This case was submitted from the online platform, with the mission from the court that to facilitate financial services. The first case of the second instance case was heard in Chongqing office, which disputes over a financial loan contract.[70] In the first instance, a bank sued and asked the borrower, Mr. Peng, to return the loan principal, interest, and attorney fees incurred in realizing the creditor's rights. After the first-instance judgment was made, a bank

[67] Ibid.

[68] Chengdu-Chongqing Financial Court, 'The full launch of Chengyu Financial Court, outlook oriental by Xinhua News Agency' (28 January 2023), http://cyjrfy.cqfygzfw.gov.cn/article/detail/2023/01/id/7113102.shtml.

[69] Ibid.

[70] Ibid.

believed that the first-instance judgment only recognized the lawyer's fee as RMB 4,000 which actually paid in the previous period, and it was an error for not recognizing the risk agency fee as agreed in the 'Entrustment Agency Agreement' into the lawyer's fee. Therefore, this bank appealed to Chengyu Financial Court with the claim of more than RMB 12,000 as the lawyer's fee.[71]

7.7 Conclusion

This chapter has examined China's new financial law courts, as it is an important decision made by the SCNPC to address the challenges and advancements in modern financial activities. It is undoubtedly a judicial innovation that addresses the evolving demands of the court system and the rapidly developing financial sector, given that China now has the largest banking industry and capital markets in the world. Before the official introduction of financial courts, the legislator considered the opinions of experts and legal scholars, as well as the voices within the judicial system and the financial industry. This comprehensive approach ensured that the establishment of financial courts incorporated valuable insights from various stakeholders, thereby enhancing the effectiveness of the judicial innovation. The launch of three financial courts in Shanghai, Beijing, and Chengdu-Chongqing tended out to be a great success as they have been dealing with tens of thousands of financial law cases each year. Leading cases on financial disputes have been published by financial courts to provide a guidance for judicial practices across the country to ensure the consistent treatment of similar commercial disputes in banking, securities, and insurance. It offers a valuable lesson for other countries in resolving commercial disputes effectively.

In China's judicial system, the establishment of financial courts, as the third category of specialized courts, brings about significant changes by providing the financial sector with dedicated expertise in case filing, hearing, and enforcement. This development contributes to a more rational, efficient, and professional court system in China. From the perspective of the financial sector, having a specialized financial court better aligns with the trend of the rapidly evolving financial industry, with judges who possess specialized knowledge and skills in the financial sector. The creation of special financial courts also reflects the proactive efforts of the Chinese authority to effectively

[71] Ibid.

respond to economic and social development. By recognizing the significance of financial activities in the modern economy and society, financial courts enhance legal protection, fostering trust, and facilitating fair dispute resolution in the financial sector. This, in turn, has positive impacts on the Chinese socialist market economy by promoting a conducive environment for conducting financial and commercial activities, encouraging financial innovation, and bolstering the confidence of participants in its dynamic financial industry.

Chapter 8
The internationalization of China's financial industry

8.1 Introduction

Chapter 8 considers how China's financial industry embarks on the road to internationalization. The level of internationalization is an important indicator of a financial superpower. All the leading financial centres in the world, such as London, New York, Frankfurt, Paris, Singapore, and Dubai, are known for their interconnectedness and attraction for global talents and capital. From the discussion in the previous chapters, we can conclude that China's financial industry is vast and well-developed at the domestic level. From the banking industry to capital markets to the latest in Fintech and CBDC, China is a leading player. Moreover, the country has built a modern financial regulatory architecture to effectively perform the regulatory tasks, as well as a financial safety net to deal with the potential crises. China has launched the specialized financial courts, as a judicial innovation, to better handle the financial law cases. Therefore, in terms of both the industry practices and the legal and regulatory environments, China's financial industry has made considerable progress in the first two decades of the twenty-first century.

The next step for China's financial industry is to increase its international connectiveness, competitiveness, and influence. That is the key to make China a true financial superpower at the international level. It will also make Beijing, Shanghai, Shenzhen, and other Chinese cities the top-tier financial centres in the world. Against this background, Chapter 8 discusses China's latest efforts to promote the internationalization of its financial industry by using some case studies of its financial industry practices and relevant regulatory reforms. Section 8.2 introduces the latest development of China's leading international financial centres (i.e. Beijing, Shanghai, and Shenzhen) and outlines their competitive advantages. Section 8.3 examines the Chinese depositary receipt (CDR) for overseas-listed corporations to obtain a secondary listing in mainland China. Section 8.4 assesses China's stock connect

Towards Financial Superpower. Lerong Lu, Oxford University Press. © Lerong Lu (2025).
DOI: 10.1093/9780198948568.003.0008

schemes linked with overseas stock exchanges to allow investors and corporations in both countries to access each other's capital markets. Section 8.5 analyses the cross-border supervision under the PRC Securities Law 2020. Section 8.6 draws a conclusion for the chapter as well as for the book and attempts to answer if and when China is becoming a financial superpower.

8.2 China's international financial centres

China's financial industry has become more internationalized over the past two decades (2000–2020), through the deepened reform and opening up of its banking sector, capital markets, and other segments of the financial industry. From Table 8.1, we can observe that China has four cities that are ranked within the top fifteen global financial centres, judging by their financial infrastructure, talent reserve, market dynamism, and regulatory frameworks. They are Hong Kong (no. 4), Shanghai (no. 6), Shenzhen (no. 11), and Beijing (no. 15). It is a remarkable achievement given that China only started its market-based economic reform in the late 1970s and opened its capital markets in early 1990s. Only the United States has more top global financial centres on the list (occupying five spots on the top fifteen list), including

Table 8.1 Global financial centres ranking (2024)

Global Financial Centre	Ranking	Rating	Change in Ranking
New York	1	764	0
London	2	747	0
Singapore	3	742	0
Hong Kong	4	741	0
San Francisco	5	740	0
Shanghai	6	739	▲1
Geneva	7	738	▲3
Los Angeles	8	737	▼2
Chicago	9	736	0
Seoul	10	735	▲1
Shenzhen	11	734	▲1
Washington DC	12	733	▼4
Frankfurt	13	732	▲1
Paris	14	731	▲1
Beijing	15	730	▼2

Source: Z/Yen Partners 'The Global Financial Centres Index 35'.

New York, San Francisco, Los Angeles, Chicago, and Washington DC. Most other highly developed countries have only one leading financial centre, such as London in the United Kingdom, Singapore as a city-state, Geneva in Switzerland, Seoul in South Korea, Frankfurt in Germany, and Paris in France.

Let us just focus on three top financial centres in mainland China as they have different expertise and competitive advantages.[1] Beijing is the capital city of China, and it is country's political, economic, educational, and cultural centre. Beijing houses the head offices of all the financial regulatory agencies that we discussed before, including the central bank (PBoC), the banking and insurance regulator (NFRA), the securities regulator (CSRC), and the State Administration of Foreign Exchange. All the industry policies and regulatory guidelines have been made in Beijing before being implemented across China. Moreover, the headquarters of the largest state-owned financial institutions are mostly in Beijing, including the big four banks. The regulatory agencies and headquarters of financial firms are clustered in the central Beijing, in particular, the Beijing Financial Street. Beijing Financial Street is considered the hub of China's financial industry, with its financial institutions holding a combined RMB 99.5 trillion in assets, representing 40% of the country's total financial holdings.[2]

Moreover, Beijing now has the latest stock exchange—Beijing Stock Exchange (BSE)—that accepts the listing of high-tech and specialized enterprises in the country. The Beijing Stock Exchange has addressed the gap of Beijing's financial industry which did not have a capital market for many decades compared with the more developed stock exchanges in Shanghai and Shenzhen. Beijing is also the headquarter of Asian Infrastructure Investment Bank (AIIB) which is a multilateral development bank and international financial institution dedicated to enhancing economic and social outcomes in Asia by financing infrastructure projects.[3] Clearly, AIIB showcases China's ambition to become a financial superpower as it has the AIIB to challenge the US-backed international financial institutions like the World Bank and International Monetary Fund. The AIIB also supports China's 'one belt, one road' initiative as a global infrastructure development project through Asia, Europe, and Africa. If China successfully becomes a financial superpower, Beijing will serve as the brain of this new superpower.

[1] For the strength of China's leading financial centres, especially their Fintech capacity, see Lerong Lu, *Global Fintech Revolution: Practice, Policy, and Regulation* (Oxford University Press, 2024), p. 52.

[2] 'Beijing Financial Street financial institutions asset scale is approaching RMB100 trillion', *ChinaNews* (29 April 2018), http://www.chinanews.com/fortune/2018/04-29/8503009.shtml.

[3] Asian Infrastructure Investment Bank (AIIB), https://www.aiib.org/en/index.html.

Shanghai is the top financial centre in mainland China in terms of capital markets. It ranks much higher than Beijing and Shenzhen as a hub for international businesses and financial institutions. The Shanghai Stock Exchange (SSE) ranks as the fourth largest stock market globally, with a total market capitalization of listed companies worth $4.59 trillion.[4] The latest star market (sci-tech innovation board) further enhances the SSE's leading position as the top platform for the listing of innovative and technological enterprises in China and beyond. Shanghai has over 1,600 financial institutions and is often the first choice for foreign institutions establishing their initial Chinese office. Shanghai is not only a key centre for securities transactions but also the hub for RMB product-dominated financial markets. As China promotes the global usage of its currency, including both physical RMB and the future CBDC, Shanghai is poised to assume a strategic position for RMB-denominated financial products. In 2023, Shanghai's financial markets achieved a record total trading volume of RMB 3,373.6 trillion.[5] The city's RMB cross-border settlement surpassed RMB 20 trillion, representing over 40% of the national total and maintaining its leading position in China.[6] As China is marching towards financial superpower, Shanghai will continue its strong position as a world top financial centre and could even challenge the top three financial centres (New York, London, and Singapore) due to its international reputation and increasing strength in securities listing, trading, and RMB products.

Shenzhen is a young city which developed from a little fishing town since the late 1970s when China started its economic reform. Now it has become the China's prime technological centre with over twelve million population. Shenzhen is the headquarter for many world-class technology companies, such as Huawei, Tencent, and BYD. The city is a global centre of electronics design and manufacturing, producing the most advanced consumer electronic products like smartphones and electric vehicles. Shenzhen is often called the Silicon Valley of China given its successful technological firms and entrepreneurial culture. Nonetheless, Shenzhen is also a leading financial centre thanks to the city's Shenzhen Stock Exchange (SZSE) and private equity firms. SZSE is the world's no. 8 largest stock exchange having a total

[4] Hong Kong Securities and Futures Commission, 'Market capitalisation of the world's top stock exchanges' (September 2019), http://www.sfc.hk/web/EN/files/SOM/MarketStatistics/a01.pdf.

[5] Shanghai Government, 'This is Shanghai—International Financial Center', https://english.shanghai.gov.cn/en-ThisisShanghai/20231207/9815a792b25f4c43bc1bbe69f61a817a.html.

[6] Ibid.

market capitalization of over $3.02 trillion.[7] As China is on its way to become a financial superpower, Shenzhen is likely to be a leading Fintech centre globally with both its high-tech industry and dynamic stock trading and investment opportunities.

8.3 Case study: Chinese depositary receipt (CDR)

This section analyses the reform of listing rules in China to further the goal of making its capital markets more international, focusing on the operating mechanism of the CDR. Most technology giants in mainland China, such as Alibaba, Tencent, Baidu, JD, and NetEase have listed their shares on overseas stock markets such as Hong Kong and New York, in order to avoid China's rigid and onerous listing rules concerning foreign ownership, variable interest entities (VIEs), weighted voting rights, and the strict profitability requirement. The China Securities Regulatory Commission (CSRC) has launched a pilot project to allow certain foreign-listed Chinese companies to issue CDRs which can be traded in the Shanghai and Shenzhen stock exchanges. Technically speaking, CDRs are not shares but they represent equity interests in foreign companies through an offshore custodian bank. The popularization of CDRs will benefit several parties. Chinese investors will be able to purchase interests in some of the top tech companies in the world. It will also lure international capital to the Chinese market and boost the valuation of issuing companies. The market scale of CDRs is estimated to be over $1 trillion, which will be a source of income for investment banks and international law firms.

8.3.1 Why did Chinese tech companies list shares overseas?

Since the early 1990s, China has established a multi-tier capital market consisting of national stock exchanges (Shanghai, Shenzhen, Beijing stock exchanges), national OTC markets (NEEQ), and regional OTC markets (equity exchange centres in each province). In total, there are over 5,000 public companies listed on the Chinese stock exchanges. Recent years have seen a high level of volatility in China's stock markets. The SSE Composite Index jumped from 2,000 points in July 2014 to a peak of 5,166.35 points in June

[7] Hong Kong Securities and Futures Commission, 'Market capitalisation of the world's top stock exchanges' (September 2019), http://www.sfc.hk/web/EN/files/SOM/MarketStatistics/a01.pdf.

2015, triggering an equity bubble that drew millions of investors to take a bet on the bullish trend.[8] However, it has been followed by a major correction and a slip into bear market territory. From 2016 to 2024, the SSE fluctuated around 3,000 points.

After a four-decade period of rapid economic growth, China now hosts some of the largest and most well-known companies in the world. For example, Alibaba, the global e-commerce giant, and Tencent, a leading social networking and online gaming company, have been included in the list of top ten most valuable brands in the world along with US companies like Google, Apple, Amazon, Microsoft, Facebook, Visa, McDonald's, and AT&T.[9] Despite the thriving stock markets, a considerable number of Chinese companies, especially high-tech firms, have chosen to list their shares overseas to avoid the legal and technical barriers to IPOs they would encounter on the mainland, as well as to gain access to international capital. The primary concern of listing overseas is centred on the registered place and foreign shareholders.

Many high-tech companies have adopted a VIE as their legal business structure. VIEs enable foreign investors to get around Beijing's restriction of foreign ownership in companies in certain industries such as the internet, finance, and education. Chinese law does not permit foreign capital to own a majority stake in internet companies. However, internet companies often raise considerable funds from foreign venture capital funds and private equity funds. For example, two of the largest shareholders of Alibaba are Softbank (Japan) and Yahoo (United States). VIE, therefore, evades the ownership limitation and allows tech firms to acquire capital from international investors. The tech firms' offshore parent companies domiciled in the Cayman Islands, British Virgin Islands, and other offshore financial centres enter a series of contracts replicating the ownership in China's operating companies.[10] However, such contractual control is inferior to proprietary rights in the event of litigation, arbitration, or insolvency proceedings. In 2014, Alibaba decided to list its shares in New York partly because its use of VIE had not been accepted by the Chinese regulators. Aside from Alibaba, other tech giants like Baidu, Tencent, Youku, and Sohu have all employed the VIE structure, and therefore, can only list shares in overseas markets, predominantly, Hong Kong and New York.

[8] Lerong Lu and Longjie Lu, 'Unveiling China's Stock Market Bubble: Margin Financing, the Leveraged Bull and Governmental Responses' (2017) 32 *Journal of International Banking Law and Regulation* 146 at 147.

[9] David Meyer, 'China now has 2 of the top 10 most valuable brands in the world for the first time', *Fortune* (29 May 2018), http://fortune.com/2018/05/29/chinese-brands-alibaba-tencent-brandz/.

[10] Charles Clover, 'Alibaba IPO shows foreign investors able to skirt restrictions', *Financial Times* (7 May 2014), http://www.ft.com/content/7a8c4816-d5df-11e3-a017-00144feabdc0.

Another controversial issue lies in the dual-class share structure (DCSS), also known as the weighted voting right. Class A shares that are sold to public investors will grant their holders one vote per share, while Class B shares that are held by company executives and private equity investors carry ten votes per share. This practice of using dual-class shares is against the traditional 'one share, one vote' principle in company law. The structure benefits the founders of tech firms who will have absolute controlling power over their companies despite not having the majority of shares. Dual-class shares have been widely used by American and Chinese tech companies, such as Google, Facebook, and Snap Inc. Richard Qiangdong Liu, the founder and chairman of Nasdaq-listed JD, a leading online B2C shopping portal, owns only 23.7% of shares in JD but has more than 80% of voting rights.[11] Although the dual-share structure is beneficial for the founders of companies, it prejudices the interests of ordinary shareholders and has raised concerns over the abuse of management power. The advocates of such a structure praise it for allowing founders to resist short-termism and to defend hostile takeover bids. For a long time, the Shanghai and Shenzhen stock exchanges did not permit the dual-class structure and consequently had lost the listing of several tech firms to the New York Stock Exchange and Nasdaq. Currently, London, Hong Kong, and Singapore have been considering introducing dual-class shares as they fear losing their prestigious status as global financial centres, and especially, in terms of attracting IPO business.[12]

Moreover, China's listing rules have been particularly strict about the issuer's profitability for decades. The PRC Securities Law (before the recent amendment) required that a company that plans to issue new shares to the public needs to demonstrate sustained profitability and good financial health.[13] The CSRC's IPO regulation further demanded that the issuer must make positive profits for the three consecutive accounting years prior to the IPO, and the accumulated profits should exceed CNY30 million.[14] In contrast, the listing rules in the United States are more lax in relation to a company's profitability. Amazon has made no profits for most quarters over its two-decade trading history.[15] Also, the electric car-marker Tesla made a series of losses after its listing.

[11] *Xinhua*, 'Tencent become the largest shareholder in JD, Liu Qiangdong still has the controlling power' (23 August 2016), http://xinhuanet.com/tech/2016-08/23/c_1119438207.htm.

[12] Fa Chen, 'Does the Dual-Class Share Structure Help Stock Markets Attract Issuers? Empirical Lessons from Global Financial Centres' (2023) 43 *Legal Studies* 159–178.

[13] PRC Securities Law 2014, Article 13(2).

[14] CSRC, *Measures for the Administration of Initial Public Offering and Listing of Stocks* (2006), Article 33(1).

[15] Jon Markman, 'The Amazon Era: No profits, no problem', *Forbes* (23 May 2017), http://www.forbes.com/sites/jonmarkman/2017/05/23/the-amazon-era-no-profits-no-problem/.

8.3.2 How do CDRs work?

CDRs are modelled on similar financial instruments such as American Depositary Receipts (ADRs) and European Depositary Receipts (EDRs) which enable US and European investors to purchase the shares of foreign incorporated companies. Depositary receipts originated in the United States in the 1920s. Under a depositary receipt arrangement, a portion of the issuing company's shares will be transferred to a custodian bank serving as the broker. The custodian bank will then sell the shares to investors on a stock exchange outside of the country of incorporation. Technically speaking, depositary receipts are not shares. They represent equity interests in foreign companies and allow investors to hold shares through the custodian bank. CDRs are the certificates issued by the custodian bank denoting a pool of foreign equities that will be traded on the Shanghai and Shenzhen stock exchanges. Figure 8.1 illustrates how CDRs operate in practice with the involvement of the issuer, custodian bank, depository bank, and securities brokers. The objective of issuing CDRs is to lure capital back to the Chinese market to drive economic growth and push forward capital market reform. It will be a convenient method for overseas-listed Chinese companies to dual-list their shares in mainland China with minimal regulatory intervention.

In addition, the issuance of CDRs will give Chinese residents more investment opportunities to purchase shares in some top-tier companies around the world. The potential market scale of CDRs could surpass $1 trillion. As well as serving listed companies, CDRs will also be utilized by unlisted tech unicorns (a tech start-up with a valuation over $1 billion). As of May 2024, there are 1,240 unicorn companies in the world with a combined valuation of $3.91 trillion.[16] The United States has 665 unicorns, while China has over 150 unicorns including Ant Group. All of these unicorns could be potential issuers of CDRs.

8.3.3 The regulation of CDR issuance

In March 2018, the CSRC formally published *Opinions for Developing Creative Enterprise Domestic IPO and Pilot Project of Chinese Depositary Receipts* ('Opinions'), which targets red-chip enterprises and innovative unicorn

[16] CB Insights, 'The complete list of unicorn companies', http://www.cbinsights.com/research-unicorn-companies.

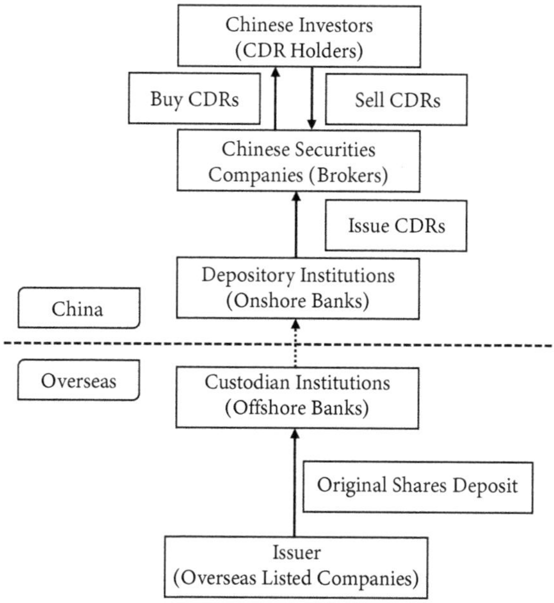

Figure 8.1 The operating mechanism of Chinese depositary receipt
Source: This figure is compiled by the author.

enterprises in high-tech industries or other emerging industries of strategic importance. It offers such businesses a dual-financing channel to trade on mainland China's stock exchanges. Red-chip enterprises refer to companies that have registered outside the territory of China but their businesses are primarily conducted within China. The pilot CDR projects have to adhere to four principles: serving the national strategy, observing existing laws and regulations, developing orderly and steadily, as well as preventing and controlling risks (protecting the benefits of small and medium investors, strengthening supervision, maintaining financial stability, and curtailing systemic risks).[17]

The *Opinions* put forward strict thresholds to filter prospective issuers. Issuing companies should conduct businesses in line with the national strategy, master core technologies, receive wide market recognition, and their businesses should fall into the following categories:

- Internet;
- Big data;

[17] CSRC, *Opinions for Developing Creative Enterprise Domestic IPO and Pilot Project of Chinese Depositary Receipts* (2018), Part 2.

- Cloud computing;
- Artificial intelligence;
- Software and integrated circuits;
- High-end equipment manufacturing;
- Biomedical science; and
- Other high-tech companies, strategically emerging enterprises, and innovative enterprises that reach certain market scales.[18]

Red-chip enterprises that have already listed in foreign stock exchanges, in light of the *Opinions*, should have a market value of at least 200 billion yuan to be qualified as a CDR issuer. For unlisted innovating enterprises including red-chip enterprises and enterprises that have registered domestically, these have to satisfy two conditions. The annual operation revenue of an innovating enterprise should be no less than CNY3 billion while the valuation of the innovating enterprise should be no less than CNY20 billion. An enterprise which meets the criteria of having a fast-growing amount of revenue, owning self-developed and internationally advanced technology, and having a comparatively dominant position in the industry will be considered by the CSRC which will form an advisory panel to assess its eligibility.

Issuing entities, apart from satisfying the basic listing rules, have to comply with the following requirements:

- The shareholding structure, corporate governance code, and operating specification can comply with the company law and relevant regulation in the jurisdiction where the issuer is incorporated, but the overall level of investor protection rules should be at least the same level of relevant rules under Chinese law; and
- If there exist weighted voting rights, the VIE, and other special arrangements, relevant risks and corporate governance issues should be sufficiently disclosed in the main sections of the prospectus of the company issuing new shares. Relevant methods to protect the interests of investors should also be addressed.[19]

In June 2018, after soliciting public opinion, the CSRC officially released *Measures for the Issuance and Trading of Chinese Depositary Receipts*.[20]

[18] CSRC, *Opinions for Developing Creative Enterprise Domestic IPO and Pilot Project of Chinese Depositary Receipts* (2018), Part 3.
[19] CSRC, *Opinions for Developing Creative Enterprise Domestic IPO and Pilot Project of Chinese Depositary Receipts* (2018), Part 5.
[20] Shenliang Liu, 'The CSRC promulgated rules on CDRs at 6 June 2018', *Xinhua* (6 June 2018), http://www.xinhuanet.com/fortune/2018-06/08/c_1122954412.htm.

Its promulgation was based on the *Opinions*, PRC Securities Law, and PRC Securities Investment Fund Law. The *Measures* further explain the policy regarding the issuance and trading of CDRs. The issuance of CDRs is considered a new IPO and the issuer has to satisfy the following requirements:

- Article 13 (1) (2) (3) of PRC Securities Law (the issuer must have a complete and well-operated organizational structure, having the capability of making profits continuously and sound financial health, and not have false records in its financial statements over the past three years and other illegal activities);
- The issuer is a legally incorporated entity that has been operating continuously for over three years. There must be no ownership disputes of the company's major assets;
- The issuer has had the same actual controlling shareholders over the past three years with no significant ownership disputes among the shareholders;
- The issuer, its controlling shareholders, and actual controllers have not conducted illegal activities jeopardizing the benefits of investors or the public interest over the past three years;
- The issuer has adopted standardized accounting rules and a sound internal control system;
- Directors, auditors, and senior managers should have a good reputation, relevant qualifications, and good credit records; and
- Other regulations of the CSRC.

8.3.4 The first group of CDR issuers

Xiaomi is said to be the first company to issue CDRs. Xiaomi is a high-tech company producing smartphones, laptops, and other smart electronic devices. In June 2018, the CSRC released Xiaomi's CDR Prospectus which plans to raise \$5 billion from the sale of depositary receipts to Chinese investors.[21] According to the Prospectus, Xiaomi will be simultaneously listed on the Hong Kong and Shanghai stock exchanges. The issuance will be based upon Class B common stocks in Shanghai, whereas the number of shares has not yet been disclosed. In 2017, Xiaomi's annual revenue and net profit were CNY114.6 billion and CNY3.95 billion, respectively, which clearly satisfy the issuing standard set by the CSRC.

[21] CSRC, 'Xiaomi—The prospectus', http://www.csrc.gov.cn/pub/zjhpublic/G00306202/201806/P020180611106685793601.pdf.

Apart from Xiaomi, there is a further group of potential red-chip businesses which could be among the first cohort of CDR issuers as each of them has a market capitalization of over CNY200 billion: Tencent (Hong Kong-listed), Alibaba (New York), Baidu (Nasdaq), JD (Nasdaq), and NetEase (Nasdaq). There is no doubt that issuing CDRs will be beneficial for issuers, investors, investment banks, and commercial law firms. Issuers can raise further capital from the dual listing in China as well as gain a higher market valuation at home. Investors can purchase shares in high-quality companies. Thus, the overall structure of China's stock markets will be significantly improved. Moreover, it is predicted that CDR issuance will generate CNY2.9–5.7 billion annual income for investment banks.[22] Clearly, this is a golden opportunity for everyone, from issuing companies to investors and stock brokers.

8.4 Case study: stock connect schemes

This is the second study to assess China's recent reforms to improve the internationalization of its financial industry. It focuses on China's stock connect schemes cooperated with overseas stock exchanges (outside mainland China). It discusses the historical development, practices, and regulatory issues of such schemes.

8.4.1 What are the stock connect schemes?

In November 2014, China launched the first stock connect scheme to link the SSE with the Hong Kong Stock Exchange (HKEX), and then in 2016 another link between SZSE and HKEX was set up.[23] The stock connect programmes are considered an important reform measure to make the Chinese capital markets more international and open to foreign investments. They enable mainland Chinese investors to purchase select Hong Kong and Chinese companies listed in HKEX, while allowing foreign investors to buy China A shares listed on the mainland in a less restrictive manner than before. The stock connect schemes effectively create a unified Chinese stock market by linking the two largest stock exchanges in mainland China (SSE and SZSE) with Hong Kong, serving as China's window to the world. It creates a win-win situation

[22] *Caijing*, 'CDR will bring over 5bn revenue for securities brokers' (9 May 2018), http://stock.caijing.com.cn/20180509/4449705.shtml.

[23] Goldman Sachs, 'The stock connect' (December 2016), https://www.goldmansachs.com/intelligence/pages/stock-connect/.

for both Chinese and international investors. For international investors, the stock connect schemes have added more than 3,000 companies (those listed in SSE and SZSE) to their investable portfolio, increasing their opportunity to invest in the world's second-largest economy. Also, the schemes help Chinese investors expand their investment collections into companies listed in Hong Kong. It is likely to enhance the trading volume for dual-listed Chinese companies and increase the likelihood of Chinese shares being included in global benchmark stock indexes (e.g. MSCI index).

Following the successful pilot of stock connect schemes with Hong Kong, China has furthered the reform to increase its global connectiveness with leading stock exchanges outside China and Asia. The international stock connect schemes allow Chinese public companies to issue Global Depository Receipts (GDRs) to be traded on a foreign stock exchange. Similarly, overseas-listed companies can issue CDRs to obtain a secondary listing on the Chinese stock exchange. In 2019, China and the United Kingdom jointly launched the Shanghai–London Stock Connect (SLSC), a groundbreaking initiative to encourage cross-border investment between the two countries and improve access to each other's capital markets.[24] In July 2022, the China–Switzerland Stock Connect Programme, established, facilitates the listing of GDRs by Chinese companies on the SIX Group, which operates Switzerland's largest stock exchange.[25]

We will use SLSC as an example to present how the stock connect works and what are their implications for global companies and investors. SLSC is a pilot cross-border financial markets listing and trading scheme which links China's SSE with the UK London Stock Exchange (LSE). The bilateral arrangement allows eligible companies listed in either the SSE or the LSE to issue depositary receipts which will be admitted to listing on the other side's stock market. The SLSC gives investors in the United Kingdom an opportunity to purchase the shares of Chinese public companies. Therefore, British and international investors can enjoy the fast growth of some of the best companies in the world's second-largest economy. Meanwhile, investors in mainland China are able to trade the shares of selected public companies listed in London. In the long term, the SLSC is said to help Chinese public companies adopt stricter information disclosure and corporate governance rules, and it could increase the overseas influence of Chinese businesses and currency. Moreover, the SLSC enhances London's status as a leading

[24] London Stock Exchange, 'London Stock Exchange Stock Connect', https://www.londonstockexchange.com/raise-finance/equity/london-stock-connect.

[25] Matthew Allen and Kai Reusser, 'Swiss stock exchange turns to China after being shunned by EU', *Swissinfo* (11 July 2023), https://www.swissinfo.ch/eng/business/swiss-stock-exchange-turns-to-china-after-being-shunned-by-eu/48648866.

global financial centre. Obviously, the SLSC will create billion-dollar business opportunities for investment banks, stockbrokers, and top commercial law firms.

8.4.2 The background and developments of Shanghai–London Stock Connect

The year 2018 marked the fortieth anniversary of China's 'reform and open-up policy' which has totally transformed the country's economy and brought China back to the world economic stage. As China vowed to further open up its economy to the rest of the world, the recently launched Shanghai–London Stock Connect (SLSC) is considered a profound initiative to open the door of Chinese capital markets to Western financial institutions and investors. Despite the US–China trade friction and other anti-globalization movements over past few years, China is determined to position the country as a leader of globalization.[26] Accordingly, it is seeking to work closely with the United Kingdom to develop a stock trading link between China and the West. The initiative displays China's great efforts to bring its stock market to the global trading system.

Previously, it had been relatively difficult for Western investors to purchase Chinese stocks, bonds, derivatives, and other financial instruments, as Beijing set strict criteria for foreign investors who intend to acquire financial assets in China. It is because the central government is wary of the stability of currency exchange rates relating to Chinese Yuan and the potential control of foreign capital over some Chinese companies in key sectors. For a long time, the only feasible method of investing in Chinese equities was to join the Qualified Foreign Institutional Investor scheme (QFII). QFII allows some licensed international investors to take part in the trading of shares, bonds, and other financial instruments listed in Shanghai and Shenzhen. However, an investment quota of up to $100 billion has been imposed on approximately 300 international investors who have been admitted to the QFII scheme.

It is not the first time for Chinese stock exchanges to establish stock links with their counterparts outside mainland China. For instance, Shanghai–Hong Kong Stock Connect and Shenzhen–Hong Kong Stock Connect have been in operation successfully since 2014 and 2016, respectively. Technically speaking, the two existing stock links with Hong Kong are fairly easy to run, since all stock exchanges involved are located in the same time zone,

[26] Emily Feng, 'China's globalisation paradox', *Financial Times* (13 July 2018), http://www.ft.com/content/4aa8ced4-7537-11e8-b6ad-3823e4384287.

and there has been close and long-term cooperation for securities regulators and financial communities in mainland China and the Hong Kong Special Administrative Region. However, stock connect initiatives with markets outside the PRC have witnessed various technical, legal, and regulatory barriers, as well as political and cultural hurdles.

In September 2015, Mr. George Osborne, the UK former Chancellor of the Exchequer, announced a landmark feasibility study into the idea of linking the Chinese and British stock exchanges together, when he attended the seventh China–UK Economic and Financial Dialogue.[27] 'I want to see our stock markets in London and Shanghai formally connected, with UK firms raising funds from Chinese savers, and Chinese firms listing in London', the Chancellor said when he visited the SSE.

In December 2017, London and Beijing restated their commitment to defend global free trade when the then British Chancellor Philip Hammond attended the ninth China–UK Economic and Financial Dialogue in Beijing.[28] The Chancellor stated, 'we have agreed to accelerate the final preparations for the London-Shanghai Stock Connect initiative and we have agreed to commence feasibility studies for a UK–China bond connect and for mutual recognition of funds between the two jurisdictions'.

From early 2018, both countries have been working on the long-awaited launch of the SLSC. From the Chinese side, the CSRC promulgated the '*Administrative Measures for the Issuance and Trading of Depository Receipts*' and '*Regulatory Provisions on the Depository Receipts under the Stock Connect Scheme between Shanghai Stock Exchange and London Stock Exchange*' which set out the listing and trading rules for the upcoming SLSC. From the UK side, the LSE issued the '*Consultations on Amendments to Issuance and Information Disclosure Standards*' which is regarded as an important prerequisite for starting the SLSC.

On 17 June 2019, Huatai Securities, one of the largest brokerages in China, became the first Chinese company to list in London via the latest SLSC pilot scheme.[29] Huatai raised $1.7 billion from the selling of 82.5 million GDRs, equivalent to 10% of its outstanding share capital. This listing formally kicked off the ground-breaking SLSC initiative as it is said to enrich investment opportunities for both sides' investors. The then Chancellor

[27] *BBC*, 'UK-China stocks link plan unveiled' (22 September 2015), http://www.bbc.co.uk/news/business-34322446.

[28] *Reuters*, 'Britain and China promise to speed up work on London-Shanghai stock connect' (16 December 2017), http://www.scmp.com/news/china/diplomacy-defence/article/2124601/britain-and-china-promise-speed-work-london-shanghai.

[29] Sarah Provan, 'Huatai securities to raise as much as $1.7bn in London listing', *Financial Times* (14 June 2019), http://www.ft.com/content/40a6eb48-8e84-11e9-a1c1-51bf8f989972.

Philip Hammond stated at the SLSC launch event that 'Stock Connect is a ground breaking initiative, which will deepen our connectivity as we look outwards to new opportunities in Asia ... London is a global financial centre like no other, and today's launch is a strong vote of confidence in the UK market'.[30] More than 260 of the 1,500 Shanghai-listed companies will be potentially eligible to participate in the project and obtain a listing in London. As for the East Bound part of the SLSC, the British bank HSBC is said to be the first UK company to apply for a listing in Shanghai.[31]

8.4.3 The practice and regulation of Shanghai–London Stock Connect

Shanghai–London Stock Connect can be divided into two sub-programmes: East Bound and West Bound, which provide the cross-border conversion of depository receipts for those listed companies which plan to obtain a second listing in the counterpart market. Regarding the West Bound issuance, Chinese A-Share companies wishing to be traded in the LSE will proceed through the issuance of GDRs. Meanwhile, East Bound issuance means that UK-listed companies will have the opportunity to list on the SSE directly by issuing CDRs. Figure 8.2 shows the operating mechanisms of both East Bound and West Bound branches of the stock connect. In theory, depository receipts are not shares but they represent equity interests in foreign

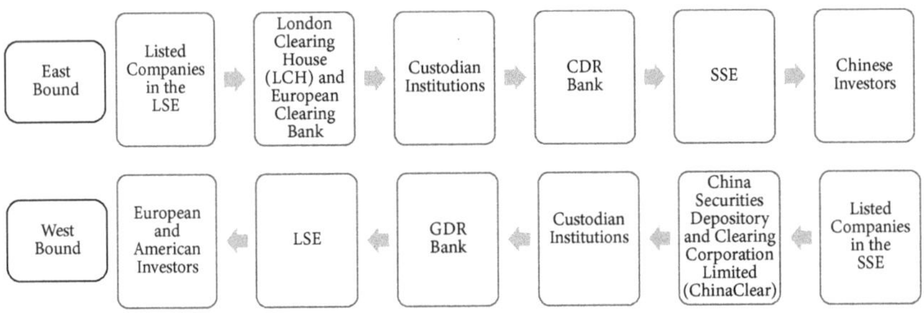

Figure 8.2 The operating mechanism of Shanghai–London Stock Connect

Source: This figure is compiled by the author.

[30] *BBC*, 'UK to launch ground-breaking China stock market link' (17 June 2019), http://www.bbc.co.uk/news/business-48658844.

[31] Don Weinland and Emma Dunkley, 'HSBC set to become first foreign company to list in China', *Financial Times* (18 October 2018), http://www.ft.com/content/e9b519b8-d28b-11e8-a9f2-7574db66bcd5.

companies through an offshore custodian bank. According to CITIC Securities, the market scale of GDR amounts to $2.9 trillion; Goldman Sachs predicted that the prospective size of the CDR market will reach over $800 billion.[32] Both West Bound and East Bound pathways are reliant on the issuance of depository receipts which have been an important financial tool in the global capital markets since the introduction of ADRs in the 1920s.

In terms of the cross-border conversion mechanism, the clearing and settlement service for CDR issuers will be served by China Securities Depository and Clearing Corporation Limited (China Clear), and the clearing service for GDR issuers will be provided by London Clearing House and the settlement will be executed via Euroclear Bank.[33] In practice, the United Kingdom has few restrictions over the selection of depository institutions and custodian institutions. However, China has introduced strict criteria in this area and allows few institutions to act as depository institutions of CDR issuers and custodian institutions of GDR issuers. For example, the depository banks for CDR issuers and custodian institutions for A-share issuers must be China Clear with issuers' subsidiaries, commercial banks, and securities companies approved by the CSRC.[34] Both sides further underscore that all trading should be in compliance with local rules, and GDR issuers should release a prospectus approved by the UK Listing Authority (UKLA) and the Financial Conduct Authority—in English. CDR issuers should open an office in mainland China to ensure information disclosure and efficient communication with Chinese investors. Given the time difference between the United Kingdom and China, both sides initially adopted the 'T+1' settlement rule, meaning that the settlement date takes place one business day after the transaction date.

The SSE and CSRC have jointly put forward thresholds for individual investors in China who wish to trade CDRs: currently, individual investors should have no less than RMB 3 million in their cash or securities accounts over twenty trading days before applying for a licence to trade CDRs; investors should also have good credit records and no criminal record. Institutional investors wishing to obtain a licence to trade CDRs should apply and submit an application to CDR cross-border conversion institutions in accordance with related rules released by the CSRC

[32] *Sina Finance*, 'CDRs are a foundation for internationalised A-shares' (8 March 2018), http://finance.sina.com.cn/stock/marketresearch/2018-03-08/doc-ifxpwyhv9413509.shtml.

[33] CSRC, *Opinions for Developing Creative Domestic IPO and Pilot Project of Chinese Depositary Receipts*, Part 3.

[34] CSRC, the *Measures for the Issuance and Trading of Depository Receipts (for Trial implementation)*, Article 26.

and the SSE. CDR holders will be treated as shareholders under Chinese company law, so they will have the right to receive share dividends, to vote on material matters, and to allocate residue assets in the event of insolvency.

Cross-border conversion institutions (also referred to as designated brokers by the LSE) will consist of securities companies that obtain a special licence to conduct business on selling and purchasing CDRs and GDRs on behalf of their clients. The SSE will be responsible for managing the procedure of how to become a cross-border conversion institution which will be the principal market makers for CDR transactions. For an LSE member broker who wishes to become a GDR cross-border conversion institution, it must appoint an SSE member broker to help it to submit the relevant application and supporting documents as required, whereas the SSE and CSRC will directly designate certain member securities companies to become CDR cross-border conversion institutions. In line with the CSRC rules, the buy-back of GDRs within 120 days is not allowed, in order to prohibit opportunistic GDR issuers from selling GDRs at a higher price but repurchase such securities at a lower price immediately (speculative arbitrage). There are, however, no restrictions on the buy-back of CDRs. To become GDR cross-border conversion institutions, securities brokers have to satisfy the following standards:

- Have a full membership of the LSE;
- Be qualified as Foreign Institutional Investor (QFII) or RMB Qualified Foreign Institutional Investor (RQFII), or be a subsidiary wholly owned by the QFII or RQFII; and
- Comply with the regulatory requirements and rules set by the SSE.

CDR cross-border conversion institutions will have to meet extra requirements imposed by the SSE and CSRC, including:

- Being approved by the SSE;
- Be approved and rated by the CSRC;
- Have a history of overseas trading;
- Be able to carry out market-making services, initial liquidity, and bilateral quotation;
- Be qualified to be involved in proprietary trading of securities;
- Be classified as securities with at least 'BBB' rating for a minimum of two years; and
- Have over three-year history in trading overseas securities.

Furthermore, both stock exchanges have set out detailed requirements for eligible companies to list their shares through the stock link programme. In comparison with the CDR issuance, it is relatively easy for GDR issuers to list on the LSE, as they have to meet the following requirements:

- Have a market value of over RMB 20 billion;
- Be listed on the SSE;
- Be approved by the CSRC;
- Allot new shares to be listed on the SSE, which will be the underlying securities to be cross-border converted as GDRs to be traded on the LSE;
- Comply with the rules of the UKLA and the LSE admission and disclosure standards; and
- Comply with the 25% free float requirement for GDR listing.

For CDR issuers, they must satisfy the following criteria:

- Have a market value of over RMB 20 billion (based on the closing price of the quoted stock 120 days ago);
- Have been listed on the LSE for over three years, with the minimum of one year in the Premium Segment of the Main Market;
- Issue at least fifty million shares of CDRs worth over RMB 500 million;
- Obtain the approval from the CSRC in line with the SSE requirements.

In addition, the CSRC has asked CDR issuers to follow the extra requirements as follows:[35]

- Have a complete and well-operated organization;
- Have the capability of making profits continuously and a sound financial status;
- Have no false record in its financial statements over the latest three years and have no other irregularity;[36]
- Have legally operated for over three years without ownership disputes over major assets;
- Have taken no illegal actions in violating the legal rights of investors and public interest;
- Have in place a standardized accounting and sound internal control system;

[35] CSRC, *Measures for the Issuance and Trading of Chinese Depositary Receipts (for trial implementation)*, Article 5.

[36] The first three provisions have reiterated Article 13(1) (2) (3) of the People's Republic of China Securities Law.

- Directors, auditors, and senior management should have a good reputation, qualifications, and good credit records; and
- Follow other rules issued by the CSRC.

Moreover, the *Measures for the Issuance and Trading of Chinese Depositary Receipts (for trial implementation)* attempts to address the conflict of laws under different jurisdictions towards existing LSE-listed companies. It requires overseas listed companies to disclose the major differences between its local company law and the Company Law of the People's Republic of China, and the relevant impacts on issuing CDRs and investor protection in the prospectus.[37] Further, companies that adopt VIE and weighted voting rights should disclose information relating to potential risks and corporate governance issues in an obvious place in the prospectus. CDR issuers are required to include a separate chapter on investor protection in the prospectus. Article 14 of the *Provisions on the Supervision and Administration of Depository Receipts under the Stock Connect Scheme between Shanghai Stock Exchange and London Stock Exchange (for trial implementation)* emphasizes that, after the CDR listing, these *Provisions* will be used for the ongoing supervision of the SLSC. However, *the Measures for Ongoing Supervision of Innovative Enterprises Following Listing of Domestically Offered Stocks or Depository Receipts (for trial implementation)* will provide alternative rules in terms of issues not mentioned in the *Provisions.*

8.4.4 Technical and regulatory difficulties of Shanghai–London Stock Connect

Given the various differences regarding trading mechanisms, laws, financial regulations, investor sophistication, and culture between China and the United Kingdom, there are multiple challenges which need to be solved by joint efforts on both sides. One main concern is the seven- to eight-hour time difference between London and Shanghai, making it difficult for traders to react to the real-time price changes in another time zone. As a response, the SSE has proposed to open an international sector during London hours to address this problem. Brexit has also cast a dark cloud over the stock link, though closer ties between Chinese and British capital markets would be welcome by London which has to protect its prestigious status as a top global

[37] CSRC, *Measures for the Issuance and Trading of Chinese Depositary Receipts (for trial implementation)*, Article 17.

financial centre. Apart from this, there are further regulatory challenges in the following areas.

One major challenge lies in the different regulatory systems between the two countries. With the rapid growth of GDR and CDR issuance in the upcoming years, it makes cross-border securities regulation and supervision an urgent task for both the CSRC and FCA. In comparison with China's heavily regulated financial markets, the United Kingdom has adopted a more market-based approach and has relatively lax rules for listed companies in many aspects. This may lead to the problem of regulatory arbitrage and improper competition arising from the deregulation process. Lax regulation in the United Kingdom could have the incentive for parties to favour their domestic UK companies over the counterparties by applying advantageous rules through deregulation. Therefore, China and the United Kingdom have been advised to establish a SLSC joint task force handling regulatory issues to try to unify the applying laws and regulatory approach.

Another problem is associated with information disclosure. At present, CDR issuers will be individually responsible for information disclosure. According to Chapter 4 of the *Measures*, CDR issuers have an obligation to release all information required by the SSE. This could make CDR issuers overburdened with various information disclosure obligations, which may hit the enthusiasm of potential CDR issuers and could jeopardize the international competitiveness of the Chinese stock market. The legal arrangements for information disclosure under ADR can offer a point of reference for the SLSC. In the United States, depository institutions as nominal issuers are responsible for the issuance, registration, and information disclosure of depository receipts, whereas, ADR issuers only need to undertake the responsibilities of issuance, registration, and information disclosure of underlying securities listed abroad.

Furthermore, there are some controversies about whether current regulations can offer good protection for investors who trade cross-border depositary receipts. Due to the different geographical locations, languages, corporate cultures, and legal systems, the classic problem of information asymmetry in the stock market is that it might be more difficult for investors to acquire the information they need to make informed investment decisions. Considering the long and complex transactional chain relating to depository receipts, the bankruptcy of any parties in the chain such as overseas listed companies, custodian institutions, or depository institutions will result in financial loss to investors who have limited remedies. In the absence of effective dispute resolution mechanisms, it would be difficult for investors to pursue litigation as they will have to overcome the difficulties of interpreting laws, collecting evidence, and enforcing claims.

8.5 Case study: the cross-border supervision of China's capital markets

This section assesses the third case study of China's efforts in improving the internationalization of its financial industry. It discusses the cross-border supervision of China's capital markets with a focus on the new provisions under the PRC Securities Law 2020.[38] It is likely to increase the extraterritorial effectiveness of the Chinese financial law and increase its international influence.

8.5.1 The Luckin Coffee incident

The introduction of cross-border supervision over Chinese capital markets, prompted by cases of fraud or misleading information disclosure by overseas-listed Chinese companies (which are commonly known as 'Chinese concept stocks' in the United States), is a significant breakthrough in the PRC Securities Law 2020. According to the latest law, if the offering and trading of securities outside mainland China disrupt the order of the domestic market and infringe upon the lawful rights and interests of domestic investors, the violator will be punished in accordance with the relevant provisions of the PRC Securities Law 2020 and will be subject to legal liability.[39] The newly established long-arm jurisdiction grants the CSRC greater authority to police and punish illegal activities in overseas securities markets where Chinese companies are listed.

The securities law has been revised in response to recent financial frauds committed by high-profile Chinese companies, such as the Luckin Coffee incident. The frequent fraudulent investigations into Chinese public companies have necessitated tougher sanctions on financial frauds and have granted the CSRC additional power to ensure compliance with securities regulations. Known as China's Starbucks, Luckin Coffee built a successful coffee empire with more than 10,000 cafes across the country. In 2019, less than two years after opening its first coffee shop, Luckin Coffee went public on NASDAQ in

[38] For the general discussion of PRC Securities Law 2020, see Chapter 5, Section 5.5 'Capital markets law reform: PRC Securities Law 2020'.

[39] PRC Securities Law 2020, Article 2(4).

the United States. In 2020, it was reported that Luckin Coffee had deliberately fabricated over $300 million in retail sales through related-party transactions.[40] Its shares were shorted by the US investment firm Muddy Waters Research LLC. Subsequently, Luckin Coffee attempted to conceal the fraud by inflating its expenses by more than $190 million, creating a fake operations database, and altering its bank records and accounting books. As a result, Luckin Coffee was fined $180 million by the SEC for conducting accounting fraud.

The Luckin Coffee scandal dominated headlines in both Chinese and US media for several weeks following the implementation of the PRC Securities Law 2020. The SEC's allegations of fraud against Luckin Coffee triggered a sell-off of the company's shares in the US markets and caused a new wave of mistrust in China concept stocks. This incident sparked intense discussions about enhancing securities regulation and information disclosure rules in China. Some argue that NASDAQ-listed Luckin Coffee should be held accountable to domestic investors in China through the CSRC's long-arm jurisdiction. Others oppose the application of long-arm jurisdiction under the securities law, citing the complexity of the legal procedure and the need for it to be claimed prudently with the principle of international comity, considering the impacts on domestic markets and investors. In practice, the United States is a major advocate for the extraterritorial effectiveness of its domestic securities law, having developed comprehensive methods for assessing jurisdictional standards over the past decades.

8.5.2 Reference to the US legal practice

The US law concerning the territorial scope of federal securities law is outlined in Sections 929P(b) and 929Y of the Dodd–Frank Wall Street Reform and Consumer Protection Act of 2010. According to the Act, courts have adopted the so-called 'conduct' and 'effect' tests on an ad hoc basis.[41] Under the 'conduct' test, courts have jurisdiction over any foreign securities fraud where 'a substantial portion of the fraud occurred in the United States and directly caused the harm abroad'. This test primarily examines whether the actions that took place in the United States are critical to the entire securities

[40] Alistair Gray, 'Luckin Coffee to pay $180m in accounting fraud settlement', *Financial Times* (16 December 2020).

[41] Erez Reuveni, 'Extraterritoriality as Standing: A Standing Theory of the Extraterritorial Application of the Securities Laws' (2009) 43 *UC Davis Law Review* 1071.

fraud activity.[42] Under the 'effect' test, courts have jurisdiction over foreign securities activities only if they have 'a foreseeable substantial effect in the United States or upon United States citizens'.[43] Therefore, the 'effect' test is similar to the one stipulated by the PRC Securities Law 2020, as both primarily focus on the impacts of the fraud on domestic capital markets and investors.

The extent to which the effect is considered 'foreseeable substantial' in such litigation can be explained through three aspects based on US judicial precedents. First, the effect should be direct and specific. In the *Bersch* case, the 'effect' test is not satisfied if the alleged fraudulent activity only has 'an adverse effect on this country's general economic interests of American security prices'.[44] In other words, a 'general effect' alone does not trigger the extraterritorial jurisdictional effects of the US Securities Law.

Second, the alleged fraudulent securities activity should have a high degree of relevance to domestic markets, such as the securities being registered in the United States or intended to be sold to US investors. In the *Leasco* case, the American plaintiff claimed he was induced to purchase securities in London by foreign defendants' fraudulent misrepresentations. The Second Circuit denied extending the application of the 1934 Securities Act to fraudulent securities activities with no connection to US stock exchanges, even though the plaintiff suffered significant losses.[45] To be more specific, if the securities in question have no relevance to domestic capital markets, it would be hard to argue that the fraudster could reasonably foresee the harmful impact on domestic capital markets when committing the fraud. Such an impact could be coincidental or accidental.

Third, the impact of fraudulent securities activity should be widespread. In the *IIT* case, involving 300 US citizens and a total claimed loss of $3 million, the Second Circuit again denied applying the long-arm jurisdiction of the 1934 Securities Act in the Bahamas. This decision was based on the fact that the losses suffered by American investors accounted for merely 0.5% of the entire trust assets, which is unlikely to constitute a material impact.[46] These three criteria can serve as references for applying the long-arm jurisdiction of the new PRC Securities Law 2020 in the context of fraudulent activities.

[42] Morrison v. Nat'l Austl. Bank Ltd., 547 F. 3d 167,171 (2d Cir.2008).
[43] SEC v. Berger, 322 F. 3d 187, 193 (2d Cir. 2003).
[44] Bersch v. Drexel Firestone, Inc., 519 F.2d 974, 993 (2d Cir. 1975).
[45] Leasco Data Processing Equip. Corp. v. Maxwell, 468 F.2d 1326, 1337 (2d Cir. 1972).
[46] IIT v. Vencap, Ltd., 519 F.2d 1001, 1016 (2d Cir. 1975).

8.6 Concluding remarks: China as a rising financial superpower

This chapter has discussed China's great efforts to become a global financial superpower in the twenty-first century. Its government and financial regulators have launched a series of reforms to increase the international connectiveness, competitiveness, and influence of the Chinese financial markets, institutions, and currencies. It has outlined the competitive advantages of three Chinese financial centres, that are Beijing, Shanghai, and Shenzhen, and predicts that they are likely to become the top-notch international financial centres like New York and London. It has used three case studies to showcase China's proactive reform to open its financial markets to international investors and corporations, as well as to increase the territorial scope of Chinese securities law. In the future, it is expected that Chinese capital will play an important role in the international financial markets. Meanwhile, more international investors, especially large institutional investors, are likely to diversify their portfolio by purchasing the stocks, bonds, and other financial instruments issued by the Chinese corporations. Global companies are also welcome to list their shares and raise funds in mainland China and get access to the abundant savings of Chinese citizens. China's increasing involvement in the global financial arena is, to a large extent, a win-win situation for China and the West if the financial resources could be allocated effectively across the world.

Throughout the analysis in this book, we have proved that China is a rising financial superpower. China has a massive and sophisticated financial industry with a sound regulatory framework and a good level of international connectiveness. From any metrics, China has quickly emerged as a strong power in the financial domain on the global stage since the start of the twenty-first century. The strength of China's financial industry is not confined to its borders, it is exerting influence globally. This could be demonstrated from the following aspects. First, China has built a sound and effective regulatory framework and legal environment for its financial industry, including the strong regulatory institutions, the financial safety net and crisis management tools, and the specialized financial courts for dispute resolution. The world-class infrastructure and regulatory framework is agile and adaptive to China's fast-evolving sector, emphasizing financial stability, prudential regulation, and consumer protection. Second, China possesses the world's largest banking industry and the second-largest capital market, as well as being a leader in Fintech innovation and AI research. The sheer size of China's financial industry makes it impossible to ignore. After four decades of economic reform, China's financial industry is highly competitive, featuring private, state-owned, and foreign institutions. This level of dynamism is rarely seen elsewhere in the world. Third, the Chinese currency, RMB or yuan, is rapidly gaining international usage. This is driven by major policy initiatives like the Belt and Road Initiative and the establishment of the AIIB, a Chinese-backed international financial organization. Additionally, China is a global leader in Fintech and CBDC experiments. The RMB, or its CBDC version, is poised to play a larger role in international finance as both a medium of exchange and a national reserve currency.

Bibliography

AIFC. 'An Introduction'. Accessed 01 July 2024. https://court.aifc.kz/en/an-introduction.

Allen, Franklin, Xian Gu, and Jun Qian. 'The People's Bank of China: From 1948 to 2016'. In Rodney Edvinsson, Tor Jacobson, and Daniel Waldenström (eds), *Sveriges Riksbank and the History of Central Banking* (Cambridge, UK: Cambridge University Press, 2018), pp. 418–453.

Allen, Matthew, and Kai Reusser. 'Swiss stock exchange turns to China after being shunned by EU'. 11 July 2023. Swissinfo. https://www.swissinfo.ch/eng/business/swiss-stock-exchange-turns-to-china-after-being-shunned-by-eu/48648866.

Angest, Henry. 'In defence of dual-class shares with different rights'. *The Financial Times*, 17 April 2019, p. 9.

Anson, Michael, David Bholat, Miao Kang, and Ryland Thomas. 'The Bank of England as lender of last resort: New historical evidence from daily transactional data' (2017). Bank of England Working Paper No. 691. https://www.bankofengland.co.uk/working-paper/2017/the-bank-of-england-as-lender-of-last-resort-new-historical-evidence-from-daily-transactional-data.

Arda, Atilla, and Mark Dobler. 'The role for deposit insurance funds in dealing with failing banks in the European Banks' (2022). IMF Working Papers. https://www.imf.org/en/Publications/WP/Issues/2022/01/07/The-Role-for-Deposit-Insurance-Funds-in-Dealing-with-Failing-Banks-in-the-European-Union-511639.

Areddy, James T. 'China to launch Beijing stock exchange to steer investment into innovation'. *The Wall Street Journal*, 02 September 2021. https://www.wsj.com/articles/china-to-launch-beijing-stock-exchange-to-steer-investment-into-innovation-11630622825.

Armour, John et al. *Principles of Financial Regulation* (Oxford, UK: Oxford University Press, 2016).

Asian Infrastructure Investment Bank. 'About AIIB'. Accessed 01 July 2024. https://www.aiib.org/en/about-aiib/index.html.

Auer, Raphael, and Rainer Böhme. 'The technology of retail central bank digital currency'. *BIS Quarterly Review*, March 2020. https://www.bis.org/publ/qtrpdf/r_qt2003j.htm.

Bank for International Settlements. 'Basel III: International regulatory framework for banks'. December 2017. https://www.bis.org/bcbs/basel3.htm.

Bank for International Settlements. 'BIS Annual Economic Report: III. CBDCs: An opportunity for the monetary system' (2021). https://www.bis.org/publ/arpdf/ar2021e3.pdf.

Bank for International Settlements. 'Central bank digital currencies for cross-border payments: Report to the G20'. July 2021. https://www.bis.org/publ/othp38.pdf.

Bank for International Settlements. 'Central bank digital currencies: Foundational principles and core features' (2020). https://www.bis.org/publ/othp33.pdf.

Bank for International Settlements. 'Multiple CBDC (mCBDC) Bridge'. Accessed 01 July 2024. https://www.bis.org/about/bisih/topics/cbdc/mcbdc_bridge.htm.

Bank of China. 'Bank of China Global Network' (2011). https://pic.bankofchina.com/bocappd/report/201104/P020110427561564499932.pdf.

Bank of Communications. 'Shareholding info'. 30 August 2023. https://www.bankcomm.com/BankCommSite/shtml/jyjr/en/2600223/2600238/2600348/list.shtml.

Bank of England. 'Financial services compensation scheme'. Accessed 01 July 2024. https://www.bankofengland.co.uk/prudential-regulation/authorisations/financial-services-compensation-scheme.

Bank of England. 'Quantitative easing'. Accessed 01 July 2024. https://www.bankofengland.co.uk/monetary-policy/quantitative-easing.

Bank of England. 'What is legal tender?'. Accessed 01 July 2024. https://www.bankofengland.co.uk/explainers/what-is-legal-tender.

Bank of Japan. 'Complementary lending facility'. Accessed 01 July 2024. https://www.boj.or.jp/en/mopo/measures/mkt_ope/len_a/index.htm.

Bank of Jiangsu. 'About us'. Accessed 01 July 2024. https://www.jsbchina.cn/EN/aboutus/aau/11040.html.

Banker, Steve. 'Apple's reliance on China poses a problem for the company'. *Forbes*, 19 January 2023. https://www.forbes.com/sites/stevebanker/2023/01/19/apples-china-problem/.

Barro, Robert J. 'Money and the price level under the gold standard' (1979). 89 *The Economic Journal* 13.

BBC News. 'Fears surface over Chinese debt amid lending practices'. 06 October 2011. http://www.bbc.co.uk/news/business-15194663.

BBC News. 'UK to launch ground-breaking China stock market link'. 17 June 2019. http://www.bbc.co.uk/news/business-48658844.

BBC News. 'UK-China stocks link plan unveiled'. 22 September 2015. http://www.bbc.co.uk/news/business-34322446.

Beijing Financial Court. '"Major debt crisis" Matter that may trigger a change in the controlling right of a company shall be regarded as insider'. 19 October 2022. https://bjfc.bjcourt.gov.cn/cac/1666162394152.html.

Beijing Financial Court. 'Court overview'. Accessed 01 July 2024. https://bjfc.bjcourt.gov.cn/cac/1615256934535.html.

Beijing Politics & Law. 'One-year overview of Beijing financial court with 6.275 cases'. 24 March 2022. https://www.bj148.org/ztk/2022nzt/bjjrfyyzn_202009/ttxw/202203/t20220329_1630981.html.

Beijing Stock Exchange. 'Welltrans Optoelectronic Co Ltd: Annual report 2020'. 26 April 2021. http://www.bse.cn/disclosure/2021/2021-04-26/1619442101_852034.pdf.

Beijing Stock Exchange. 'Welltrans Optoelectronic Co Ltd: Semi-annual report 2021'. 27 August 2021. http://www.bse.cn/disclosure/2021/2021-08-27/1630054790_168417.pdf.

Bernanke, Ben S. *The Federal Reserve and the Financial Crisis* (New Jersey: Princeton University Press, 2013).

Bertrand, Astrid, Winston Maxwell, and Xavier Vamparys. 'Do AI-Based Anti-Money Laundering (AML) systems violate European fundamental rights?' (2021). 11 *International Data Privacy Law* 276.

Bloomberg. 'China drafts bank deposit insurance in move to free rates'. 30 November 2014. https://www.bloomberg.com/news/articles/2014-11-30/china-drafts-deposit-insurance-in-move-to-free-interest-rates.

Bloomberg. 'China's epic battle with capital flows is more intense than ever'. 06 April 2021. https://www.bloomberg.com/news/articles/2021-04-06/china-s-epic-battle-with-capital-flows-is-more-intense-than-ever.

Bloomberg. 'There are now more stock traders in China than Communist Party Members'. 30 June 2015. https://www.bloomberg.com/news/articles/2015-06-30/in-communist-china-stock-market-capitalists-now-rule.

Boar, Codruta, Henry Holden, and Amber Wadsworth. 'Impending arrival—A sequel to the survey on central bank digital currency'. BIS Papers No. 107, January 2020. https://www.bis.org/publ/bppdf/bispap107.pdf.

Bordo, Michael D. 'Rules for a lender of last resort: A historical perspective' (2014). 49 *Journal of Economic Dynamics & Control* 126.

Buckley, Ross P., et al. 'Sovereign digital currencies: Reshaping the design of money and payments systems' (2021). 15 *Journal of Payments Strategy & Systems* 7.

Byrd, William. *The Market Mechanism and Economic Reforms in China* (New York: Routledge, 1991).

Caijing. 'CDR will bring over 5bn revenue for securities brokers'. 09 May 2018. http://stock.caijing.com.cn/20180509/4449705.shtml.

Campbell, Andrew. 'Insolvent banks and the financial sector safety net-lessons from the northern rock crisis' (2008). 20 *Singapore Academy of Law Journal* 316.

Campbell, Peter. 'Geely builds $9bn stake in Mercedes owner Daimler'. *The Financial Times*, 24 February 2018. http://www.ft.com/content/68c57048-18c1-11e8-9376-4a6390addb44.

Canaves, Sky. 'China property bubble, 1990s style'. *The Wall Street Journal*, 17 March 2010. https://www.wsj.com/articles/BL-CJB-7835.

Carr, Winston Keith. 'Measures to promote effective interrelationships among financial safety net participants' (2006). 8 *Journal of Banking Regulation* 73.

Cayman Islands Judicial Administration. 'Financial services division'. Accessed 01 July 2024. https://www.judicial.ky/courts/grand-court/financial-services-division.

CB Insights. 'The complete list of unicorn companies'. Accessed 01 July 2024. http://www.cbinsights.com/research-unicorn-companies.

Central Huijin Investment Ltd. 'About us'. Accessed 01 July 2024. http://www.huijin-inv.cn/huijineng/About_Us/index.shtml.

Chen, Fa. 'Does the dual-class share structure help stock markets attract issuers? Empirical lessons from global financial centres' (2023). 43 *Legal Studies* 159.

Chen, Ting, Zhenyu Gao, Jibao He, Wenxi Jiang, and Wei Xiong. 'Daily price limits and destructive market behaviour' (2019). 208 *Journal of Econometrics* 249.

Chengdu-Chongqing Financial Court. 'Chengdu-Chongqing Financial Court held its first press conference'. January 2023. http://cyjrfy.cqfygzfw.gov.cn/article/detail/2023/01/id/7086361.shtml.

Chengdu-Chongqing Financial Court. 'Court introduction'. Accessed 01 July 2024. http://cyjrfy.cqfygzfw.gov.cn/article/detail/2023/11/id/7615653.shtml.

Chengdu-Chongqing Financial Court. 'Media paid close attention to the first press conference of Chengyu financial court'. 04 January 2023. http://cyjrfy.cqfygzfw.gov.cn/article/detail/2023/01/id/7086414.shtml.

Chengdu-Chongqing Financial Court. 'The full launch of Chengyu Financial Court, Outlook oriental by Xinhua News Agency'. 28 January 2023. http://cyjrfy.cqfygzfw.gov.cn/article/detail/2023/01/id/7113102.shtml.

China Court. 'The Beijing High Court held a press conference on the retrial and review of private lending disputes'. 26 December 2023. https://www.chinacourt.org/chat/chat/2023/12/id/53196.shtml.

China Daily. 'Science and technology innovation board'. 07 November 2018. http://www.chinadaily.com.cn/a/201811/07/WS5be23110a310eff303286fda.html.

China Development Institute. 'The China Financial Center Index (CFCI)'. 27 December 2022. http://www.cdi.com.cn/Article/Detail?id=18078&cid=160.

China Economic Weekly. 'Before and after the Wenzhou Private Financing Regulation'. 09 December 2013, p. 58.

China Economy Net. 'Xinwang Bank was fined 6.3 million yuan: Transactions with unidentified customers'. 26 July 2021. http://www.ce.cn/cysc/newmain/yc/jsxw/202107/26/t20210726_36751717.shtml.

China Securities Regulatory Commission. 'About CSRC'. Accessed 01 July 2024. http://www.csrc.gov.cn/csrc_en/c102023/common_zcnr.shtml.

ChinaNews. 'Beijing financial street financial institutions asset scale is approaching RMB100 Trillion'. 29 April 2018. http://www.chinanews.com/fortune/2018/04-29/8503009.shtml.

ChinaNews. 'The launch of new third board to nationwide. Listed enterprises up to more than 2000'. 07 November 2013. https://www.chinanews.com.cn/stock/2013/11-07/5473975.shtml.

Chinese Government. 'Bank deposit insurance program launched'. 31 March 2015. http://english.www.gov.cn/premier/news/2015/03/31/content_281475080793833.htm.

Chinese Government. 'Loan prime rate centralised quotation and release mechanism officially launched'. 25 October 2013. https://www.gov.cn/jrzg/2013-10/25/content_2515184.htm.

Chinese Government. 'The new FSDC held the first meeting'. 03 July 2018. http://www.gov.cn/guowuyuan/2018-07/03/content_5303229.htm.

Chinese Government. 'The plan for the development of the Chengdu-Chongqing economic circle'. 21 October 2021. http://www.gov.cn/zhengce/2021-10/21/content_5643875.htm.

Chinese Government. 'We will give policy support to small and medium-sized enterprises'. 01 April 2021. http://www.gov.cn/zhengce/2020-04/01/content_5497938.htm.

Chinese Government. 'Xi Jinping Chairs the 17th meeting of the central committee for comprehensively deepening reform and delivers an important speech'. 30 December 2020. http://www.gov.cn/xinwen/2020-12/30/content_5575462.htm.

Chiu, Iris H-Y, and Joanna Wilson. *Banking Law and Regulation* (Oxford, UK: Oxford University Press, 2019).

Chong, Koh Ping, and Alexander Osipovich. 'NYSE to Delist Chinese telecom carriers after rejecting appeals'. *The Wall Street Journal*, 07 May 2021. https://www.wsj.com/articles/nyse-to-delist-chinese-telecoms-carriers-after-rejecting-appeals-11620394719.

Clover, Charles. 'Alibaba IPO shows foreign investors able to skirt restrictions'. *The Financial Times*, 07 May 2014. http://www.ft.com/content/7a8c4816-d5df-11e3-a017-00144feabdc0.

Coin Market Cap. 'Bitcoin price today'. Accessed 01 July 2024. https://coinmarketcap.com/currencies/bitcoin/.

Companies Market Cap. 'Largest companies by market cap'. Accessed 01 July 2024. https://companiesmarketcap.com/.

Credit Suisse. 'China: Shadow banking—Road to heightened risks'. Securities Research & Analytics. February 2013.

CSRC. 'Xiaomi—The prospectus'. Accessed 01 July 2024. http://www.csrc.gov.cn/pub/zjhpublic/G00306202/201806/P020180611106685793601.pdf.

Desai, Susan. 'A regional comparison of China's new deposit insurance system' (2016). *FED Bank of San Francisco Pacific Exchange Blog*. https://www.frbsf.org/banking/asia-program/pacific-exchange-blog/regional-comparison-chinas-new-deposit-insurance-system/.

Dobler, Mark, Simon Gray, Diarmuid Murphy, and Bozena Radzewicz-Bak. 'The lender of last resort after the Global Financial Crisis' (2016). IMF Working Paper. https://www.imf.org/external/pubs/ft/wp/2016/wp1610.pdf.

Domanski, Dietrich, and Vladyslav Sushko. 'Rethinking the lender of last resort' (2014). BIS Papers No. 79. https://www.bis.org/publ/bppdf/bispap79.htm.

Dong, Emma, and Simon Rabinovitch. 'China's lending laboratory'. *The Financial Times*, 23 May 2012. http://www.ft.com/intl/cms/s/0/90e7f67a-a41b-11e1-a701-00144feabdc0.html.

Dongguan Rural Commercial Bank. 'About us'. Accessed 01 July 2024. https://www.drcbank.com/drcbank_news/gywx60/bxjj/index.html.

Dunkley, Emma. 'Ten years after Northern Rock: Has UK banking changed?'. *The Financial Times*, 12 September 2017. https://www.ft.com/content/d05c3ea4-97bf-11e7-a652-cde3f882dd7b.

Dyer, Geoff. 'China authorises "massive" stimulus package'. *The Financial Times*, 10 November 2008. http://www.ft.com/content/6e89710e-ae91-11dd-b621-000077b07658.

Eastmoney. 'The latest shareholding structure of JD.com revealed'. 10 May 2019. http://stock.eastmoney.com/a/201905091118284644.html.

Egan, Matt. 'After Historic 1.000-point plunge. Dow Dives 588 points at close'. *CNN*, 25 August 2015. http://money.cnn.com/2015/08/24/investing/stocks-markets-selloff-china-crash-dow/.

Engbith, Lily S. 'China: 1999 Asset Management Corporations' (2021). 3 *Journal of Financial Crises* 485.

Enoch, Charles, Peter Stella, and May Khamis. 'Transparency and ambiguity in Central Bank Safety Net Operations' (1997). IMF Working Papers. https://www.imf.org/external/pubs/ft/wp/wp97138.pdf.

European Banking Authority. 'Deposit guarantee schemes data'. Accessed 01 July 2024. https://www.eba.europa.eu/regulation-and-policy/recovery-and-resolution/deposit-guarantee-schemes-data.

European Central Bank. 'A digital euro'. Accessed 01 July 2024. https://www.ecb.europa.eu/paym/digital_euro/html/index.en.html.

European Central Bank. 'Exploring anonymity in central bank digital currencies'. December 2019. https://www.ecb.europa.eu/paym/intro/publications/pdf/ecb.mipinfocus191217.en.pdf.

European Central Bank. 'Standing facilities'. Accessed 01 July 2024. https://www.ecb.europa.eu/mopo/implement/sf/html/index.en.html.

European Central Bank. 'What is a lender of last resort?' (2019). https://www.ecb.europa.eu/ecb/educational/explainers/tell-me-more/html/what-is-a-lender-of-last-resort.en.html.

Federal Deposit Insurance Corporation. 'A brief history of deposit insurance in the United States' (1998). https://www.fdic.gov/bank/historical/brief/brhist.pdf.

Federal Reserve Board. 'Open market operations'. Accessed 01 July 2024. https://www.federalreserve.gov/monetarypolicy/openmarket.htm.

Feng, Emily. 'China's globalisation paradox'. *The Financial Times*, 13 July 2018. http://www.ft.com/content/4aa8ced4-7537-11e8-b6ad-3823e4384287.

Ferran, Eilís, and Look Chan Ho. *Principles of Corporate Finance Law* (2nd edn, Oxford, UK: Oxford University Press, 2014).

Financial Stability Board. 'Enhancing cross-border payments: Stage 3 roadmap'. 13 October 2020. https://www.fsb.org/wp-content/uploads/P131020-1.pdf.

Financial Stability Board. 'Evaluation of the effects of too-big-to-fail reforms—Consultation report'. 28 June 2020. https://www.fsb.org/wp-content/uploads/P280620-1.pdf.

Freeman, Scott. 'Rediscounting under aggregate risk' (1999). 43 *Journal of Monetary Economics* 197.

Fung, Hung-Gay, Alan Guoming Huang, Qingfeng Wilson Liu, and Maggie Xiaoqin Shen. 'The development of the real estate industry in China' (2006). 39 *The Chinese Economy* 84.

Gaspar, Vitor. 'Introductory remarks to the fiscal monitor press conference'. IMF, 11 October 2023. https://www.imf.org/en/News/Articles/2023/10/11/introductory-remarks-to-the-fiscal-monitor-press-conference-vitor-gaspar.

Georgieva, Kristalina. 'The time is now: We must step up support for the poorest countries'. 31 March 2023. IMF Blog. https://www.imf.org/en/Blogs/Articles/2023/03/31/the-time-is-now-we-must-step-up-support-for-the-poorest-countries.

Gillespie, Alisdair, and Siobhan Weare. *English Legal System* (9th edn, Oxford, UK: Oxford University Press, 2023).

Global Times. '1st trading week of Beijing Stock Exchange meets expectations with 340.000 new investors coming online'. 21 November 2021. https://www.globaltimes.cn/page/202111/1239536.shtml.

Global Times. 'China launches sci-tech innovation board, stressing further financial opening-up amid trade war'. 13 June 2019. http://www.globaltimes.cn/content/1154078.shtml.

Global Times. 'IPOs to enter era of full registration, delisting process to be normalized'. 01 November 2020. http://www.globaltimes.cn/content/1205330.shtml.

Global Times. 'New Securities Law takes effect, targets overseas activity'. 01 March 2020. http://www.globaltimes.cn/content/1181185.shtml.

Gobat, Jeanne. 'Banks: At the heart of the matter'. IMF. Accessed 01 July 2024. https://www.imf.org/en/Publications/fandd/issues/Series/Back-to-Basics/Banks.

Goldman Sachs. 'The stock connect'. December 2016. https://www.goldmansachs.com/intelligence/pages/stock-connect/.

Goodhart, Charles, and Dirk Schoenmaker. 'Should the functions of monetary policy and banking supervision be separated?' (1995). 47 *Oxford Economic Papers* 539.

Gore, Lance L P. 'China's central commission on comprehensively deepening reforms: seven years on'. EAI Background Brief No. 1581, 18 March 2021. https://research.nus.edu.sg/eai/wp-content/uploads/sites/2/2021/03/EAIBB-No.-1581-Chinas-Central-Commission-7-yrs-on-exsum.pdf.

Gorton, Gary B, and Andrew Metrick. 'Regulating the shadow banking system'. Brookings Papers on Economic Activity, Fall 2010, p. 261.

Gorton, Gary B, and Jeffery Y Zhang. 'Taming wildcat stablecoins' (2023). 90 *The University of Chicago Law Review* 909.

Gorton, Gary. 'Clearing houses and the origin of central banking in the United States' (1985). 45 *The Journal of Economic History* 277.

Gray, Alistair. 'Luckin Coffee to pay $180m in accounting fraud settlement'. *The Financial Times*, 17 December 2020. https://www.ft.com/content/4db3b074-829f-4f1c-a256-11c7e28a31d1.

Griffoli, Tommaso Mancini, et al. 'Casting light on central bank digital currency' (2018). IMF Staff Discussion Notes No. 18/08. https://www.imf.org/en/Publications/Staff-Discussion-Notes/Issues/2018/11/13/Casting-Light-on-Central-Bank-Digital-Currencies-46233.

Gropp, Reint, and Jukka Vesala. 'Deposit insurance, moral hazard and market monitoring'. February 2004. European Central Bank Working Paper Series No. 302. https://www.ecb.europa.eu/pub/pdf/scpwps/ecbwp302.pdf.

Grundy Jr, Thad. 'Practical aspects of the deposit insurance system' (1988). 44 *Business Lawyer* 169.

Gunter, Frank R. 'Why China lost about $3.8 trillion to capital flight in the last decade'. *Forbes*, 22 February 2017. http://www.forbes.com/sites/insideasia/2017/02/22/china-capital-flight-migration/.

Haentjens, Matthias, and Bob Wessels. 'Three paradigm shifts in recent bank insolvency law' (2016). 7 *Journal of International Banking Law and Regulation* 396.

Hancock, Tom, and Lucy Hornby. 'China conglomerates suffer different fates in Beijing crackdown'. *The Financial Times*, 23 February 2018. http://www.ft.com/content/8ed61466-186e-11e8-9376-4a6390addb44.

Harvey, David. *A Brief History of Neoliberalism* (New York: Oxford University Press, 2005).

Hauser, Andrew. 'Lender of last resort operations during the financial crisis: seven practical lessons from the United Kingdom' (2014). BIS Working Paper No. 79. https://www.bis.org/publ/bppdf/bispap79e.pdf.

He, Dong. 'Digitalization of cross-border payments' (2021). 14 *China Economic Journal* 26.

He, Laura. 'Australia's exports to China hit record high as relations thaw'. *CNN*, 05 May 2023. https://edition.cnn.com/2023/05/05/economy/australia-china-exports-record-intl-hnk/index.html.

He, Laura. 'Bitcoin mining: China's government is cracking down'. *CNN*, 24 May 2021. https://edition.cnn.com/2021/05/24/investing/bitcoin-mining-china-crackdown-intl-hnk/index.html.

He, Xinrong, and Linlin Wang. 'Loss of deposit? Shanghai CPPCC foretell the Shanghai Financial Court'. *People*, 24 January 2015. http://finance.people.com.cn/n/2015/0124/c1004-26443897.html.

Hong Kong Monetary Authority. 'Policy statement on the role of the Hong Kong Monetary authority as lender of last resort'. *Quarterly Bulletin*, 8/1999. https://www.hkma.gov.hk/media/eng/publication-and-research/quarterly-bulletin/qb9908/fa04.pdf.

Hong Kong Securities and Futures Commission. 'Market capitalisation of the World's top stock exchanges'. September 2019. http://www.sfc.hk/web/EN/files/SOM/MarketStatistics/a01.pdf.

Huang, Robin Hui. *Fintech Regulation in China: Principles, Policies and Practices* (Cambridge, UK: Cambridge University Press, 2021).

Humphrey, Thomas M. 'Lender of last resort: The concept in history' (1989). 75 *FRB Richmond Economic Review* 8.

Hurun. 'Hurun Global Unicorn List 2019'. Accessed 01 July 2024. http://www.hurun.net/CN/Article/Details?num=E7190250C866.

IADA. 'Evaluation of differential premium systems for deposit insurance' (2020). https://www.iadi.org/en/assets/File/Papers/Approved%20Research%20-%20Discussion%20Papers/DPS_Paper_final_16June2020_Final.pdf.

IADA. 'Glossary—Implicit protection'. Accessed 01 July 2024. https://www.iadi.org/en/core-principles-and-guidance/glossary/implicit-protection/.

ICBC. 'Overseas branches'. Accessed 01 July 2024. https://big5.icbc.com.cn/en/column/1438058479532523524.html.

ICBC. 'Particulars of shareholding of the top 10 ordinary shareholders of the bank'. 31 December 2021. https://www.icbc-ltd.com/ICBCLtd/Investor%20Relations/Share%20Information/Shareholding%20Structure/.

IMF. 'An overview of the legal, institutional, and regulatory framework for bank insolvency' (2009). https://www.imf.org/en/Publications/Policy-Papers/Issues/2016/12/31/An-Overview-of-the-Legal-Institutional-and-Regulatory-Framework-for-Bank-Insolvency-PP4327.

IMF. 'IMF data mapper—China, People's Republic of'. Accessed 01 July 2024. https://www.imf.org/external/datamapper/profile/CHN.

IMF. 'IMF staff completes 2024 Article IV mission to the People's Republic of China'. 28 May 2024. https://www.imf.org/en/News/Articles/2024/05/28/pr24184-china-imf-staff-completes-2024-art-iv-mission.

IMF. 'World economic outlook'. 11 April 2023. https://www.imf.org/en/Publications/WEO/Issues/2023/04/11/world-economic-outlook-april-2023.

International Association of Deposit Insurers. 'IADI core principles for effective deposit insurance system' (November 2014). https://www.iadi.org/en/assets/File/Core%20Principles/cprevised2014nov.pdf.

Ji, Siqi. 'China GDP to surpass US around 2035, years later than previously expected, Goldman Sachs predicts'. *South China Morning Post*, 09 December 2022. https://www.scmp.com/economy/china-economy/article/3202752/china-gdp-surpass-us-around-2035-years-later-previously-expected-goldman-sachs-predicts.

Jiang, Xueqing. 'Deposit insurance to improve competition'. *China Daily*, 01 December 2014. https://www.chinadaily.com.cn/cndy/2014-12/01/content_19000665.htm.

Jones, Kenneth, and Barry Kolatch. 'The federal safety net, banking subsidies, and implications for financial modernization' (1999). 12 *FDIC Banking Review* 1.

Jones, Marc. 'Over $315.000 in digital yuan used every day at Olympics, PBOC official says'. *Reuters*, 16 February 2022. https://www.reuters.com/technology/around-300-mln-digital-yuan-used-every-day-olympics-pboc-official-says-2022-02-15/.

Kaufman, George G. 'Lender of last resort: A contemporary perspective' (1991). 5 *Journal of Financial Service Research* 95.

Ketcha Jr, Nicholas J. 'Deposit insurance system design and considerations' (1999). 7 *BIS Policy Papers* 221.

Klee, Elizabeth. 'The first line of defense: The discount window during the early stages of the financial crisis' (2021). 17 *International Journal of Central Banking* 143.

Kosmetatos, Paul. 'Last resort lending before Henry Thornton? The Bank of England's role in containing the 1763 and 1772-1773 British credit crises' (2018). 23 *European Review of Economic History* 299.

Kydland, Finn E, and Edward C Prescott. 'Rules rather than discretion: The inconsistency of optimal plans' (1977). 85 *Journal of Political Economy* 473.

Labonte, Marc. 'Federal reserve: Oversight and disclosure issues' (2017). Congressional Research Service. https://sgp.fas.org/crs/misc/R42079.pdf.

Laeven, Luc. 'Pricing of deposit insurance'. July 2002. World Bank Policy Research Working Paper 2871. https://documents1.worldbank.org/curated/en/917821468739467603/106506322_20041117162012/additional/multi0page.pdf.

Lastra, Rosa, 'Northern Rock, UK bank insolvency and cross-border bank insolvency' (2008). 9 *Journal of Banking Regulation* 165.

Lastra, Rosa, and Andrew Campbell. 'Definition of bank insolvency and types of bank insolvency proceedings'. In Rosa Lastra (ed.), *Cross-Border Bank Insolvency* (Oxford, UK: Oxford University Press, 2011).

Lastra, Rosa, and Geoffrey Wood. 'Bank insolvency in the context of crisis management'. In Rosa Lastra (ed.), *Cross-Border Bank Insolvency* (Oxford, UK: Oxford University Press, 2011), pp. 17–22.

Lauria, Vinnie. 'Instant replay: Naspers-Tencent echoes the SoftBank-Alibaba story'. *Forbes*, 17 July 2019. https://www.forbes.com/sites/vinnielauria/2019/07/17/instant-replay-naspers-tencent-echoes-the-softbank-alibaba-story/.

Law, Fiona, Prudence Ho, and Shayndi Raice. 'Bank of America exits China Bank Stake'. *The Wall Street Journal*, 03 September 2013. https://www.wsj.com/articles/SB1000142 41278873244324045t79052401692576092.

Lee, Amanda. 'China's financial overhaul continues with banking veteran Li Yunze named party chief of new regulatory body'. *South China Morning Post*, 10 May 2023. https://www.scmp.com/economy/china-economy/article/3220080/chinas-financial-overhaul-continues-banking-veteran-li-yunze-named-party-chief-new-regulatory-body.

Leng, Cheng, and Edward White. 'China's biggest four banks feel property pinch from failing loans'. *The Financial Times*, 07 September 2022. https://www.ft.com/content/2f0eb985-ac20-4b09-8955-3be8925f1a12.

Li, Keqiang. 'Government work report 2015'. National People's Congress, 05 March 2015.

Liu, Shenliang. 'The CSRC promulgated rules on CDRs at 6 June 2018'. *Xinhua*, 06 June 2018. http://www.xinhuanet.com/fortune/2018-06/08/c_1122954412.htm.

London Stock Exchange. 'London stock exchange stock connect'. Accessed 01 July 2024. https://www.londonstockexchange.com/raise-finance/equity/london-stock-connect.

Lu, Lerong, and Anat Keller. 'Is it China's Lehman Brothers moment? Unveiling Evergrande debt crisis, financial risks, and regulatory implications' (2022). 16 *Law and Financial Markets Review* 133.

Lu, Lerong, and Hang Chen. 'Digital Yuan: The practice and regulation of China's central bank digital currency' (2021). 36 *Butterworths Journal of International Banking and Financial Law* 601.

Lu, Lerong, and Jiujing Ye. 'Beijing stock exchange and multi-tier capital markets: How China alters share listing and trading rules to promote SME finance?' (2022). 43 *Company Lawyer* 233.

Lu, Lerong, and Lingsheng Zhang. 'China experiments with cross-border payments of central bank digital currencies'. 17 December 2021. *Columbia Law School's Blog on Corporations and Capital Markets.* https://clsbluesky.law.columbia.edu/2021/12/17/china-experiments-with-cross-border-payments-of-central-bank-digital-currencies/.

Lu, Lerong, and Lingsheng Zhang. 'Could the "Dragon" now fly beyond borders? Contextualizing regulatory aspects and risks for China's CBDC cross-border use' (2022). *14:S Tsinghua China Law Review* 19.

Lu, Lerong, and Lingsheng Zhang. 'Regulating fintech corporations amidst Covid-19 pandemic: An analysis of Ant Group (Alipay)'s suspension of IPO and business restructuring' (2021). 42 *Company Lawyer* 341.

Lu, Lerong, and Longjie Lu. 'Unveiling China's stock market bubble: Margin Financing, the leveraged bull and governmental responses' (2017). 32 *Journal of International Banking Law and Regulation* 146.

Lu, Lerong. 'Bitcoin: Speculative bubble, financial risk and regulatory response' (2018). 33 *Butterworths Journal of International Banking and Financial Law* 178.

Lu, Lerong. 'Black Swans and Grey Rhinos: Demystifying China's financial risks and the financial regulatory reform' (2018). 33 *Butterworths Journal of International Banking and Financial Law* 594.

Lu, Lerong. 'Decoding Alipay: Mobile payments, a cashless society and regulatory challenges' (2018). 33 *Butterworths Journal of International Banking and Financial Law* 40.

Lu, Lerong. 'Financial technology and challenger banks in the UK: Gap fillers or real challengers?' (2017). 32 *Journal of International Banking Law and Regulation* 273.

Lu, Lerong. 'Private banks in China: Origin, challenges and regulatory implications' (2016). 31 *Banking and Finance Law Review* 585.

Lu, Lerong. 'Reforming corporate share-listing rules in China: understanding the rationale and advantages of the registration-based IPO regime' (2021). 42 *Company Lawyer* 236.

Lu, Lerong. 'Shadow banking for cash-strapped entrepreneurs: A study of private lending agreements under Chinese contract law' (2018). *Journal of Business Law* 215.

Lu, Lerong. *Global Fintech Revolution: Practice, Policy, and Regulation* (Oxford, UK: Oxford University Press, 2024).

Lu, Lerong. *Private Lending in China: Practice, Law, and Regulation of Shadow Banking and Alternative Finance* (Abingdon, UK: Routledge, 2018).

Lu, Shen. 'China to set up Beijing Stock Exchange'. *Protocol*, 02 September 2021. https://www.protocol.com/bulletins/china-to-set-up-beijing-stock-exchange.

Ma, Guonan, and Ben S C Fung. 'China's asset management corporations' (2002). BIS Working Papers No. 115. https://www.bis.org/publ/work115.pdf.

Ma, Nan, and Gabriel Wildau. 'Beijing's visible hand lies heavy on China IPOs'. *The Financial Times*, 26 March 2015, p. 18.

Markman, Jon. 'The Amazon era: No profits, no problem'. *Forbes*, 23 May 2017. http://www.forbes.com/sites/jonmarkman/2017/05/23/the-amazon-era-no-profits-no-problem/.

Martin, Will. 'Deutsche Bank: A major financial crisis is almost twice as likely in China as anywhere else in the world'. *Business Insider UK*, 11 December 2017. http://uk.businessinsider.com/deutsche-bank-china-debt-financial-crisis-probability-2017-12.

McCulley, Paul. 'Teton reflections'. September 2007. PIMCO Global Central Bank Focus.

McMorrow, Ryan, Sun Yu, and Tom Mitchell. 'China's Didi to delist from New York and switch to Hong Kong'. *The Financial Times*, 03 December 2021. https://www.ft.com/content/c30cf911-51da-4b40-a969-161351de6f04.

McVea, Harry. 'What's wrong with insider dealing?' (1995). 15 *Legal Studies* 390.

Meltzer, Allan H. 'Regulatory reform and the federal reserve' (2009). The US Senate Committee on Banking. https://www.banking.senate.gov/imo/media/doc/MeltzerTestimony72309.pdf.

Meyer, David. 'China now has 2 of the top 10 most valuable brands in the World For the first time'. *Fortune*, 29 May 2018. http://fortune.com/2018/05/29/chinese-brands-alibaba-tencent-brandz/.

Miller, Geoffrey P. 'Deposit insurance for economies in transition' (1997). 2 *Yearbook of International Financial and Economic Book* 103.

Ministry of Industry and Information Technology. 'China industry development and industry policy report (2011)'.

Minsky, Hyman P. *Stabilizing an Unstable Economy* (New York: McGraw Hill, 2008).

Mitchell, Tom. 'Xi's four-point plan gives reason for optimism'. *The Financial Times*, 15 November 2013. http://www.ft.com/intl/cms/s/0/4469ec2c-4e06-11e3-8fa5-00144feabdc0.html.

Mo, Jingxi. 'Xi highlights key national security tasks'. *China Daily*, 31 May 2023. https://www.chinadaily.com.cn/a/202305/31/WS647654d7a3107584c3ac2f92.html.

Mo, YK. 'A review of recent bank reforming in China'. *BIS Working Paper* (1999). https://www.bis.org/publ/plcy07d.pdf.

Morris, Stephen, James Fontanella-Khan, and Arash Massoudi. 'How the Swiss "Trinity" forced UBS To save credit Suisse'. *The Financial Times*, 20 March 2023. https://www.ft.com/content/3080d368-d5aa-4125-a210-714e37087017.

Mu, Changchun. 'Reflection on controlled anonymity CBDC'. *Sina Finance*, 25 March 2021. http://finance.sina.com.cn/zl/china/2021-03-25/zl-ikknscsk1349458.shtml.

Nakamoto, Satoshi. 'A peer-to-peer electronic cash system' (2008). https://bitcoin.org/bitcoin.pdf.

Nanfang Daily. 'Guangzhou seized the establishment of the North Exchange opportunity to listed enterprises one-time capital subsidies' (24 November 2021).

National Equities Exchange and Quotations. 'About NEEQ'. Accessed 01 July 2024. http://www.neeq.com.cn/en/about_neeq/overview.html.

National Financial Regulatory Administration. 'Institution introduction'. Accessed 01 July 2024. https://www.cbirc.gov.cn/cn/view/pages/jigougaikuang/jigougaikuang.html.

National Financial Regulatory Administration. 'NAFR, PBOC, and CSRC issued typical cases on the protection of financial consumers' rights and interests'. 10 October 2023. https://www.cbirc.gov.cn/cn/view/pages/ItemDetail.html?docId=1130937&itemId=4099.

National Financial Regulatory Administration. 'NFRA issues the rules on capital management of commercial banks'. 01 November 2023. https://www.cbirc.gov.cn/en/view/pages/ItemDetail.html?docId=1142371.

National Financial Regulatory Administration. 'Total banking assets, total liabilities 2023 (quarterly)'. 21 February 2024. https://www.cbirc.gov.cn/cn/view/pages/ItemDetail.html?docId=1109300&itemId=954.

Nelson, William. 'Lessons from lender of last resort during the crisis: The Federal Reserve experience' (2014). BIS Papers No 79. https://www.bis.org/publ/bppdf/bispap79d.pdf.

Ninebot Limited. 'CDR public offering prospectus'. April 2019. http://static.sse.com.cn/stock/information/c/201904/6cb9b97495db4b80aeeb99eac8e35c49.pdf.

O'Connell, Dominic. 'The collapse of Northern Rock: Ten years on'. *BBC*, 12 September 2017. https://www.bbc.co.uk/news/business-41229513.

OuYang, Shi Jia, and Zhou Lan Xu. 'Draft law on financial stability targets risks'. *China Daily*, 29 December 2022. https://www.chinadaily.com.cn/a/202212/29/WS63acedfaa31057c47eba6bff.html.

PBoC, et al. 'The action plan on building Shanghai International Financial Centre (2018-2020)'. http://www.shanghai.gov.cn/nw2/nw2314/nw2315/nw4411/u21aw1360150.html.

PBoC. '2021 report on RMB internationalization'. http://www.pbc.gov.cn/goutongjiaoliu/113456/113469/4344602/2021091814193942128.pdf.

PBoC. 'A brief history of the people's bank of China'. Accessed 01 July 2024. http://www.pbc.gov.cn/en/3688066/3688089/index.html.

PBoC. 'Announcement on loan prime rate (20 May 2020)'. http://www.pbc.gov.cn/en/3688229/3688335/3883798/4054582/index.html.

PBoC. 'Balance sheet of monetary authority'. January 2024. http://www.pbc.gov.cn/diaochatongjisi/resource/cms/2024/01/2024011616021539705.htm.

PBoC. 'China financial stability report 2023'. pp. 17–18. http://www.pbc.gov.cn/jinrongwendingju/146766/146772/5177895/2023122217072818365.pdf.

PBoC. 'Financial stability law of the People's Republic of China (Draft)'. 6 April 2022. http://www.pbc.gov.cn/goutongjiaoliu/113456/113469/4525742/index.html.

PBoC. 'Former Governors'. Accessed 01 July 2024. http://www.pbc.gov.cn/en/3688066/3688086/index.html.

PBoC. 'Interim measures for the administration of emergency loans of the People's Bank of China'. Yinfa [1999] No. 407. http://www.pbc.gov.cn/zhengcehuobisi/125207/125213/125437/125815/2835315/index.html.

PBoC. 'Introduction to structural monetary policy instruments (by the end of September 2023)'. http://www.pbc.gov.cn/en/3688229/3688335/4738114/5241680/index.html.

PBoC. 'LPR'. Accessed 01 July 2024. http://www.pbc.gov.cn/en/3688229/3688335/3883798/index.html.

PBoC. 'Macroprudential goals, implementation and cross-border communication'. 2017. BIS Paper No. 94. https://www.bis.org/publ/bppdf/bispap94h.pdf.

PBoC. 'Management team'. Accessed 01 July 2024. http://www.pbc.gov.cn/en/3688066/3688083/index.html.

PBoC. 'Medium-term lending facility'. Accessed 01 July 2024. http://www.pbc.gov.cn/en/3688229/3688335/3730282/index.html.

PBoC. 'MLF operations in February 2024'. http://www.pbc.gov.cn/en/3688229/3688335/3730282/5260695/index.html.

PBoC. 'Notice on further preventing and resolving the risks of virtual currency trading and speculation'. 15 September 2021. http://www.pbc.gov.cn/en/3688253/3689012/4353814/index.html.

PBoC. 'Open market operations'. Accessed 01 July 2024. http://www.pbc.gov.cn/en/3688229/3688335/3730267/index.html.

PBoC. 'People's Bank of China decides to raise reserve requirements ratio (23 August 2023)'. http://www.pbc.gov.cn/english/130721/2830889/index.html.

PBoC. 'Progress of research & development of E-CNY in China (Whitepaper)'. July 2021. http://www.pbc.gov.cn/en/3688110/3688172/4157443/4293696/2021071614584691871.pdf.

PBoC. 'PSL operations in January 2024'. http://www.pbc.gov.cn/en/3688229/3688335/3730285/5238337/index.html.

PBoC. 'Purposes and functions'. Accessed 01 July 2024. http://www.pbc.gov.cn/en/3688066/3688080/index.html.

PBoC. 'Required reserves'. Accessed 01 July 2024. http://www.pbc.gov.cn/en/3688229/3688335/3730270/index.html.

PBoC. 'Shanghai financial operation report (2022)'. http://shanghai.pbc.gov.cn/fzhshanghai/113589/4599988/2022070814444473871.pdf.

PBoC. 'SLF operations in January 2024'. http://www.pbc.gov.cn/en/3688229/3688335/3730279/5238313/index.html.

PBoC. 'Standing lending facility'. Accessed 01 July 2024. http://www.pbc.gov.cn/en/3688229/3688335/3730279/index.html.

PBoC. 'The PBoC increased reloan and rediscount quota by 300 Billion Yuan this year to support the financing of small and micro businesses and private enterprises'. 23 October 2018. http://www.pbc.gov.cn/english/130721/3650283/index.html.

PBoC. 'The White Paper on the research and development of China's Digital Yuan'. July 2021. http://www.pbc.gov.cn/goutongjiaoliu/113456/113469/4293590/2021071614200022055.pdf.

Peck, Sally. 'The truth about Chinese travellers'. *The Telegraph*, 25 July 2017. http://www.telegraph.co.uk/travel/destinations/asia/china/how-chinese-tourists-travel-etiquette-and-money/.

People. 'ICBC: 2022 net profit exceeded 360 billion yuan with growth rate of 3.1%'. 31 March 2023. http://finance.people.com.cn/n1/2023/0331/c1004-32655126.html.

People. 'Preventing and defusing financial risks requires a good grasp of two relationships'. 06 November 2023. http://theory.people.com.cn/n1/2023/1106/c40531-40110869.html.

People's Daily. '35 years, Chinese economy keep rising'. 21 November 2013, p. 4.

People's Daily. 'Effectively prevent financial risks'. 17 July 2017. http://opinion.people.com.cn/n1/2017/0717/c1003-29407958.html.

People's Daily. 'Let specialized special new small and medium enterprises thrive'. 19 October 2021. http://www.gov.cn/xinwen/2021-10/19/content_5643541.htm.

Provan, Sarah. 'Huatai securities to raise as much as $ 1.7bn in London listing'. *The Financial Times*, 14 June 2019. http://www.ft.com/content/40a6eb48-8e84-11e9-a1c1-51bf8f989972.

QianLong. 'The performance of Beijing Financial Court'. 31 December 2021. https://beijing.qianlong.com/2022/1231/7945973.shtml.

Qiao, Zheng, and Yangshu Liu. 'Open market operation effectiveness in China' (2017). 53 *Emerging Markets Finance and Trade* 1706.

Rabinovitch, Simon. 'Treasure piles up for Alibaba as depositors desert China's banks'. *The Financial Times*, 20 December 2013. https://www.ft.com/content/58dfd7ce-63d8-11e3-98e2-00144feabdc0.

Ramzy, Austin. 'A credit crisis in China's most enterprising city is making the Country Nervous'. *Time*, 28 November 2011. http://content.time.com/time/magazine/article/0.9171.2099675.00.html.

Relbank. 'World's Largest Banks by assets 2019'. 20 October 2019. https://www.relbanks.com/worlds-top-banks/top-world-banks-by-assets-2019.

Ren, Daniel. 'Tesla's Shanghai factory delivers fewer electric cars as upgrade ahead of new Model 3 launch disrupts production'. *South China Morning Post*, 09 October 2023. https://www.scmp.com/business/china-business/article/3237342/teslas-shanghai-factory-delivers-fewer-electric-cars-upgrade-ahead-new-model-3-launch-disrupts.

Reuters. 'Britain and China promise to speed up work on London-Shanghai stock connect'. 16 December 2017. http://www.scmp.com/news/china/diplomacy-defence/article/2124601/britain-and-china-promise-speed-work-london-shanghai.

Reuters. 'China bans financial, payment institutions from cryptocurrency business'. 18 May 2021. https://www.reuters.com/technology/chinese-financial-payment-bodies-barred-cryptocurrency-business-2021-05-18/.

Reuters. 'China issues draft financial stability law to prevent systemic risks'. 06 April 2022. https://www.reuters.com/world/china/china-issues-draft-financial-stability-law-prevent-systemic-risks-2022-04-06/.

Reuters. 'China's He Lifeng named to key post in Central Financial Commission'. 06 November 2023. https://www.reuters.com/world/china/china-appoints-he-lifeng-head-office-central-financial-commission-cbank-2023-11-06/.

Reuters. 'Chinese regulator to take over Baoshang Bank due to credit risks'. 24 May 2019. https://www.reuters.com/article/us-china-banks-regulator-baoshang-bank-idUSKCN1SU1DN.

Reuters. 'Cutting ties with China is "unthinkable", Mercedes-Benz CEO tells Bild am Sontag'. 29 April 2023. https://www.reuters.com/business/autos-transportation/cutting-ties-with-china-is-unthinkable-mercedes-benz-ceo-tells-bams-2023-04-29/.

Reuveni, Erez. 'Extraterritoriality as standing: A standing theory of the extraterritorial application of the securities laws' (2009). 43 *UC Davis Law Review* 1071.

Rutkowski, Ryan. 'Too big to fail: Deposit Insurance and Chinese State Banks' (2013). Peterson Institute for International Economics. https://www.piie.com/blogs/china-economic-watch/too-big-fail-deposit-insurance-and-chinese-state-banks.

S & P Global. 'The World's 100 largest banks 2023'. https://www.spglobal.com/market intelligence/en/news-insights/research/the-world-s-100-largest-banks-2023.

Savills. 'China dominates global city rankings for house price growth'. 12 February 2018. http://www.savills.co.uk/insight-and-opinion/savills-news/228041-0/china-dominates-global-city-rankings-for-house-price-growth.

Schwartz, Anna J. 'Origins of the financial crisis of 2008' (2009). 29 *The Cato Journal* 19.

Securities Times. 'Over 17.000 cases in five years, the disputes in securities industry greatly exceed banking and insurance'. 24 August 2023. https://www.stcn.com/article/detail/957115.html.

Shanghai Financial Court. 'Introduction to the Shanghai Financial Court'. Accessed 01 July 2024. http://www.shjrfy.gov.cn/jrfy/English/about.jsp.

Shanghai Financial Court. 'Work report on trial activities of from 2018 to 2021'. Accessed 01 July 2024. http://61.129.132.51/jrfy/gweb/xx_view.jsp?pa=aaWQ9NjU0OAPdcssPdcssz.

Shanghai Financial Court. 'Xu et al. v. Shanghai Potevio Co. Ltd. concerning dispute over liability for misrepresentation in the securities market.' 11 June 2020. http://61.129.132.51/jrfy/English/news_view.jsp?pa=aaWQ9NTAwNQPdcssPdcssz.

Shanghai Government. 'Brief introduction of Shanghai stock exchange'. 18 July 2023. https://www.shanghai.gov.cn/nw47986/20200824/0001-47986_108559.html.

Shanghai Government. 'This is Shanghai—International Financial Center'. Accessed 01 July 2024. https://english.shanghai.gov.cn/en-ThisisShanghai/20231207/9815a792b25f4c43bc1bbe69f61a817a.html.

Shanghai Securities News. 'NAFR Chief Li Yunze: The three main tasks in financial sector'. May 2023. https://news.cnstock.com/news.bwkx-202305-5062916.htm.

Shanghai Stock Exchange. 'Listing on SSE'. Accessed 01 July 2024. http://www.sse.com.cn/services/list/listedinsse/bluechips/a/20170825/b254004db4002ca4bd105c017adb374a.pdf.

Shanghai Stock Exchange. 'Regulations of launching the star market and experimenting registration-based IPO'. Accessed 01 July 2024. http://www.sse.com.cn/lawandrules/sserules/tib/.

Shen, Samuel, and John Ruwitch. 'Baoshang failure takes a toll in China's interbank markets as contagion fears grow'. *Reuters*, 21 June 2019. https://www.reuters.com/article/us-china-markets-baoshang-idUSKCN1TM11T.

Shen, Wei. 'Shadow banking system in China—Origin, uniqueness and governmental response' (2013). 28 *Journal of International Banking Law and Regulation* 20.

Sina Finance. 'CDRs are a foundation for internationalised A-shares'. 08 March 2018. http://finance.sina.com.cn/stock/marketresearch/2018-03-08/doc-ifxpwyhv9413509.shtml.

Sohu. '50 good proposals from members of CPPCC'. 21 December 2022. https://www.sohu.com/a/619521214_120119476.

Song, Xuetao. 'What is the historical significance of sci-tech innovation board?' *TF Securities*, 02 March 2019. http://pdf.dfcfw.com/pdf/H3_AP201903041302384303_1.pdf.

South China Morning Post. 'China bonds to bail out banks'. 02 March 1998. https://www.scmp.com/article/231741/china-bonds-bail-out-banks.

Spencer, Mimosa, and Silvia Aloisi. 'LVMH flags strong Chinese rebound, U.S. slowdown'. 13 April 2023. https://www.reuters.com/business/retail-consumer/lvmh-sales-lifted-by-strong-chinese-rebound-first-quarter-2023-04-12/.

State Administration of Foreign Exchange. 'Official reserve assets'. 07 February 2022. https://www.safe.gov.cn/safe/2022/0207/20625.html

State Council of China. 'China establishes national financial regulatory administration'. 18 May 2023. https://english.www.gov.cn/news/202305/18/content_WS6465bd1ac6d03ffcca6ed27f.html.

State Council of China. 'China's central bank steps up financial support to agriculture, small firms'. 30 June 2023. https://english.www.gov.cn/news/202306/30/content_WS649ed7c4c6d0868f4e8dd642.html.

Statista. 'Largest stock exchange operators worldwide as of September 2023, by market capitalization of listed companies'. https://www.statista.com/statistics/270126/largest-stock-exchange-operators-by-market-capitalization-of-listed-companies/.

Statista. 'Most active currency for international payments in 2021, based on transaction value'. https://www.statista.com/statistics/1189498/share-of-global-payments-by-currency/.

Statista. 'Most used currency in the world for international payments in SWIFT from January 2019 to July 2023, based on share in total transaction value'. https://www.statista.com/statistics/1189498/share-of-global-payments-by-currency/.

Statista. 'Total assets of the banking sector in select countries worldwide 2022, by country'. https://www.statista.com/statistics/875144/banking-sector-assets-worldwide-by-country/.

Statista. 'Total deposits of large state-owned commercial banks in China from 2014 to 2021'. https://www.statista.com/statistics/1171187/china-total-deposits-of-large-state-owned-banks/.

Steer, George. 'The inside story of Credit Suisse's collapse, by Credit Suisse'. *The Financial Times*, 24 April 2023. https://www.ft.com/content/857567b8-775c-496a-8578-c7b6419c9c96.

Study in the UK. 'International Chinese student guide to UK universities'. 28 March 2023. https://www.studyin-uk.com/study-guide/chinese-student-guide-uk-universities/.

Supreme People's Court. 'First-of-its-kind financial court gets down to work in Shanghai'. 22 August 2018. http://english.court.gov.cn/2018-08/22/content_36806558.htm.

Supreme People's Court. 'Opinions of the Supreme People's court on providing judicial services to safeguard the development of the Chengdu-Chongqing Economic Circle'. 13 January 2021. https://lawinfochina.com/display.aspx?id=35000&lib=law.

Supreme People's Court. 'Several provisions of the Supreme People's court on the trial of civil cases for damages for the tort of misrepresentation in the securities market' (2022). http://www.lawinfochina.com/display.aspx?id=37627&lib=law.

Swiss National Bank. 'The monetary base and the M1, M2 and M3 monetary aggregates'. February 2007. https://www.snb.ch/en/mmr/reference/histz_geldmengen_book/source/histz_geldmengen_book.en.pdf.

Taleb, Nassim Nicholas. *The Black Swan: The Impact of the Highly Improbable* (New York: Random House, 2007).

The Economist. 'A premium for risk: A scheme to protect savers exposes Chinese banks to useful uncertainty'. 04 December 2014. https://www.economist.com/finance-and-economics/2014/12/04/a-premium-for-risk.

The Economist. 'China's economy: Coming down to Earth'. 18 April 2015. http://www.economist.com/news/briefing/21648567-chinese-growth-losing-altitude-will-it-be-soft-or-hard-landing-coming-down-earth.

The Economist. 'China's economy: Hitting the Kerb'. 22 October 2011. http://www.economist.com/node/21533412.

The Economist. 'China's stock market: A crazy casino'. 26 May 2015.

The Economist. 'Entrepreneurship in China: Let a million flowers bloom'. 10 March 2011. https://www.economist.com/briefing/2011/03/10/let-a-million-flowers-bloom.

The Economist. 'Financing Europe's small firms: Don't bank on the banks'. 16 August 2014. http://www.economist.com/news/finance-and-economics/21612251-small-businesses-seek-alternatives-banks-leave-them-lurch-dont-bank.

The Economist. 'The age of the Appacus: Fintech in China'. 25 Feb 2017. 65.

The Economist. 'The rapid rise and fall of the Anbang empire'. 23 February 2018.

The Federal Reserve Bank of Richmond. 'The note issue function of Central Banks'. *Monthly Review*, July 1962. https://fraser.stlouisfed.org/files/docs/publications/frbrichreview/pages/65387_1960-1964.pdf.

The Federal Reserve. 'Availability of credit to small businesses'. October 2022. https://www.federalreserve.gov/publications/2022-october-availability-of-credit-to-small-businesses.htm.

The Federal Reserve. 'Discount window lending'. Accessed 01 July 2024. https://www.federalreserve.gov/regreform/discount-window.htm.

The Federal Reserve. 'Federal reserve board releases discussion paper that examines pros and cons of a potential U.S. Central Bank Digital Currency (CBDC)'. January 2022. https://www.federalreserve.gov/newsevents/pressreleases/other20220120a.htm.

The Financial Times. 'China property: Accelerating meltdown threatens other markets'. 25 September 2023. https://www.ft.com/content/790ceab3-3169-445f-aade-733daa50bb07.

The Wall Street Journal. 'What's behind China's decision to launch deposit insurance'. 31 March 2015. https://www.wsj.com/articles/BL-CJB-26388.

Tomasic, Roman. 'Creating a template for banking insolvency law reform after the collapse of northern rock'. In Paul Omar (ed.), *International Insolvency Law* (Abingdon, UK: Routledge, 2013), pp. 115–144.

Tor-Inge, Harbo. 'The function of the proportionality principle in the EU law' (2010). 16 *European Law Journal* 158.

Tsai, Kellee S. 'The political economy of state capitalism and shadow banking in China'. The Hong Kong University of Science and Technology IEMS Working Paper No. 2015-25.

Tse, Alice, and Julianna Wu. 'Why "Made in China 2025" triggered the wrath of President Trump'. *South China Morning Post*, 11 September 2018. http://multimedia.scmp.com/news/china/article/made-in-China-2025/index.html.

Wang, Yongli. 'What changes will digital RMB bring?'. *Sina Finance*, 09 November 2020. https://finance.sina.com.cn/blockchain/coin/2020-11-09/doc-iiznctke0425584.shtml.

Wei, Shang-Jin, and Tao Wang. 'The Siamese twins: Do state-owned banks favor state-owned enterprises in China?' (1997). 8 *China Economic Review* 19.

Weinland, Don, and Emma Dunkley. 'HSBC set to become first foreign company to list in China'. *The Financial Times*, 18 October 2018. http://www.ft.com/content/e9b519b8-d28b-11e8-a9f2-7574db66bcd5.

Wildau, Gabriel, and Yizhen Jia. 'Collapse of Chinese peer-to-peer lenders sparks investor flight'. *The Financial Times*, 22 July 2018. https://www.ft.com/content/75e75628-8b27-11e8-bf9e-8771d5404543.

Wildau, Gabriel. 'China's first online-only lender launched'. *The Financial Times*, 06 January 2015. p. 16.

World Bank. 'Belt and road initiative'. 29 March 2018. https://www.worldbank.org/en/topic/regional-integration/brief/belt-and-road-initiative.

World Bank. 'Gross domestic savings (% of GDP)-China'. Accessed 01 July 2024. https://data.worldbank.org/indicator/NY.GDS.TOTL.ZS.

World Intellectual Property Organisation. 'IP facts and figures'. Accessed 01 July 2024. https://www.wipo.int/en/ipfactsandfigures/patents'.

WTO. 'China—Member information'. Accessed 01 July 2024. https://www.wto.org/english/thewto_e/countries_e/china_e.htm.

Wu, Yujian, Zhang Yuzhe, and Denise Jia. 'PBOC sets up depository insurance fund management company'. *Caixin*, 30 May 2019. https://www.caixinglobal.com/2019-05-30/pboc-sets-up-deposit-insurance-fund-management-company-101421410.html.

Wucker, Michele. *The Gray Rhino: How to Recognize and Act on the Obvious Dangers We Ignore* (New York: St. Martin's Press, 2016).

Xinhua. 'Beijing releases full text of new city plan'. 29 September 2017. http://www.xinhuanet.com/english/2017-09/29/c_136649259.htm.

Xinhua. 'Central financial work conference is held'. 01 November 2023. https://english.news.cn/20231101/e027c8d2e7994fd590957c7152d4f4fa/c.html.

Xinhua. 'China unveils regulation on securities, futures violations. 30 November 2021. http://en.people.cn/n3/2021/1130/c90000-9926128.html.

Xinhua. 'Focusing on NPC and CPPCC'. 02 March 2015.

Xinhua. 'From zero start. China now has the second largest capital market in the world'. 08 October 2019. http://www.xinhuanet.com/fortune/2019-10/08/c_1210303693.htm.

Xinhua. 'ICBC profit expands in 2022'. 02 April 2023. https://english.news.cn/20230402/836f4f2c288e4b22b0cb0acc3cc20856/c.html.

Xinhua. 'Number of listed companies in China reaches 5.346 by end of 2023'. 04 February 2024. https://www.chinadaily.com.cn/a/202402/04/WS65bef4cfa3104efcbdae98c9.html.

Xinhua. 'Nuoqi's share slumping reason: Chairman Ding Hui missing'. 26 July 2014. http://news.xinhuanet.com/fortune/2014-07/26/c_126799805.htm.

Xinhua. 'Private lending disputes became China's second largest civil litigation type; The Supreme Court issued new judicial interpretation'. 06 August 2015. http://news.xinhuanet.com/legal/2015-08/06/c_1116171913.htm.

Xinhua. 'Registration-based IPO reform of ChiNext a boon for innovative enterprises'. 17 June 2020. http://www.xinhuanet.com/english/2020-06/17/c_139146066.htm.

Xinhua. 'Tencent become the largest shareholder in JD, Liu Qiangdong still has the controlling power'. 23 August 2016. http://xinhuanet.com/tech/2016-08/23/c_1119438207.htm.

Xinhua. 'The first week of sci-tech innovation board: how the first 25 listing companies performed?'. 27 July 2019. http://www.xinhuanet.com/fortune/2019-07/27/c_1210216065.htm.

Xinhua. 'The second group of companies obtained listing in sci-tech innovation board'. 07 August 2019. http://www.xinhuanet.com/fortune/2019-08/07/c_1210232152.htm.

Yang, Zeyi. 'The new Beijing Stock Exchange's companies are older and less tech-forward than Promised'. *Protocol*, 14 November 2021. https://www.protocol.com/china/beijing-stock-exchange-old-nontech.

Yao, Qian. 'Experimental study on prototype system of central bank digital currency' (2018). 29 *Journal of Software* 2716.

Ye, Ningyao, and Lerong Lu. 'Building a Eurasian capital market: Understanding the operating mechanism and legal framework of Shanghai-London Stock connect' (2020). 35 *Journal of International Banking Law and Regulation* 67.

Ye, Ningyao, and Lerong Lu. 'How to harness a unicorn? Demystifying China's reform of share listing rules and Chinese Depositary Receipts (CDRs)' (2019). 30 *International Company and Commercial Law Review* 454

Yip, Martin. 'Death for Fraud: China debates Wu Ying's sentence'. *BBC News*, 24 February 2012. http://www.bbc.co.uk/news/world-asia-china-17071311.

Yu, Xie. 'Why is Kangmei Pharmaceutical, found to have committed one of China's biggest financial frauds. rallying?'. *South China Morning Post*, 23 August 2019. https://www.scmp.com/business/companies/article/3024084/why-kangmei-pharmaceutical-found-have-committed-one-chinas.

Z/Yen Group. 'The Global Financial Centres Index 35'. 21 March 2024. https://www.longfinance.net/publications/long-finance-reports/the-global-financial-centres-index-35/.

Zhang, Chunlin. 'How much do state-owned enterprises contribute to China's GDP and employment?'. World Bank, 15 July 2019. https://documents1.worldbank.org/curated/en/449701565248091726/pdf/How-Much-Do-State-Owned-Enterprises-Contribute-to-China-s-GDP-and-Employment.pdf.

Zhang, Yuyan. *Reform, Opening-up and China's Changing Role in Global Governance* (Singapore: Springer, 2021).

Zhou, Lanxu. 'NEEQ to ease funding woes of small firms'. *China Daily*, 28 July 2020. https://www.chinadailyhk.com/article/138272.

Zhou, Lanxu. 'New fund to strengthen financial safety net, smooth market slumps'. *China Daily*, 28 September 2022. http://www.chinadaily.com.cn/a/202209/28/WS63339dcaa310fd2b29e7a208.html.

Zhou, Xiaochuan. 'The evolution principles of currencies and payments in the digital age'. *Sina Finance*, 02 December 2020. http://finance.sina.com.cn/zl/china/2020-12-02/zl-iiznctke4306697.shtml.

Zhou, Xin. 'China's super financial regulator headed by vice-premier more powerful than ministries'. *South China Morning Post*, 08 November 2017. http://www.scmp.com/news/china/economy/article/2119001/chinas-super-financial-regulator-headed-vice-premier-more.

Zhou, Yi. 'Establishing a deposit insurance system in China: A long-awaited move toward deepening financial reform' (2016). 16 *Chicago-Kent Journal of International & Comparative Law* 46.

Zhu, Julia. 'The personal information protection law: China's version of the GDPR?'. 14 February 2022. *The Bulletin Blog—Columbia Journal of Transnational Law*. https://www.jtl.columbia.edu/bulletin-blog/the-personal-information-protection-law-chinas-version-of-the-gdpr.

Zhu, Jun. 'Closure of financial institutions in China' (1999). BIS Working Paper. https://www.bis.org/publ/plcy07u.pdf.

Index

For the benefit of digital users, indexed terms that span two pages (e.g., 52–53) may, on occasion, appear on only one of those pages.

Note: The following abbreviations have been used –*f* = figures; n = footnote; *t* = table. All Chinese personal names are in the format of family name followed by given names with no comma between.